Alison Light – Inside History:
From Popular Fiction to Life-Writing

The Feminist Library
Series editors: Jackie Jones, Alison Light, Gill Plain

Published
Alison Light – Inside History: From Popular Fiction to Life-Writing
Alison Light

Forthcoming
Cora Kaplan – Double Crossings: Feminism, Race, the Popular
Cora Kaplan

Alison Light – Inside History

From Popular Fiction to Life-Writing

Alison Light

EDINBURGH
University Press

Edinburgh University Press is one of the leading university presses in the UK. We publish academic books and journals in our selected subject areas across the humanities and social sciences, combining cutting-edge scholarship with high editorial and production values to produce academic works of lasting importance. For more information visit our website: edinburghuniversitypress.com

Edinburgh University Press Ltd
The Tun – Holyrood Road
12(2f) Jackson's Entry
Edinburgh EH8 8PJ

First published in hardback by Edinburgh University Press 2022

Typeset in 10.5/13 Bembo by
IDSUK (DataConnection) Ltd

A CIP record for this book is available from the British Library

ISBN 978 1 4744 8155 7 (hardback)
ISBN 978 1 4744 8172 4 (paperback)
ISBN 978 1 4744 8156 4 (webready PDF)
ISBN 978 1 4744 8157 1 (epub)

Contents

The Feminist Library: Classic Essays in Literary and Cultural Criticism

Series Editors' Preface

Libraries are a vital part of culture and community. They celebrate the written word, safeguard its history, and make knowledge available to all. This series aims to be just such a library, building an archive of recent feminist scholarship and making it newly accessible in lasting print and digital form. The Feminist Library will publish incisive and thought-provoking essays by influential contemporary critics working across the intersections of gender, class, race and sexuality; it will illustrate feminism's complex encounters with history, popular culture and the canon; and it will offer to readers, new and old, exemplary instances of what it means to read and write as a feminist.

Each volume of essays will be selected and introduced by its author, permitting personal and critical reflection on the value of thinking as a feminist. The collections will range from challenging think-pieces to classic yet often out-of-reach articles to new work and new directions, reflecting the suppleness of feminist thought and its capacity to engage across radically different contexts and forms. In this sense, the volumes in this library are also handbooks or, perhaps, intellectual autobiographies. They dissolve the distinction between the academic and the activist, the personal and the political, to demonstrate what a life of feminist enquiry might look like and the diverse, protean forms it might take.

Feminism is, of necessity, always a work in progress. The ideas, questions and debates explored in the volumes of The Feminist Library will mean new things to a new generation of readers, and will be put to new purposes, but they will also act to remind us of our history.

The social, political and intellectual challenges of the recent past have not gone away, and earlier feminist interventions can enrich our engagement with those of the present. The Feminist Library brings into focus twentieth-century questions that the twenty-first century cannot afford to ignore; but it also has another purpose. Libraries do not just inform, they seduce, liberating the imagination and generating pleasure. To that end, The Feminist Library collects eloquent, incisive, provocative writing with the simple aim of enabling rich, rewarding reading.

Jackie Jones
Alison Light
Gill Plain

Acknowledgements

I would like to thank Dr Jackie Jones at Edinburgh University Press for proposing the idea of *The Feminist Library* series and for encouraging me to submit a pilot volume. Both she and Professor Gill Plain at the University of St Andrews have been exemplary co-editors and a great pleasure to work with. They and the whole team at EUP – Susannah Butler, Fiona Conn and Caitlin Murphy – have made the production process smooth and congenial – almost as if we were meeting in person rather than working long-distance during a global pandemic. Thanks also go to Amanda Speake for her meticulous index.

I hope I was generous with my original acknowledgements for the older essays and reviews collected here but I would like to thank the editors of the *London Review of Books* and of the *Kenyon Review* for the opportunity to re-print the more recent pieces. Finally, as ever, I have relied on my husband, John O'Halloran, for all manner of support and understanding.

Introduction: Reading Oneself Backwards

An introduction like this one, looking back over nearly thirty-five years of work, is bound to be deceptive. Thought does not travel in a straight line; ideas are seeded and gestate or lie dormant for decades; others fall by the wayside or on stony ground. Work is always work in progress. Realising too, as I get older, how much I am always 'inside history', has meant acknowledging that my work, however much it feels original, is also representative, forged in the crucible of time, fashioned in a culture and a place, owing much to others. One's self is only ever known in social relations and such relations, like time, do not stand still. 'I' am a crowd. If the self is a kind of flow, the knowledge of one's own historicity, accrues like silt.

A life, in other words, is not a curriculum vitae with its forged, purposive path and its fantasy of the individual cutting a swathe into the future, a lonely intellect working in isolation. Yet that fantasy, call it ego, is a mobilising one and necessary for survival. Indeed one of the pleasures of writing, perhaps the most crucial, lies in creating the illusion – if only for the length of a sentence – that one is authoring one's life. Perhaps this is why, sorting through my past essays and articles, I found myself beset by mournfulness as if I was already posthumous. This feeling that the owl of Minerva is ready to fly out at one's own twilight is an effect of arranging the selection chronologically. The person who wrote these essays is impossible to find; she is already scattered to the winds, and yet she is speaking to you now. The moment of writing is forever slipping away. The reader recreates it in their present.

An edited collection such as this is a privilege but it also resembles a 'Festschrift' of the kind presented by one's colleagues at the end of an academic career, part-celebration, part-obituary. I am not about to retire; indeed I am hardly in a position to do so since I have not been in a full-time academic

post since 1995 and have spent as many years as a freelance writer as I have
as a teacher. But I am now retirement age, and with a retrospective survey, I
feel the pressure to present my personal past as a life-thesis, a sort of summation. I mean to resist this. With this in mind, the middle section of this book,
'Short Cuts' might be the place for the reader to start. The articles here, mostly
free-floating journalism, encapsulate some of the arguments and themes in the
longer essays or anticipate those which emerged, often much later, in book
form. ('On Mourning', for instance, waited nearly twenty years to become a
book.) From here the reader might go backwards into the 1980s or forwards
into the 2000s.

Each revisiting, each spiralling of thought back round on itself, nonetheless
brings something different in its train. To take, for instance, the slender piece,
reprinted here, which I wrote in 1989 for an opinion column called 'Stand'
in the British weekly the *New Statesman*. Its pretext – the hook, as journalists
would call it – was the fifty years anniversary of the outbreak of the Second
World War. It opens with memories of the war which I was too young to
experience but which dominated my childhood. Growing up in the late 1950s
in an English city which had been heavily blitzed, 'the war' was a staple of the
stories we heard from parents and relatives, of the songs that were still sung or
broadcast, of the films we watched. It was the imaginary backdrop to games
we played in the street or on old bombsites. I was intrigued by the mismatch
between the shapes given to the public narratives of history - the idea of a generation, and indeed of the anniversary, are examples – and the way the fluidity
of memory collapses time and offers its own inside history.

Fast forward twenty years. In 2009, I wrote a longer memoir, also included
here, 'A Child's Sense of the Past'. It took the form of reverie and was published
in a special issue on 'Life-writing' in the academic journal *New Formations*. It
too moved, as memoir can, between history and memory and the different
experiences of time but it was also trying more self-consciously to understand
what it might mean, in my case, to come from the English working-classes,
the particular childhood world where writing and the printed word was far
less important than speech. My parents and grandparents, my eight aunts and
uncles, their friends and workmates constantly made a theatre, an entertainment, of the travails of the past by telling stories, joking, gesticulating, singing.
In the article I suggested a contrast between the idea of a generic 'pastness'
conjured by reverie or nostalgia which corresponded to my child's vision and a
historical imagination which is distancing, which keeps one's own experience
at arm's length and sees it as representative: the self displaced from the centre
of the narrative and experience no longer the sole guarantor of meaning. This
piece, like the diary 'In Portsmouth' published in the fortnightly literary paper

the *London Review of Books*, was also the beginning of the search for a more precise account of my family's history, a history as it turned out of the migrant poor. That account eventually became *Common People* (2014), a mix of social history, memoir and reflections on the writing of history.

The title of the first section of this volume, 'From Fiction to Nation', might suggest that an increasingly historical turn has taken me away from the interpretation of 'texts' – novels, plays, poetry – to scouring original documents in local archives, the historian's staple, from which narratives are produced and arguments made. But the opposition between literary texts on the one hand and history on the other is a false one, as I hope these essays show. Literature is no more a handmaiden serving history, bending to its superior commands or mimicking its concerns, than history is simply 'background' to the work of art which magically transcends the society from which it issued. Equally, historical evidence is not value-free; it needs to be sifted and interpreted and read between the lines. Learning about my own past, for instance, has also meant trying to make sense of the fictions of national identity which are part of 'the myths we live by'.[1] 'From fiction to nation' is not a one-way street. Nor have I ceased to write as a species of literary critic.

What strikes me now –with hindsight – as consistent throughout is the urge to engage listeners directly and personally. It obviously owes something to my upbringing and to my own love of performance and singing (lecturing is always theatre). Talking to an audience, with plenty of jokes and ad-libbing, rather than presenting an academic paper, is my preferred mode. All the longer articles in this volume apart from the essays for the *London Review of Books* began life as talks from notes, with questions and discussion to follow. They were later written up and revised for publication (and I have not tinkered with any of them again for publication here). Experiments in other forms of writing, some of which are included – the opinion column, the literary diary, prefaces to other people's memoirs, obituaries, re-readings of works that mattered to me in my growing up – allowed me to make my 'voice' as the author, as now, the connecting path through the writing.

This impulse was also stimulated by the emphasis on what was called 'self-expression' in the way I was taught English at grammar school after the age of eleven. Writing one's own verses or imaginative compositions; writing short plays and acting them out, was encouraged, alongside personal responses to what was read. What used to be called 'appreciation' generally meant expressing a view about one's reading and often a judgement on it, usually without any sense of historical context at all. The reader, in the case of plays or novels, was asked to identify with the characters (be they Lady Macbeth or David Copperfield), making sense of the characters' inner lives and emotions (girls were meant to be especially good at this), explicating their actions. English, a compulsory subject in British schools, soon bifurcated into two 'O' or Ordinary levels in England – literature and language. While English literature 'A' or Advanced level relied on similar responses, it also concentrated on how literary works got their effects: paying attention to syntax, rhythm, imagery, tone and so on, learning how a poem or a sentence was put together and annotating difficult vocabulary. I have never regretted this training in 'close reading'. The writing of one's own stories or poetry, though, was relegated to the sidelines of school work (writing for the school magazine, say). Although I left school a keen (perhaps a too keen) poet, I wrote not a line at university. But then at eighteen I had no plans 'to be a poet' – an idea as preposterous, *more* preposterous, than becoming Prime Minister. I knew no-one going about their business in the literary world, actually living as a writer, publisher, editor or journalist. That world was, as it is for the majority of the public, a closed shop.

I came from a highly articulate, un-bookish home. Both my parents had left school before the age of fourteen, had no official qualifications and in their different ways revered learning and literature. The ways I learnt to speak and write in school and college were for me, as for many, many others, a kind of exile from the language and culture of home. Education, although hugely enabling, was a form of loss of connection to my family and to the world in which I had grown up. One of the excitements of the women's movement as I encountered it was the chance to be part of a new communality of readers and writers. It was where I could begin to talk and write about and measure the distance I had travelled. My prompt for leaving paid work to be a student again nearly ten years after my first degree was joining a 'women's writing' class in London in 1979, run by the novelist Zoe Fairbairns[2]. I was experimenting again with fiction, poetry and short essays, though I did not yet know what I wanted to say.

Making myself present in the moment of writing, trying to span what felt like a gulf between where I came from and where I now found myself, meant writing self-consciously about 'class', that blunt instrument of a word, for the first time. As these essays suggest, writing about class, and trying to understand its meanings, became a way of disrupting consensus, wedging open any assumptions as to what women as a whole might share and thinking about power between women. In an academic context it questioned what might constitute a literary sensibility and what might count as worthy of study. Many of the articles here, especially in the first section of the book, sought to challenge any purely celebratory view of 'women's writing' by asking how literary works created the meaning of differences between women, shoring up those differences as well as re-imagining them. I have always been interested in the sticking-points of the imagination, the internal conflicts from which writers write, the conservatisms which tether them as well as their flights of fancy.

★

The essays in the first section of this volume belong to the '80s and '90s when the idea of feminist cultural politics was first being aired. The impact of the so-called 'second wave' of the women's movement from the late 1970s on the cultural sphere of the arts is hard to overestimate. What we could read in Britain was utterly changed by the great outpouring of work by women from the independent feminist presses, including Virago, Onlywomen, the Women's Press, Sheba and Pandora, to name only the best known of them: volumes of history, politics and sociology; of contemporary poetry, plays and fiction, travel-writing, essays and translations – the list goes on – as well as the reprinting of an astonishing raft of writers whose works had been forgotten or neglected (a baker's dozen taken at random from my shelves of green-spined Virago Modern Classics: Antonia White, Willa Cather, Dorothy Richardson, Radclyffe Hall, Zora Neale Hurston, Ann Petry, Tillie Olsen, Elizabeth Taylor, Charlotte Mew, Christina Stead, Charlotte Perkins Gilman, Sylvia Townsend Warner, Rosamund Lehmann, all by the mid-'80s). A plethora of journals appeared, including *Women: A Cultural Review, Women Writing, Red Rag,* and the most popular, *Spare Rib,* a monthly magazine which brought together feminist politics and creative work in the arts and culture at large. I wrote a handful of film and television reviews for them and published extracts from the beginnings of a novel.

The opening section of articles circle many of the questions then asked as to what 'women's writing', a still-outlandish term in the early '80s, might be. Feminists in the US had led the way.[3] Did women writers write differently? If so, how? Did women offer different insights from their male contemporaries and come at literary forms and genres from another perspective, or did they have more in common with their contemporaries writing in similar genres than with female writers in the past? How might their works have been treated differently by those who reviewed them? Clearly these questions went beyond a close reading of the words on the page and beyond looking at literary traditions to exploring the conventions and assumptions of the society in which women wrote and the definitions of femininity. They were questions which also inspired experiments in contemporary writing. At new national gatherings, like that of the 'Women's Writing Network', novelists, poets and dramatists – Angela Carter, Michele Roberts and Liz Lochhead, for instance –shared the platform with critics and scholars, elaborating their views or reading from their work.

(This was also before the standardising collective term 'academics' became common parlance, a later reflex of the marketing culture taking hold of higher education in the UK, I think.)

My first analytical article for a wider audience – on Daphne du Maurier and romance fiction, reprinted here – found a home in the quarterly *Feminist Review*, set up in 1979. Whilst being more academic in its tendencies, *Feminist Review* also carried pieces referring to national and international campaigns and activism, articles on sexual politics, lesbianism and race, as well as poetry and cartoons in the manner of countercultural magazines of the 1960s. It was not a professional journal aimed at a disciplinary subject area, 'research-driven' (the phrase did not exist), or indeed hoping to advance careers. Run by an all-female 'collective', not an official board, its first editorial announced that its members were all feminists and socialists. *Feminist Review* would 'bridge the gap between theory and practice', marking a difference from the more university-based 'women's studies' gathering pace in the US. My article appeared alongside others on sado-masochism and feminism; on the women's movement and the Labour Party in Britain, which took the form of a lengthy group interview with Party members; and on feminism and the family.[4]

Working on popular fiction was not part of my official postgraduate study. It allowed me to write about girlhood reading and books which were central to women's lives, but it was well below the radar of mainstream literary studies in the early '80s. My arguments for taking this reading seriously were aimed largely at left-wing male critics who sneered at the genre rather than at the literary establishment. It felt daring at the time but it was also part of a Zeitgeist. The team at Birmingham's Centre for Contemporary Cultural Studies, a maverick offshoot of the English Department led by Stuart Hall in the 1970s, had already published extensively on the idea of popular culture, especially on the question of its post-war 'Americanisation' and on working-class subcultures in Britain. An adult education course on popular culture was underway at The Open University (running from 1982–7). Thinking about class meant thinking about the term 'popular': did it only signal the indigenous products and cultural activities of 'the people', whoever they were, often assuming some notion of the authenticity of that culture and of its resistance to the powers that be? Was modernity an increasing process of degradation, the hijacking of this culture by the market and the mass media, with its commercial products produced *for*, rather than *by*, 'the people' – the bestseller, the soap opera, the record industry, and so on? Could these definitions of 'popular' be reconciled? Should they be?[5] In 1985 I joined a Popular Literature Reading Group to discuss these questions and to put on events around them (including workshops on 'Popular Romance', 'Detective Fiction', 'Autobiography' and 'Children's

Literature'). It was a tributary of the 'History Workshop' movement, with its huge national assemblies of historians of every stripe from inside and outside educational institutions. The 'Pop Lit' group met in London in the kitchen of Raphael Samuel. A socialist and historian, Raphael had long taught adults at Ruskin College Oxford, the trade union college where History Workshop had been launched and where the first British 'Women's Liberation' conference was held in 1970.[6] (Reader, I married him.)

Living with and working with Raphael, who was a generation older than me and from an internationalist Jewish and quondam Communist family, brought my own Englishness home to me.[7] Raphael was the instigator of a series of workshops on 'History, the Nation and the Schools' held at Ruskin in the late '80s, a response to the idea of a core national curriculum in schools and the more strident assertions of national unity from Prime Minister Margaret Thatcher's conservative government. 'National history: for and against', 'Four nations or one?', 'Islam and Christianity', 'The British Empire' were among the topics debated, with traditionalists also putting their views.[8] A two day workshop on 'patriotism' and British national identity at London's Institute for the Contemporary Arts was followed by a 'two-day teach-in and conference' at Ruskin on 'The Future of English' in June 1991 in which I was heavily involved.[9] Over four hundred attended, mostly schoolteachers, but also policy-makers and lecturers from across the sectors. It opened with a plenary panel on 'Firing the Canon: for and against the idea of an *English* Literature' while the forty odd sessions included pedagogic discussions of current practice and recent government policy as well as panels on the history of how English, in all its varieties, had been and was being taught: primary school English, 'feminism and English literature', 'media Teaching', 'race and reading in the classroom', 'nineteenth century Shakespeare', the history of literacy teaching and more. The event was hugely enjoyable but was virulently attacked by the right-wing press. The *Daily Telegraph* deemed the conference 'devoted to the mechanics of subversion'.[10]

In these years what was often called 'continental theory' brought its own sense of renovation or rejuvenation to the subject of English, as echoed in the title of the 'New Accents' series, which included the influential *Critical Practice* (1980) by Catherine Belsey, intended as the antithesis of 'practical criticism'. In English departments the apparent disinterestedness of literary criticism with its idea of a universal reader un-located in time and place was under attack, but as histories of English were written, they also showed that it had long been a protean subject and frequently a radical one.[11] Emerging in the 1880s in the working-class mechanics institutes and as a subject women might be eligible to study, English was the modern and more democratic alternative to the stranglehold exercised by Classics at the ancient universities. English, in other words, was often in crisis and renewed itself frequently. Witness 'the New English', for instance, of the 1960s in schools, with its determinedly child-centred pedagogy. I myself was the beneficiary of the ideals behind a liberal education with its emphasis upon expressivity and growth and a history of 'missionary work' among the poor and in inner city schools. It was important not to caricature that history.[12]

'Theory' was good to think with. In particular it was a way of making strange what seemed natural or familiar in the culture (Roland Barthes's *Mythologies* was an early key text). I was puzzling my way into understanding the English middle classes and found the idea of anthropologising these other tribes, their habits and values, very sympathetic. Several pieces here – on Agatha Christie, Anita Brookner *et al* – belong to this inquiry, which became my first book.[13] Alternately, being able to theorise meant putting my experience at arm's length, querying the notion of a fixed or unified identity, and refusing to see either as the automatic grounds for moral superiority, as if being a woman was a vindication in itself (writing on Stevie Smith, I explored the ambivalent strategies of women poets who were deemed 'outside' history).[14] But 'Theory' reified and used only by a professional clerisy among themselves did not interest me very much; it ossified too quickly into formulaic or automatic phrases, a jargon or at worst a dogma.

I can only gesture here towards a cultural history which needs to be written. In the first place it would look to the margins, to informal collaborative efforts and events where teachers in schools, in further education and adult education, as well as the universities and polytechnics, intermingled. Reading groups like 'Literature Teaching Politics' were part of a national network of teachers and students who produced their own journals for national circulation. My article on Alice Walker's *The Color Purple* drew on my teaching adults but was part of a group presentation by members of the Sussex University LTP. The piece on Stevie Smith originally appeared, in *English*, produced by the English Association, which was – and is - open to English teachers across the board, parents and other interest groups. The Inner London Education Authority ran annual summer schools for sixth form pupils on which I also taught. 'Against Empathy' was a talk given to a schools conference; it appeared in *The English Review*, a subscription magazine edited within the Oxford English Faculty but whose material was 'monitored' by schools and colleges with whom they liaised. Schools were often in the vanguard of change. I am struck by the fact that the front cover of another issue, also nearly thirty years ago, carried a photograph of Alice Walker. It flagged an article by Andrea Ashworth on African-American writers with the headline 'No Longer Hidden'.[15]

Feminist cultural politics generated a confidence and an alertness to the reception of work by women in cultural institutions and in the media. Slowly the addition of writing by women challenged the content of curricula, the boundaries of literary periodisation and the assumptions of literary criticism. In adult education an adventurous ten week syllabus might be designed by a single teacher – or co-taught – a few weeks in advance; the Workers' Education Association put on courses for adults with only slightly more supervision of content. In tertiary education the polytechnics moved somewhat faster than the snail's pace of a British university administration where the idea of a single discipline was often deep-rooted. In 1984 my first full-time job as a lecturer in English in the Humanities Department at Brighton Polytechnic meant teaching a degree in 'British Studies', working with philosophers, historians and geographers and looking beyond these islands to Europe, the Commonwealth and the break up of Empire. 'The canon', at least in this context, did not exist. But I was equally happy to teach Wordsworth or Dickens or T. S. Eliot. I wanted to expand, not curtail, the students' experience and their reading. What inspired me was a more generous conception of literary culture as a whole and, in turn, realising that 'literature' was only part of a far wider world of language use and literacy, of different reading publics whose interest in, or access to, print culture is hugely various.

These were years of discovery rather than consolidation. But in the polytechnic where I worked it was a far from euphoric time. The 1980s saw an unprecedented round of funding cuts to higher education implemented by an aggressively modernising Tory government, committed to the long-term monetising of education. The next stage, an expansion of student numbers, looked like democratising but wrong-footed many of us by introducing market mechanisms and new versions of 'accountability' drawn from the business model (heads of institutions were to re-imagine themselves as CEOs, with concomitant salaries). The so-called 'upgrading' of the polytechnics to university status in 1992 was presented as a levelling up, while in reality creating new research and teaching league tables, squeezing out anomalous institutions and courses if they could not conform to these new imperatives. And structures of employment, especially in the more traditional institutions, were resistant to change. In the '80s very few women were teaching; fewer still were black or from ethnic minorities. A conversation in the early '90s, with a well-meaning and supportive colleague at one of the colleges of London university stays in my mind. 'What percentage of women would you be happy with, would you like to see on the staff?', he asked me mildly. I still remember the shock on his face when I said '50%'. It seemed to him an exorbitant demand.

★

If the thirty-something woman of the '80s and '90s conjured here is charac-
terised by reading groups, collective projects, marriage to a socialist, teaching,
how outgoing and busy she seems! Yet it was not, of course, a time free of
argument and even acrimony and during this time I also left jobs in order to
work on my own. That other phantom – the writer – flitting in and out of
this account gradually took on more flesh. In the first place, writing for the
press meant speaking to a broader readership and expanding what I could write
about – film, for instance in *Sight and Sound*, a monthly magazine produced by
the British Film Institute. Journalism is an apprenticeship in economy: a strict
word length and a pressing deadline is a good discipline, accepting that one's
prose can be cut and amended, having a cherished article 'spiked' by editors,
means cultivating a workmanlike attitude to one's precious outpourings. From
1999 I also began to write for the *London Review of Books*, mostly essays of
3,500 to 5,000 words, long enough to think about pace and cadence, to vary
punctuation and the length of sentences; to play with effects and create the
drama of a paragraph.

In the years spanned by this volume, three books were written and a fourth
conceived. They are the absent presences shadowing these essays. At book-
length, writing can be more interested in itself, in an architecture that has
its own power; it has room for more formal experiments with structure or
technique or narrative devices, like switching tenses or using imagery from the
senses. It becomes a composition; more of an art; and it allows for more ampli-
tude of thought. Writing becomes re-writing over years, rather than weeks or
months. In my forties, after Raphael's death in 1996, writing became a daily,
central activity, not least because I had more financial security. The writer's
point of view is more to the fore in the essays in the final section of this
volume. But what does that mean?

Creative works – novels, poems, films and so on – offer their own complex
'inside history', speaking to their readers' dreams and desires, re-imagining the
possibilities of the social world whose values they also inevitably reproduce.
The cultural critic teases out the contradictions from which a work of art is
made; the tensions which give it a dynamic and which complicate its meaning. But I have often found myself arguing against the kind of reductive reading which sees literature as mere content, art as simply a repository of social
attitudes judged by one's own concerns. 'Against Empathy', a short polemic,
deliberately intended to stir up seventeen year olds at a schools conference,
emphasised the anarchic in art – 'the imaginable but unmanageable' – and
argued against the idea of 'relevance' as the main reason for reading. It fell on
stony ground. *The English Review* printed some of their responses, nearly all
hostile to the idea that literature should not be read as a hall of mirrors, reflecting

the reader's concerns or feelings. Partly I was playing devil's advocate, but I wanted to remind them how much reading and viewing relies on our losing of our selves and our bearings – and what a delight that is. Literature is much larger than life. It is also the place of the shocking, the appalling and the difficult, even the disgusting, which can be another kind of pleasure.

Feminists have long had particular trouble with the pleasures of art. Mary Wollstonecraft famously inveighed against 'the reveries of the stupid novelists' corrupting the minds and hearts of the women of her time.[16] The suspicion that art is a wayward fabrication, that the artist is both a maker and a liar, troubles modern-day puritans. But writers and artists stubbornly insist on the freedom of the imagination – or the operation of the unconscious – and on the centrality of the material or stuff with which they work, how it shapes what they are able to imagine; how its language speaks them. The sculptor Maggie Hambling's defence of her much-criticised abstract statue dedicated to Wollstonecraft took this line in an interview: 'I am not in control of what I do. The subject speaks through me when I work', she maintained, calling her way of working 'an erotics of the studio'.[17] Writers may see writing as a game or art as a solace, or strenuously wish to be freed from the shackles of interpretation; writing can release us from the passage of time, be 'a form of redemption', as W. G. Sebald put it;[18] it can seek to dissolve the ties of identity, as in Alice Oswald's reworking of Greek myths in her long poetic sequence, *Nobody*.

In the '80s and '90s the work of Virginia Woolf, perhaps more than any other twentieth-century author, was a focus for feminist discussion of this tension, put crudely, between art and politics. She looms large in the final section of this book. Before the early '80s Woolf's work was barely discussed in British universities where she was chiefly known as an experimental novelist (the influential Cambridge critic, F. R. Leavis, had famously dismissed her as 'a slender talent', excluding her work from 'the great tradition' of the British novel). Following on from Quentin Bell's revelatory biography of Woolf (1972) and wider interest in 'Bloomsbury', Woolf's semi-fictionalised essay of 1929 *A Room of One's Own*, arguing for female intellectual freedom and financial independence, was reprinted in paperback in the UK. It became one of the founding texts of second wave feminism and of feminist literary criticism. As Woolf's several volumes of diaries appeared, edited by Anne Olivier Bell and published between 1977 and 1984, and the full extent of Woolf's *Collected Essays* were published by 1986, the sheer scope of her writing and her utter commitment to it emerged. Woolf was pre-eminently a writer of fiction but she was also a biographer, critic and essayist whose reading took in centuries of English literature, a champion too of the so-called lesser genres, such as letters, memoirs and diaries.

In the UK Michele Barrett's *Virginia Woolf: Women and Writing* published by the Women's Press in 1979 was a pioneering collection. It assembled a number of Woolf's essays reclaiming other women writers, often pointing up the social and sexual constraints on their creativity. Yet as Barrett pointed out, Woolf remained attached to a Romantic, even mystical, vision of beauty and of the integrity of the work of art, transcending society. She frequently repudiated anger in her writing – it marred Charlotte Brontë's *Jane Eyre*, in her view; she disliked the label 'feminist' and typically, in a talk to the Artists International Association in 1936, she took the line that to mix art and politics was to 'adulterate' the former.[19]

As a postgraduate at Sussex University in 1981, I first encountered Woolf through *A Room of One's Own* and her diaries. How could someone who privately held such spiteful and vitriolic views of the women who worked for her be claimed as a feminist? My Woolf was always a profoundly English Woolf, riddled with all the insular attitudes of her sheltered upbringing. And yet the risks she took as a writer! Few writers could face as she did the failings which torment them, analysing her hateful feelings, probing the place of fear and aggression in her life. *Three Guineas* saw all forms of masculine authority as shading into authoritarianism (a position also taken up by radical feminists in the 1970s), yet how dangerous to believe, as she appeared to, that she wrote from a kind of obliteration; from a position of utter passivity. Writing was the place where a self might be temporarily composed but where the writer must also remain invisible, efface herself and eschew authority. Be an outsider, she urged herself, full of contempt for any kind of honour or celebrity.

Woolf's works received a feminist imprimatur in the UK when they came out of copyright in 1991 and were reprinted by both Penguin Classics and Oxford University Press World Classics with women scholars at the helm as editors. I was intrigued that *Flush*, her most popular book, was initially omitted. Her spoof-biography of Elizabeth Barrett Browning's spaniel is hard to categorise. It was meant as a joke and became a shaggy dog story which ran away with itself. Shamelessly escapist and about escape, Flush is released from his Englishness, from the obsession with breeding and status and ultimately from the constraints of gender (though Woolf was not so lucky; *Flush* was deemed 'exquisite' and seen, as she knew it would be, and her most 'ladylike' book). Woolf could play with biography – and history from below – by giving us an affectionate and mocking relation to the Victorians. As he questions the concept of identity, Flush becomes a Canine Modernist.

Animals represented for Woolf what she called 'the play-side of life'. They embody a kind of wishfulness for human beings trapped in their histories and cultures, a desire to escape what defines them, including language. But they also represent bestiality – the animal within. In Woolf's ideal world Flush escapes the body altogether; he becomes 'nothing', a non-entity. One of my justifications for including in this volume my own lengthy introduction to *Flush* is that it allowed me to write about the escapism of art but also Woolf's fraught relation to writing about the body, the way that the threat of 'animality' surfaces in her perceptions of class and racial differences. There is another 'dogsbody' in *Flush*: the troubling presence of the servant whose life, Woolf felt, she could not write. *Flush* took me further into writing the lives of these 'real people', including the servants who worked for Virginia Woolf. And it was my return to life after Raphael's death.

Like Flush, biography is a mongrel. Once seen as extraneous to literary studies, as amateur or dilettante, writing lives is now a respectable activity in academic departments. Indeed, ironically, 'life-writing' as a term has signalled both an opening up to every kind of life and how it is recorded, and its potential academicisation. The final article in this volume was a talk given at a Centre for Life-writing at Wolfson College, Oxford, to practitioners of different kinds: those writing about young children or considering the dilemmas of documenting the lives of refugees, recording the memories of activists on rent strikes, writing their own memoirs or analysing testimonies of different kinds. I had begun a memoir of my own, using my diaries as 'evidence' toward writing a history of my first marriage. What was I to make of the life of Raphael's mother, Minna, an ardent Communist in the '30s and '40s, who firmly believed, as the Party dictated, that the personal life should be subordinated to the greater good and that the very idea of the individual self might be a corrupting malformation? Does the life need the self? Isn't the individualism of our culture part of the problem? How, I asked, were we to write group lives conveying the force of a generation or a collective politics? And what of those cultures which do not share the European notion of individuality or where the notion of privacy makes no sense?

The essay also reflects on Woolf's memorable invention of 'Shakespeare's sister' in *A Room of One's Own*. Shakespeare's sister, in Woolf's imagining, is both a martyr and a victim, a frustrated woman artist and a lonely genius battling against oppressive circumstances. Her sister under the skin is the heroine. Both are today the staple of endless biopics and girls still grow up – as I did – 'in training for a heroine', looking for role models. (Maggie Hambling's abstract statue was partly meant to avoid the monumentalising of Woollstonecraft.) A belief in the fiction of individual self-fulfillment, the Romantic idealisation of the writer as a unique individual can motivate but also paralyse (as it did the avid diarist Jean Lucey Pratt, whom I write about here). And the language of ownership is far from neutral and not entirely appealing. No room, no self, exists outside history. Language is always shared and social as well as personal: one of Woolf's social class could never have committed the solecism of writing 'a room of *your* own'. Virginia Woolf made no bones about the financial underpinning of writerly independence. She suggested £500 a year at a time when the average wage was not much more than £70. Feminists sometimes forget that she was referring to a private income, that is, from stocks and shares or rents, not a job. Her honesty does not diminish her as a writer in my eyes. Quite the reverse. And as a person she remains human, not a heroine.[20]

★

In one's late sixties the urge to pontificate is strong and must be resisted. I have written my last three books largely outside the academy but this has not been a matter of mastering institutions so much as sidestepping them, sometimes fleeing them altogether. I have never applied for promotion; my recent professorships have been honorary; and my emoluments – a lovely word derived from the payment for the grinding out of corn! – have dwindled until they have now petered out altogether. I have loathed the marketisation of the university, but there has been, I think, a self-protective timidity, a hatred and fear of competition, as well as a cussedness in my needing to move on. Perhaps a fantasy of fecklessness is closer to my heart than that which fuels the work ethic; or perhaps, conversely, I harbour the old proletarian ambition of being my own boss. In whatever battered form, I hang on to the remnants of childhood values which were not money values. I can call myself a writer nowadays without demur because that too, thanks to the internet, is far less grand than it used to be. The romance that once made the word fragrant now barely lingers.

But this, I remind myself, is not to be a credo or apologia. It is only a brief exercise in what the cultural critic, Walter Benjamin, called 'reading oneself backwards', his description of how memory works to build up a self from the fragmentary nature of what is remembered. History and memory may be irreconcilable. Woolf put it provocatively in her diary, 'But indeed nothing happens at one moment rather than another. The history books will make it much more definite than it is'.[21] She was pondering the different temporalities within which we live – inside history but a history which is always made up of present moments where our sense of time fluctuates and follows different rhythms. In much of her work Woolf wanted to capture the indeterminacy of the present before it is shaped into the story we tell of ourselves or is made into a history, the story of a shared past. And that mournfulness of mine, what is it but grief at the way the past comes to seem inevitable in our telling of it?

How we organise our accounts of the past and of ourselves depends on the vista granted to us by what Woolf called in her memoirs, 'the platform of the present'. I imagine the platform of the present, the moment of writing, as a pier or a landing stage, flimsily built and precariously jutting out over the waves. I can look through its wooden slats at the sunlit water swirling mysteriously beneath, as I did when I was child, and we caught a local ferry from Portsmouth to Hayling Island across Langstone Harbour, or over to Gosport across the Solent. Yet wherever I stood, and no matter from where I looked back, I could never see the whole picture. So much remained in the shade.

★

I would like to thank Simon Cooke, Erica Carter, Gill Plain and John O'Halloran, for their help with this piece.

NOTES

1. The phrase is owed to oral history: *The Myths We Live By*, eds, Raphael Samuel and Paul Thompson (1990).
2. Zoe Fairbairns's first novel, *Benefits*, a feminist dystopia where the patriarchal state uses the social security system to repress women, was published by Virago in 1979.
3. Most influential were Ellen Moers, *Literary Women* (1976); Elaine Showalter, *A Literature of Their Own* (1977); and Tillie Olsen, *Silences* (1978) but see also Rosalind Coward, 'Are Women's Novels Feminist Novels?', *Feminist Review* 5 Summer 1980.
4. *Feminist Review* 16 Summer 1984. I was a member of the collective 1988–1993.
5. *People's History and Socialist Theory* (1981), ed. Samuel, is a useful way into these debates.
6. 'History Workshop' became both a series of national and international meetings, with up to two thousand attendees and a journal, the latter still publishing. For documents, memoirs and critique relating to its history, see *History Workshop: A Collectanea 1967–1991*, ed. Samuel (1991).
7. I have written about this at more length in *A Radical Romance: A Memoir of Love, Grief and Consolation* (2019).
8. Key texts for these debates included Beverley Bryan, Stella Dadzie, Suzanne Scafe, *The Heart of the Race: Black Women's Lives in Britain* (1985); Paul Gilroy's *There Ain't No Black in the Union Jack: The Cultural Politics*

of Race and Nation (1987); Stuart Hall's *The Empire Strikes Back: Race and Racism in 70s Britain* (1992).

9. See the three volumes of *Patriotism: The Making and Unmaking of British National Identity,* ed. Samuel (1989).

10. *The Daily Telegraph*, 20 June 1991.

11. See *Rereading English*, ed. Peter Widdowson (1982); Raymond Williams, *Writing in Society* (1983); Chris Baldick, *The Social Mission of English Criticism, 1848–1932* (1983); Bryan Doyle, *English and Englishness* (1989).

12. I explored this further in 'Two Cheers for Liberal Education', in *Dialogue and Difference: English into the Nineties*, eds Peter Brooker and Peter Humm (1989).

13. *Forever England: Femininity, Literature and Conservatism between the Wars* (1991).

14. Despite the first woman Prime Minister in Britain being a Tory, little was written about conservatism and women, Beatrix Campbell's *The Iron Ladies: Why Do Women Vote Tory?* (1987) being the exception.

15. *The English Review*, Vol. 3 Issue 3 February 1993. This issue, featuring women as 'creators and creations', also carried an article by a male sixth-form teacher about teaching Margaret Atwood's *A Handmaid's Tale* in a boy's boarding school.

16. *A Vindication of the Rights of Woman* (1792), Part I chapter 13.

17. Interview with Maggie Hambling, *The Guardian*, 16 December 2020.

18. W. G. Sebald, *The Emergence of Memory*, ed. L. S. Schwartz (2010).

19. 'Why Art Today Follows Politics', *Daily Worker*, December 1936.

20. T. S. Eliot wrote pointedly to Emily Hale in 1932, 'Virginia's *Room of One's Own* irritates me; and I have wanted to tell her that I have never had £500 a year of private (unearned) income or anything like it, and that I have never had a room of my own except a bedroom at a Lausanne pension for month where I wrote most of *The Waste Land*.', cited Paul Keegan, *London Review of Books*, 22 October 2020.

21. Walter Benjamin, *A Berlin Chronicle* (1932); Woolf *Diary*, 18 February 1921.

PART I
FROM FICTION TO NATION

1

'Returning to Manderley': Romance Fiction, Female Sexuality and Class*

Last night I dreamt I went to Manderley again.

Thus opens Daphne du Maurier's *Rebecca*, published in 1938. With thirty-nine impressions and translations into twenty languages in as many years, *Rebecca* was and still is an enormous bestseller. Hitchcock made a film of the novel in 1940, its latest TV serialization was only a couple of years ago and even more recently it has been the subject of an opera. Whilst one study of its initial success claims that 'every good historian should read it in tandem with contemporary newspapers' (Beauman, 1983: 178), it's clear that *Rebecca* speaks as much to readers in the 1980s as it did to those in the 1940s. The story of the plain, genteel orphan girl – we never learn her name – who marries the aristocratic widower has got everything a romance needs and more: jealously, mystery, adultery and murder.

Jealousy and envy of her husband's first wife – the beautiful, upper-class Rebecca – propels the nameless heroine down the dark corridors of Rebecca's past. But in unlocking the secrets of Rebecca's character, the girl gets more than she bargained for: her husband turns out to have murdered Rebecca himself. All is not lost, however, for the heroine's bourgeois virtue triumphs and in the end she manages to save both her husband and her marriage. *Rebecca* is a rewrite of *Jane Eyre* amidst a nostalgia for the waning of the British Empire and the decline of its aristocracy. It's a lingering farewell to the world of Monte Carlo and of paid companions, to splendid breakfasts and devoted servants, the ease and arrogance of life in a stately home like Manderley, the Cornish mansion of the suave gentleman-hero, Maximilian de Winter. Obviously, it is

---

* First published in *Feminist Review* 16, Summer 1984.

a ripping yarn. But apart from that how do feminists and socialists account for the continued popularity and appeal of a book like this?

In the aftermath of Charles and Di, a lot of critical attention has been turned toward romance and its fictions, from Mills and Boon to 'bodice rippers' and the latest high-gloss consumerist fantasies (see, for example, Batsleer, 1981; Margolies, 1982; Harper, 1982). At the centre of the discussion has been the question of the possible political effects of reading romances – what, in other words, do they do to you? Romances have on the whole, been condemned by critics on the Left (although Janet Batsleer's piece is a notable exception). They are seen as coercive and stereotyping narratives which invite the reader to identify with a passive heroine who only finds true happiness in submitting to a masterful male. What happens to women readers is then compared to certain Marxist descriptions of the positioning of all human subjects under capitalism.[1] Romance thus emerges as a form of oppressive ideology, which works to keep women in their socially and sexually subordinate place.

I want to begin by registering the political dangers of this approach to romance fiction and then to suggest that we should come at the question of its effects rather differently. David Margolies, for example, (Margolies, 1982:9) talks in highly dubious ways when he refers to women readers being 'encouraged to sink into feeling' and 'to feel without regard for the structure of the situation'. 'Romance', he continues, 'is an opportunity for exercising frustrated sensitivity . . . inward-looking and intensely subjective', it is 'retrogressive' as a form of 'habitual reading for entertainment'. Such an analysis slides into a puritanical Left-wing moralism which denigrates readers. It also treats women yet again as the victims of, and irrational slaves to, their sensibilities. Feminists must baulk at any such conclusion which implies that the vast audience of romance readers (with the exception of a few up-front intellectuals) are either masochistic or inherently stupid. Both text and reader are more complicated than that. It is conceivable, say, that reading Barbara Cartland could turn you into a feminist. Reading is never simply a linear con-job but a process of interaction, and not just between text and reader, but between reader and reader, text and text. It is a process which helps to query as well as endorse social meanings and one which therefore remains dynamic and open to change.[2]

In other words, I think we need critical discussions that are not afraid of the fact that literature is a source of pleasure, passion *and* entertainment. This is not because pleasure can then explain away politics, as if it were a panacea existing outside of social and historical constraints. Rather it is precisely because pleasure is experienced by women and men within and despite those constraints. We need to balance an understanding of fictions as restatements (however mediated) of a social reality, with a closer examination of how literary texts might function in our lives as imaginative constructions and interpretations. It is this meshing of the questions of pleasure, fantasy and language which literary culture takes up so profoundly and which makes it so uniquely important to women. Subjectivity – the ways in which we come to express and define our concepts of our selves – then seems crucial to any analysis of the activity of reading. Far from being 'inward-looking' in the dismissive sense of being somehow separate from the realities of the state or the marketplace, subjectivity can be recognized as the place where the operations of power and the possibilities of resistance are also played out.

A re-emphasis on the imaginative dimensions of literary discourse may then suggest ways in which romance, as much because of its contradictory effects as despite them, has something positive to offer its audience, as readers and as *women* readers. It must at the very least prevent our 'cultural politics' becoming a book-burning legislature, a politics which is doomed to fail since it refuses ultimately to see women of all classes as capable of determining or transforming their own lives.

Romance fiction deals above all with the doubts and delights of heterosexuality, an institution which feminism has seen as problematic from the start. In thinking about this 'problem' I myself have found the psychoanalytic framework most useful since it suggests that the acquisition of gendered subjectivity is a process, a movement towards a social 'self', fraught with conflicts and never fully achieved. Moreover, psychoanalysis takes the question of pleasure seriously, both in its relation to gender and in its understanding of fictions as fantasies, as the explorations and productions of desires which may be in excess of the socially possible or acceptable. It gives us ways into the discussion of popular culture which can avoid the traps of moralism or dictatorship.

What I want to do in this article is to focus some of these points by a close study of du Maurier's *Rebecca*, a text which seems to me to provide a classic model of romance fiction while at the same time exposing many of its terms. Crucially, because, *Rebecca* concentrates on femininity as it is regulated and expressed through class difference, it illustrates and also investigates the psychic, social and fictive conditions necessary for a successful bourgeois romance.

A ROMANTIC THRILLER

Rebecca is in fact a tale in two genres – crime and romance. Both of these have been dominated by women writers in this last century (interestingly, Agatha Christie – 'the Queen of Crime' – also wrote romance fiction under the name of Mary Westmacott). The girl's romance and whirlwind marriage, however, only occupy about one eighth of *Rebecca*. Although this is the chronological starting point of the girl's story – the plot – it is not the starting point of the novel, or narrative proper. The opening chapter and a half of *Rebecca* are chronologically the story's epilogue, an epilogue in which the girl narrator and her unnamed husband are in exile abroad, homeless and disinherited.[3] The entire novel and clearly the romance take the form of a flashback. *Rebecca* takes the conventional romance story as its setting and as its own prologue; all the rest of the action takes place *after* marriage, after what traditionally constitutes the happy ending of romance fiction. Instead, the bulk of the text revolves around the girl's jealous pursuit of Rebecca's character and of her death. Once these enigmas have been solved they will explain the curious situation of the couple as expatriates which opens the story and will bring it full circle. I want to follow this structural movement of displacement and return, as it is narrated by the girl. I want to argue that through it *Rebecca* can investigate the terms and conditions of romance for women, both fictionally and socially. The novel becomes a thriller which goes behind the scenes of the romance drama.

'*I'm asking you to marry me, you little fool.*' This irresistable proposal (du Maurier, 1975: 36) is the climax of the romance between the 'red-elbowed and lanky haired' girl (20) and 'the man who owns Manderley', as Maxim is first designated in the dining-room of the Monte Carlo hotel where they meet. Their marriage – which takes place against all odds, and much to everyone's amazement – would itself have furnished the standard plot of a contemporary Berta Ruck or Barbara Cartland romance (Anderson, 1974). Yet it is this category of romance that the girl immediately begins to question and that is as troubling as it is reassuring:

> Romantic, that was the word . . . Yes, of course. Romantic. That was what people would say. It was all very sudden and romantic . . .(61).

From here she is led on to compare her 'raw ex-schoolgirl' dream to the adult love-story she imagines took place between Maxim and Rebecca. What makes the girl insecure about 'romance' is not simply her youth and lack of sexual experience, but crucially its expression in the class difference between her and Maxim, her and Rebecca. Much is made of her dowdy and inelegant clothes, of exactly how much she earns, of her down-at-heel middle-class niceness. Obviously their marriage is not one of social equals. Maxim makes this explicit in a comparison which demonstates how class interprets and regulates sexual behaviour and expectations:

> instead of being companion to Mrs Van Hopper you become mine, and your duties will be almost exactly the same (58).

Not surprisingly, the girl finds this both comforting and profoundly depressing. Thus her initial jealousy of Rebecca is one of her confident social and sexual place, since for women the one must secure and define the other. Where Rebecca was 'mistress of Manderley' the girl 'is no great lady' (79). And more importantly the girl begins to imagine that Rebecca's aristocratic lineage allowed her a passionate and equal sexuality which her own bourgeois model of femininity, with its stress on companionship and duty, does not. Rebecca's class difference makes her seem more mature, more adult, both socially and sexually. In the course of the novel the girl idealizes her as the expression of all the other possible versions of female sexuality which her own middle-classness excludes. Rebecca disrupts the girl's romantic model and leads her to search for a 'successful' marriage which will also legitimize female sexual desire. For the girl to find a secure social identity (a name) as Maxim's wife, Rebecca's difference must be reinterpreted. From being the girl's imaginary ideal, she has to become her nightmarish enemy. No longer the perfect wife, hostess and lover, she is to branded by the end of the novel as lesbian and whore.

So the key question of romance that the girl asks – does Maxim really love her? – comes to depend on the answer to an earlier question – did Maxim love Rebecca? If so, how can he love both, so different? This then raises the question of the nature of Rebecca's difference – what was Rebecca like? On returning to Manderley, the girl begins to pick up clues which lead to the discovery of Rebecca's mysterious death. It is no coincidence that the exploration of Rebecca's sexuality is imaginatively recast in the novel as a crime story. The text shifts between a fiction which idealizes and constructs harmonious models for human relations – romance – and one which starts from the violent disruption of the social – crime. This shifting marks out the distance which the girl and the reader have to travel in coming to understand Rebecca's significance as a seductive but ultimately tabooed expression of femininity. What is more *Rebecca* is a who-dunnit with a difference. Not only does the culprit get away with murder and ostensibly with the reader's approval too, but the innocent witness is called upon to become an accomplice. The girl agrees to keep secret the facts of Rebecca's murder in order to find true romance with the criminal, finally to get her man.

The problem is that in pursuing Rebecca the girl has identified with her as a positive alternative to herself. What then is dramatized is a scenario of extraordinary force and suspense. It is nothing less than an enactment of the power relations upon which successful bourgeois marriage depends, and upon which the institution of its oppressed female heterosexuality turns. What the girl has to attempt, and what she must compulsively repeat in the telling of the tale, is a kind of self-murder. It is a violent denial of those other versions of female sexuality which Rebecca has come to represent.

Rebecca, then, is the focus of the novel's conflicting desires for and descriptions of the feminine. She is the character through whom the fiction of romance is undermined and whose murder will rescue and re-establish its norms. She jeopardizes the given social categories by existing outside them. And it is from this point of social and sexual disruption that the novel and its narrator must always draw back. From the outset, the novel acknowledges that the regulation of female sexuality finds its weapon in the expression of class difference. In so doing, it threatens to expose the social construction of all sexuality and the inherent instability of *all* those class and gender definitions. The narrative's circular structure thus tries to mop up and gloss over the disorder at its centre. It constantly disproves the girl's opening assertion – 'we can never go back' (8). Going back is precisely what *Rebecca* is all about: returning to Manderley, to the primal scene of the acquisition of femininity.

Becoming a good bourgeois woman is shown in *Rebecca* to be a perilous process, one which can never be either fictionally or socially completed. *Rebecca* begins with the dream of a return and so it anticipates its own narrative strategies. It gestures too toward the dream of all romance fiction: toward a resolution of all the tensions within fictionality itself. It gestures to an imaginary realm in which the conflicts of class and gender differences might be transcended by an unproblematic and full female subjectivity. But as the story of *Rebecca* comes full circle it is doomed to expose as a failure the myth, which is at the centre of all bourgeois ideology, and is its ultimate romance – that of a unified and coherent self.

WHO IS REBECCA?

As the girl finds out about Rebecca in the first part of the novel, she herself begins to fade. Her fragile security as married woman, and indeed as woman, crumbles until she is brought to the point of collapse and almost of self-destruction. This is the first movement of the plot and it charts Rebecca's ascendancy. Slowly the girl collects the signs of Rebecca's difference: the raincoat (Rebecca's height and slenderness), the handwritten cards and accounts (Rebecca's elegance and efficiency as wife), the cambric handkerchiefs, silk lingerie and perfume which suggest her sensual and delicate nature, as well as her expensive tastes. Maxim's grandmother testifies to Rebecca's amiability and Frank Crawley testifies to her beauty. Rebecca was fearless and energetic, rode difficult horses and sailed boats single-handed, even in rough weather. The girl, who doesn't hunt, shoot or sail, likes sewing and doing the

odd sketch. Gradually the text sets up a binary opposition between the two
kinds of femininity which the girl and Rebecca represent. Virginal Lily and
sensuous dark-haired Rose; the girl occupies the East wing overlooking the
domesticated flower garden whilst the West wing, Rebecca's, is dominated
by the sight and sound of the sea, restless and disturbing. Rebecca emerges as
an aristocratic mix of independent and 'essential' femininity, a strong physical presence, a confident and alluring sexuality. The girl emerges as literally a
girl, immature by Rebecca's standards.

But these conventional oppositions are recast in an important way. For it
is crucial that Rebecca is wholly a figment of the girl's imagination, invented
from a sense of her own social and sexual limitations. 'Rebecca' is a projection
of her own desires which both help to produce and to ratify the girl's feelings
of inadequacy. Rebecca is in fact only the most complete moment and expression of the girl's longing for a secure place, socially and sexually. The narrative
is made up of a series of fantasies which the girl projects, all of which function
as an imaginary commentary on her lack of a fixed identity. She constantly
slides away from her real location in time and space to invent scenarios, for
example, between Maxim and the servants, which points up her failure to
become a proper grown woman and wife, to be a Mrs de Winter.

But whilst the reader is invited to share this process of disintegration which
the young romantic undergoes, she is also offered something else. There is
another twist. The girl herself is only a remembered and invented persona –
relayed back to us by the older-woman narrator with whom we started the
novel. The narrator is already projecting back into the feelings and thoughts
of an imaginary younger self. The reader knows then from the beginning that
the girl makes it, becomes that adult woman, 'older, more mature' (49). But
this twist means also that we can be given clues about Rebecca which the
girl misses and which come from the hindsight of the older woman. Thus
'Rebecca' the novel and 'Rebecca' the woman, are being simultaneously written and revised. The 'editorial' position of the older self and the insecure persona of the young girl are both available for the reader.

Our very first intimations of an alternative Rebecca come from the opening pages of the novel, from that dream-return to Manderley which finds it
overgrown and wild. 'Nature', we are told,

> had come into her own again . . . things of culture and grace . . . had gone
> native now, rearing to monster height without a bloom, black and ugly . . .
> The rhododendrons . . . had entered into an alien marriage with a host
> of nameless shrubs, poor, bastard things . . . conscious of their spurious
> origin (5–6).

The English garden has been overrun by natives in a kind of horticultural anarchy in which the proper order of class, family and Empire has been flouted. The passage neatly expresses social and racial disruption in terms of sexual – 'natural' – excess. This symbolism is given more force when the heroine is startled by the same rampant rhododendrons on arrival at Manderley. This time her homily on the politics of gardening is clearly linked to definitions of femininity. The shrubs are

> slaughterous red, luscious and fantastic . . . something bewildering, even shocking . . . To me a rhododendron was a homely, domestic thing, strictly conventional . . . these were monsters . . . too beautiful I thought, too powerful; they were not plants at all (70).

It turns out that these had been planted by Rebecca, her pride and joy. The lesson of an 'over-natural' and therefore deviant female sexuality is being mapped out.

Two processes are at work then in the narrative. As the appeal of Rebecca mounts, the girl begins to be dissatisfied with the romance between her and Maxim – bourgeois companionship now seems mere paternalism on his part, doglike devotion on hers. Rebecca becomes the figure which reveals the girl's unfulfilled desires. She is what is missing from the marriage; she is body to the girl's endless cerebration, the absent centre around which the narrative and its definitions of femininity turn. But even as the girl finds herself lacking, the older-woman narrator begins to hint darkly at Rebecca's 'real nature' and to signal to the reader that the distance between Rebecca and the girl is in fact proof-positive of the girl's superior femininity and true worth. *Rebecca* thus offers the reader the chance to have her cake and eat it, to slide like the girl between possible sexual identities, but unlike the girl to be in the know all along. The reader can have the pleasure of finding Rebecca desirable *and* of condemning her in advance. I want to argue this position is an androcentric one and fraught with difficulty for the woman reader. It is difficult because it offers a control of the discourses that define femininity, which women, since they themselves remain subject to those discourses, can never wholly enjoy. The reader, like the girl, wants to be like Rebecca, but dare not. And yet once that process of identification with Rebecca has been set in motion its effects can never be fully contained nor its disruptive potential fully retrieved. This narrative of wishful projection and identification, displacement and repulsion is then the story of all women, of what we go through in the constructing and maintaining of our femininity.

In fact the hints at Rebecca's deviancy become so obvious that the girl's social and sexual purity is only just about believable. When Ben, the local 'idiot', says, for example, 'You're not like the other one. . . . She gave you the feeling of a snake' (162). One wonders how the girl is still able to ignore the negative connotations of Rebecca's phallic sexuality. The point of this 'innocence' *is*, however, that it is almost wilful. The girls's inability to see Rebecca as deviant slowly becomes a *refusal* to do so, so caught up is she in the development of her own fantasy of a powerfully sexual and autonomous female subjectivity.

Of course it is Mrs Danvers, Rebecca's devoted housekeeper, who acts as catalyst and midwife here. She actively feeds the girl's sense of herself as 'a second-rate person' (80) until the fantasy of that other self takes over and actually begins to direct the girl's behaviour. In an extraordinary scene in the West wing Mrs Danvers acts out Rebecca's seduction of the girl, inviting her to touch Rebecca's lingerie, put her hands inside her slippers, to imagine her waiting in bed. Importantly, though, the girl has already performed these actions, if timidly: Mrs Danvers merely ratifies her desires. Shortly afterwards the girl day-dreams an incident between Maxim and Rebecca, with herself cast as Rebecca. Maxim who has watched her silent reverie comments that she looked 'older suddenly, deceitful' (210).

This desire of the girl to be like Rebecca reaches its full expression when, misled by Mrs Danvers, she unknowingly copies a fancy dress costume identical to one worn by Rebecca. This is the moment of her most complete social and sexual confidence as mistress of Manderley and as Mrs de Winter:

> Everybody looked at me and smiled. I felt pleased and flushed and rather happy. People were being nice . . . It was suddenly fun, the thought of the dance, and that I was to be the hostess (218).

'Being Rebecca' leads of course to her social and sexual disgrace, to the novel's crisis when it seems that the girl's marriage is all but destroyed. The girl wrongly interprets Maxim's horror at her appearance as evidence of her inadequacy, believing that her difference is her tragedy. Significantly alone in bed (Maxim fails to join her after the ball incident) she submits to Rebecca's triumph:

> There was nothing quite so shaming, so degrading as a marriage that had failed. . . . Rebecca was still mistress of Manderley. Rebecca was still Mrs de Winter. . . . I should never be rid of Rebecca. Perhaps I haunted her as she haunted me (242–244).

The boundaries which shored up the girl's identity have now been dissolved. The projection of her desire which the imaginary Rebecca represents now threatens to undermine not just the basis of her marriage but also to jeopardize the girl's only known route into acceptable middle-class womanhood and into being a person, a self.

This is when the girl decides to return to the West wing and when she hears the truth about Rebecca from Mrs Danvers. Tellingly du Maurier's description of Rebecca's childhood cruelty and ostensible heartlessness is shot through with envy and admiration. It is unmistakeably appealing:

> She was never one to stand mute and still and be wronged. 'I'll see them in hell, Danny,' she'd say. . . . She had all the courage and spirit of a boy. . . . She ought to have been a boy. . . . She did what she liked, she lived as she liked. She had the strength of a little lion. . . . She cared for nothing and for no one (253–5).

The key moment in Mrs Danvers's account of Rebecca's unnaturalness, of her refusal to be a good girl and a proper wife, comes when she describes Rebecca's relation to sexual pleasure – 'It was like a game to her. Like a game.' This is the giveaway, the telltale sign of Rebecca's criminality for which she was punished with death. The girl, however, is so immersed in her fantasies of Rebecca as a *positive* alternative to her own imagined failure as wife and woman that she refuses to listen. Her need to endorse other approved versions of sexuality leads her to contemplate suicide. Either she or Rebecca must survive – the two sexualities cannot co-exist.

This is the book's crisis. Now every attempt must be made to separate Rebecca out from the girl's and the reader's identification with her. Rebecca must be externalized, taken out of the realm of imaginary projections of subjectivity and put back into the world. This means that in terms of the text. she must be forcibly reinscribed within that range of social discourses which will condemn *her* difference and so legitimate the girl's. At this climax the girls is saved from suicide by the ships' hooters sounding a shipwreck. They also signal the return of Rebecca in person, as it were. Her body is about to be found in her sabotaged boat – 'Je Reviens' – and her coming back leads to Maxim's confession of murder. From now on the text runs all downhill in its rewriting of who Rebecca was. Maxim's final testimony needs only to be compared with that of Mrs Danvers quoted above, to gauge the disproportionate force with which the text reasserts its allegiance to a bourgeois morality, whereby women's pursuit of sexual pleasure outside of marriage must be brutally tabooed.

> She was vicious, damnable, rotten through and through. We never loved each other, never had one moment of happiness together. Rebecca was incapable of love, of tenderness, of decency. She was not even normal (283).

But this diatribe is a measure too of Rebecca's disruptive force: of what is at stake, fictionally and socially, that she needs to be so profoundly denigrated. This devaluation suggests too that for the girl and the reader once to have fallen for Rebecca is never to be free of the possibilities she offers. Perhaps after all Rebecca will have the last word.

REBECCA'S MURDER

What then is the significance of Rebecca's murder? To know this we have to know her crime. Rebecca refused to obey the law whereby women exchange their bodies for social place. Moreover, by treating sex as a game, she exposed the ways in which femininity is powerfully over-determined – definitions of female sexuality are not just saturated with class meanings, but produce them and ensure their continuation. Rebecca's sins have therefore been against the whole fabric of the social order – against family (her lover, Jack Favell, was her cousin), against class (she even made overtures to the workmen), against property (turning Manderley into a 'filthy den' (287)), and most importantly against her husband. Rebecca's most heinous crime, which drove Maxim to shoot her, was, of course, to taunt him with a future heir of Manderley who might not be his. What is at stake in her murder is the continuance of male authority and of masculinity itself, as it is defined through ownership and the power of hierarchy. The sexual and the social underpin each other.

Maxim's only attempt to mitigate or excuse his actions is via an appeal to a kind of aristocratic patriotism which offers itself as a moral discourse transcending the considerations of gender and class, even though the language of his sentiments is obviously steeped in them:

> I thought about Manderley too much. . . . Christ said nothing about stones, and bricks, and walls, the love that a man can bear for his plot of earth, his soil, his little kingdom (286).

Manderley here is Little England as well as Little Eden. Both are lost through the love of a woman. It is a measure of the social support du Maurier must have felt she could rely on that this crime of Maxim's can not only be forgiven but actually celebrated. Emphatically, the confession chapter ends:

> If it had to come all over again I should not do anything different. I'm glad I killed Rebecca. I shall never have any remorse for that, never, never (313).

Importantly, Maxim's revelations are recorded by the girl not in a mood of sober consideration (for after all, what kind of man remarries six months after murdering his first, and as he believed, pregnant wife?) but of heady joy. For a vital sleight of hand is taking place which will shift our attention from the crime back to the questions of romance, and in so doing establish the girl once and for all as model wife and woman.

Maxim's confession has a revealing sequence. It is not enough for him to admit to murder, he must also stress that he never loved Rebecca, that the crime was one of hatred not of passionate jealousy. Thus the girl's relief at Maxim's emotional 'freedom' can replace the problem of his guilt. Maxim's crime becomes a statement of his love for the girl and can then be recast as a test of her love for him. Now it seems she has the chance to be happily married after all, if she will agree to be complicit in the murder:

> I had listened to his story, and part of me went with him like a shadow in his tracks. I too had killed Rebecca, I too had sunk the boat there in the bay. . . . All this I had suffered with him . . . but the rest of me sat there on the carpet . . . caring for one thing only, repeating a phrase over and over again, 'He did not love Rebecca. . . .' Now at the ringing of the telephone, these two selves merged and became one again. I was the self that I had always been. I was not changed. But something new had come upon me that had not been before (297).

The girl, in becoming narrator of the crime, transfers her identification from Rebecca to Maxim, and invites the reader to do the same. Her own identity solidifies and secures itself around this endorsement of murder. She is no longer torn in loyalties between Maxim and Rebecca, between different femininities. The murdering of Rebecca is the price the girl must pay to guarantee the success of her marriage and to take on the status of good middle-class woman. She is rewarded with the identity of Mrs de Winter, the security of belonging to the male, but only at the cost of underwriting his definitions of what femininity should be. In order to become a social subject – to think of herself *as* a self – she learns to accept the regulation of female heterosexuality through class differences which themselves necessitate sexual competition between women.[4]

Yet for the girl to learn about Rebecca is in some measure to repeat Rebecca's fall, to lose her own sexual innocence. Maxim's cry of no regrets is immediately followed by his mourning of the girl's entry into womanhood. She no longer has that 'young, lost look'; she has finally got hold of that 'knowledge', which Maxim warned her earlier, must 'be kept under lock and key' (211) by fathers and husbands. If Rebecca's crime was to be too 'natural', too much of a woman, how then can the girl be both sexual and different from her? The text's confusion at this point is worth noting. Up until now

Maxim's and the girl's sexual relations have either been played down or literally written out of the text – their honeymoon takes place between chapters. Now that the girl has lost her symbolic virginity they are able to become real lovers: 'He had not kissed me like this before' (279). At the same time, their new happiness must not be misconstrued as *simply* sexual – 'there was', we are assured 'nothing feverish or urgent about this'. Nevertheless du Maurier must still add that their lovemaking 'was not like stroking Jasper, Maxim's dog, anymore'! This coy ambivalence points to the fact that, having discovered the joys of sex, the second Mrs de Winter must take pains to see that she does not end up murdered too. If Maxim found his first wife dispensable because of her sexuality, what is to stop him from finding his second equally flawed? Hence the remorseless logic of a Bluebeard. Women are all the potential victims of a femininity which is not just endlessly defining us in terms of sexual status – we are wives, mothers, virgins, whores – but which marks us as representing 'the sexual' itself. Where women's sexual desirability is competitively organized around male approval and social reward, there will always be a Rebecca who is both an idealized alternative to our elusive subjectivity and a radical undermining of it.

What saves the girl is her middle-classness. This is also what commits her to a cycle of repression and denial. Those other possiblities for female sexuality which exist outside the perimeters of middle-class femininity, and which had, in the figure of Rebecca, all but seduced her, she must now firmly repress:

> something . . . that I wanted to bury for ever more deep in the shadows of my mind with old forgotten terrors of childhood . . . (263).

And yet it is clear that Rebecca can never be forgotten since she is the condition for the girl knowing 'who she is'. As the girl's femininity is defined against Rebecca's, Rebecca becomes more, not less, important. It is their difference from each other that gives each meaning. The girl and Rebecca need each other in order to *mean* at all. In imagining the drama of romance as a murder, the novel shows successful heterosexuality to be a construct, not a natural given. Correct femininity has to be learnt, and whilst Rebecca's murder recalls all the discourses which condemn her, it cannot do so without revealing their social and therefore arbitrary order. Within such a system of differences the girl is equally a deviant Rebecca and this for the reader could be a potentially revolutionary reversal.

For the girl in *Rebecca* the impulse from which the story-telling originates is the desire, not to forget, but to remember. Her act of repression can be seen as one of definition and expression – the unconscious literally making sense

of the conscious in a dynamic, not a static relation. As older-woman narrator she looks back and relives the trauma of her marriage, within a narrative
whose structure is circular. For she must constantly refabricate the illusion of
her coherent social and sexual identity. As the ambiguity of the opening sentence suggests, she has dreamt of a return to Manderley and this dream keeps
on coming back:

Last night I dreamt I went to Manderley again. She becomes a kind of Ancient
Mariner of her story of middle-class femininity, as much the victim as the
producer of its fictionality. The more she tries to control her own life, tell her
own story, the more she is brought back to Rebecca who has disrupted and
defined both. It is Rebecca who is the named subject of the novel, she who
dictates its movement, pushes epilogue to prologue, and structures the impossibility of its ending.

It was Rebecca, of course, who originally drew me to write. It seemed to
me that there was a whole alternative narrative to be written from her point
of view. Bold, independent, cooped up with her stuffed shirt of a middle-
aged playboy husband, in the middle of nowhere, in a house surrounded by
grasslands and sea, Rebecca is the wife who refuses to go mad. The force for
my identification came though from du Maurier's own, from the image of a
confidently sexual woman which she herself could not resist,

> Rebecca seizing life with her two hands; Rebecca, triumphant, leaning
> down from the minstrel's gallery with a smile on her lips (284).

Rebecca's fictional come-uppance underlines all the more her dangerous
appeal. She has to be more than murdered. Not only does Maxim escape
freely and get a new adoring wife into the bargain, he is finally vindicated.
The dénouement reveals that far from growing a baby inside her, Rebecca was
growing a cancer. She would have died of her sins anyway, so there was no
harm in making sure. And then the final, brutally gratuitous touch: the doctor's X-rays, we are told, indicated a malformed uterus:

> which meant she could never have had a child; but that was quite apart, it
> had nothing to do with the disease (383).

Don't the forces of social and fictional retribution seem just a might excessive?
Even with all this overkill Rebecca refuses to stay dead. There *is* to be no going
back, but not in the sense intended by the new Mrs de Winter. There can be
no undoing of the crime she commits against herself in order to find a name.
Her middle-class femininity is to be her punishment as well as her salvation.

For middle-class readers in the 1930s Rebecca's murder appears to offer an ideal fictive solution to those all too seductive deviant femininities. It is less than simple, however. Rebecca is no longer 'out there', the wife in the attic of the Gothic text, but *inside* the female subject, the condition of its existence. The process of identification which the novel depends upon is, in more ways than one, fatal. For Rebecca does, after all, get what she wants. She lures Maxim into killing her and thereby alters forever the balance of his authority and power. Ultimately, she robs him of his place. For we know from the very first page that something goes wrong with Maximilian de Winter's *second* marriage. That initial and final mystery has still to be solved – the mystery of Maxim and his child-bride finding themselves homeless, countryless, and childless.

HAPPY EVER AFTER?

I want to stress that it is the ways in which class intersects with gender priorities that determine the denouement and leave it finally unresolved. The 'psychic' cannot therefore be seen as somehow existing ouside history or the 'social' but is in fact its material. Class and gender differences do not simply speak to each other, they cannot speak *without* each other. What is at stake in *Rebecca* is for the girl to become both wife of Maxim and mistress of Manderley, and it is the latter which she must forego. For if Manderley cannot be ruled or even haunted by Rebecca then it is inconceivable, within the imaginative model of social relations in the text, for the girl to take Rebecca's place. The problem of their sexual identification has to be dealt with equally forcibly in the arena of class differences. Notably, the girl's first action as a newly confident Mrs de Winter is to bully the housemaid and dismiss Mrs Danvers's stale menu. Both acts make her the mistress. Her new-found sexual status and her superior class position differentiate and strengthen each other.

The problem is of course that the girl's actions are here too Rebecca-like for comfort. On arrival at Manderley she had in fact deplored the wastefulness of its aristocratic kitchens – though typically the text dwells lingeringly on the breakfast spread before condemning it. Now she is throwing bourgeois thrift to the winds. The girl cannot stay within this ambiguous class position and yet it is equally impossible to imagine a happy ending for the de Winters within that original bourgeois romanticization of marriage. One cannot see Maximilian de Winter settling down to a cosy, middle-class existence, the model for which is provided by the cameo sketch of Dr Baker near the end of the novel and whose domesticity is felt to be both appealing and trite. The proto-type for Maximilian was in fact called 'Henry' (du Maurier, 1981); like Brontë's

Rochester, he ended up physically crippled and maimed. Daphne du Maurier decided after all not to call her hero 'Henry' and in so doing made it impossible for him to find true happiness pottering about the herbaceous borders with a wife busy sewing on the boys' nametapes – a fate suitable for many of the adorably dull husbands in the novels of the war-years to come.

Thus Maxim's loss of place, of Manderley itself, is a social, psychic and fictional necessity within the terms set up by the girl's assumption of Rebecca's position. It is interesting to see just how over-determined their self-imposed exile is. For it is certainly not 'realistically' necessary. After all, once Rebecca's cancer has been discovered and the verdict of her suicide accredited, what is to stop the couple, if not re-building Manderley, then finding another mansion house in the West country, or at least in the parklands of Surrey? Why do they have to leave England altogether? The point of asking these questions, which are of the 'how-many-children-had-Lady-Macbeth?' variety, is to see how certain possibilities are not imaginable within the text. Maxim and the girl must be left without a place. All kinds of necessities are met by their exile. Firstly, the text can invoke a compensatory moral discourse which equates Maxim's economic loss with a psychological crippling, and can therefore atone for his crime. Losing your stately home is a fair cop for murdering your wife. Secondly, the couple can be placed literally outside of the English class system and the problem of whose class position is to be endorsed, is neatly avoided. And this can then be the price that the new Mrs de Winter has to pay. Reading *Country Life* and listening to the World Service can thus be shown to be both a far sadder and a greater thing than to be mistress of Manderley. Notably, Mrs de Winter lacks those sons who would so obviously need a Home (see pp 74-75 for details), so again the problem of class inheritance and of competing notions of the family are sidestepped. The couple's exile is also used to appeal to a 'universal' Englishness and their position made poignant by relying on a mildly jingoistic patriotism with its dislike of 'abroad' and of foreigners, which had all the more force in 1938, with the Empire on the wane. The logic of Maxim's crime is, of course blurred and it seems that Rebecca is responsible for his loss of home, authority and even for the sunset of the Empire. Through her fall, the couple are exiled from their little Eden, leaving the garden of England to become overgrown by social and racial anarchy.

This epilogue is placed, though, as I have said, at the beginning of the novel. By the end of *Rebecca* the reader may well have forgotten these details and their relation to the plot. The text actually closes with the burning of Manderley, apparently instigated by Mrs Danvers (though we do not know this for sure; the conflagration is also a kind of spontaneous combustion). This is a far more ambivalent ending since it is impossible to mourn the loss of

Manderley without mourning too the loss of Rebecca who made it what it was – 'the beauty of Manderley . . . it's all due to her, to Rebecca' (287). The death of Manderley is in a way brought home as the real tragedy, as a place untouched by the demands of capital, a site of feudal freedom, which like Rebecca herself could at least operate outside of an encroaching bourgeois hegemony of social and sexual values.

Manderley has to burn to keep the whole range of readers happy, to leave Maxim and his new wife finally unplaced, free-floating outside of the allegiances of class and family. This is both the end and the beginning of the girl's story – where in fact we came in. Interestingly, unlike Jane Eyre, the girl does not find family and social place at the end of her story. She ends as she began, abroad, a paid companion. But the last page of the novel also ends with a dream, a dream of discovery which again has murderous consequences:

> Back again into the moving unquiet depths. I was writing letters in the morning-room. . . . But when I looked down to see what I had written it was not my . . . handwriting. . . . I got up and went to the looking-glass. A face stared back at me that was not my own. . . . The face in the glass stared back at me and laughed. And then I saw that she was sitting on a chair . . . and Maxim was brushing her hair. . . . It twisted like a snake, and he took hold of it with both hands and smiled at Rebecca and put it round his neck (396).

The dream points exactly to the act of writing as the moment of danger. For the girl in *Rebecca*, the narrating is both a making safe and opening up of subjectivity, a volatile disclosure which puts her 'self' at risk. Rebecca acts out in this dream what the girl also desires. Perhaps, then, the de Winters *do* need to go abroad to save Maxim's skin – not from the scaffold, but from his wife. Perhaps the whole of the narrative should be seen as a kind of displaced revenge, a revenge which the ordinary middle-class girl dare not acknowledge as her own, and which only feminism would allow her to speak.

REBECCA'S STORY – TO BE CONTINUED

The ending of *Rebecca* resists a simple resolution in favour of the middle-class reader. If the ordinary girl triumphs, that triumph involves a deep sense of loss. Du Maurier, herself a displaced aristocrat, was perhaps drawn to query that shifting of values which historically was taking place. The texts of the 1930s are full of these dying houses. *Rebecca* is unique, however, in using its aristocratic class mythology to interrogate bourgeois definitions of femininity. There is no straight-forward model for social mobility in the novel because what is central to it is the question of female sexual pleasure. However much Rebecca is finally condemned as a deviant woman, the text still does foreground the problem for women of desiring an autonomous sexuality. No doubt the novel is a snobbish farewell to Manderley but looking into the 1940s it also registers, I think, a collective gritting of the teeth by those women who suspected that so be a 'Mrs Miniver' would be a lesser thing than to be a Rebecca de Winter.[5] In the war years that followed, romance began to move into a more conservative terrain, one which tabooed the erotic and minimized the conflict between the demands of middleclass marriage and femininity, and the desire for sexual excitement and pleasure (Harper, 1982; Anderson, 1974).

Rebecca marks an outpost in the late 1930s, a transitional moment historically and fictionally, when the demands of middle-class femininity could be discussed and even dismantled within a public and popular form like romance. It demarcates a feminine subjectivity which is hopelessly split within bourgeois gendered relations. The girl's autobiography of gendered experience dramatizes the contradictory pressures which middle-class sexual ideologies were to place upon women, pressures which were in some measure to be responsible for their politicization some thirty years later.

Much of the popular fiction of the 1940s and '50s can therefore be seen as a space where women as writers and readers seek to resolve and secure a gendered and desirous subjectivity by celebrating a staunch British middle-classness, with differing degrees of inevitable failure. Like Freud's hysteric 'suffering from reminiscences' their writing continually makes visible the tensions within the social construction of femininity whose definitions are never sufficient and are always reminders of what is missing, what could be.

The continuation of Rebecca's disruptive story can be glimpsed and sometimes openly followed in the novels which in the 1950s began to centre on the pressures and contradictory demands of middle-class femininity. The bleak and abrupt closures of the early novels of Elizabeth Taylor, the comic refusal of Barbara Pym to write novels about 'a full life', describing instead the lives of elderly or single women, the silences and madnesses of writers like Antonia White, Jean Rhys and Pym herself, have to be understood also as responses to the decade's regulation of acceptable femininity through its public discourses on marriage, motherhood and home (Weeks, 1981; Wilson, 1977 and 1980; Birmingham Feminist History Group, 1979). It is not until the 1960s, with its renewed emphasis on sexual pleasure and with the happy housewives themselves breaking into print, that personal and marital collapse become openly the subject of many literary narratives. The shift from the Gothic 'Other' of female sexuality to its resiting within the individualized trauma of the gendered subject can no longer be contained. Jean Rhys rewrites both *Jane Eyre* and *Rebecca* in her own dramatic comeback, *Wide Sargasso Sea* (1966). This time the revenant mad wife tries to tell her own story and finishes it by coming down from the attic to set fire to the house. It would be wrong, however, to characterize this moment as one of social rebellion pure and simple. For within literary discourse, 'the return of the repressed' (Wilson 1980) is imagined by white, middle-class writers as actually maddening. Anna, in Doris Lessing's *Golden Notebook* (1962), finds a personal artistic freedom which is also a private hell, as much a place of individualized confinement as of sexual protest. Perhaps then it is not too fanciful to suggest that it is only from inside the collectivity of a feminist politics that Rebecca's story could ever be imagined without fear of social, psychic or fictive retribution.

POSTSCRIPT: THE FICTION OF ROMANCE

How then does *Rebecca* say anything at all about the formulaic fiction in which frail flower meets bronzed god? I would like to see *Rebecca* as the absent subtext of much romance fiction, the crime behind the scenes of Mills and Boon. For it seems to me that perhaps what romance tries to offer us is a 'triumph' over the unconscious, over the 'resistance to identity which lies at the very heart of psychic life' (Rose, 1983:9) *Rebecca* acts out the process of repression which these other texts avoid by assuming a fully-achievable, uncomplicated gendered subject whose sexual desire is not in question, not produced in struggle, but given. Above all, romance fiction makes heterosexuality easy, by suspending history in its formulae (whether costume, hospital or Carribean drama) and by offering women readers a resolution in which submission and repression are not just managed without pain or humiliation but managed at all.

Thus although women are undoubtedly represented as sexual objects, there might be a sense in which women are also offered unique opportunities for reader-power, for an imaginary control of the uncontrollable in the fiction of romance. Within that scenario of extreme heterosexism can be derived the pleasure of reconstructing any heterosexuality which is not 'difficult'. Romance offers us relations impossibly harmonized; it uses unequal hetero-sexuality as a dream of equality and gives women uncomplicated access to a subjectivity which is unified and coherent *and* still operating within the field of pleasure.

Perhaps then the enormous readership of romance fiction, the fact that so many women find it deeply pleasurable, can be registered in terms other than those of moralizing shock. Romance is read by over fifty per cent of all women, but it is no coincidence that the two largest audiences are those of young women in their teens and 'middle-aged housewives'. (See Anderson, 1974, for discussion of readership patterns and responses and Euromonitor for more recent data.) I would suggest that these are both moments when the *impossibility* of being successfully feminine is felt, whether as a 'failure' ever to be feminine enough – like the girl's in *Rebecca* – or whether in terms of the gap between fulfilling social expectations (as wife and mother) and what those roles mean in reality. That women read romance fiction is, I think, as much a measure of their deep dissatisfaction with heterosexual options as of any desire to be fully identified with the submissive versions of femininity the texts endorse. Romance imagines peace, security and ease precisely because there is dissension, insecurity and difficulty. In the context of women's lives, romance reading might appear less a reactionary reflex or an indication of their victimization by the capitalist market, and more a sign of discontent and a technique for survival. All the more so because inside a boring or alienating marriage, or at the age of fifteen, romance may be the only popular discourse which speaks to the question of women's sexual pleasure. Women's magazines, for example, do at least prioritize women and their lives in a culture where they are usually absent or given second place.

Patterns of romance reading are also revealing. Readers often collect hundreds, which are shared and recycled amongst friends. Reading romance fiction means participating in a kind of subculture, one which underlines a collective identity as women around the issue of women's pleasure and which can be found outside a political movement. As Janet Batsleer has pointed out, romances are not valued because like 'Great Art' they purport to be unrepeatable stories of unique characters, they are valued precisely as ritual and as repetition. It is difficult then to assume that these narratives are read in terms of a linear identification – it is not real and rounded individuals who are being presented and the endings are known by *readers* to be a foregone conclusion. Romance offers instead of closure a postponement of fulfillment. They are addictive because the control they gesture toward is always illusory, always modified and contained by the heterosexuality which they seek to harmonize. In a sense the activity of reading repeats the compulsion of desire and testifies to the limiting regulation of female sexuality. Romances may pretend that the path to marriage is effortless (obstacles are there to be removed) but they have to cry off when the action really starts – after marriage. The reader is left in a permanent state of foreplay, but I would guess that for many women this is the best heterosexual sex they ever get.

I want to suggest then that we develop ways of analysing romances and their reception as 'symptomatic' rather than simply reflective. Romance reading then becomes less a political sin or moral betrayal than a kind of 'literary anorexia' which functions as a protest against, as well as a restatement of, oppression. Their compulsive reading makes visible an insistent search on the part of readers for more than what is on offer. This is not, of course, any kind of argument for romance fictions being somehow progressive. Within the realities of women's lives, however, they may well be *trans*-gressive. Consumerist, yes; a hopeless rebellion, yes; but still, in our society, a forbidden pleasure – like cream cakes. Romance does write heterosexuality in capital letters but in so doing it is an embarrassment to the literary establishment since its writers are always asking to be taken seriously. Their activity highlights of course the heterosexism of much orthodox and important Literature. For, leaving aside the representation of femininity, what other models are available *anywhere* for alternative constructs of masculinity? Romance is not being wilfully different in its descriptions of virility as constituted around positions of authority, hierarchy and aggression. Male, left-wing critics might do well to address themselves to projects which set out to deconstruct 'normal' male heterosexuality – a phenomenon which does after all exist outside war-stories and cowboy books.

To say, as I have, that subjectivity is at stake in the practices of reading and writing is not to retreat into 'subjectivism'. It is to recognize that any feminist literary critical enterprise is asking questions about social and historical formations, not just as they operate 'out there', but as they inform and structure the material 'in there' – the identities through which we live, and which may allow us to become the agents of political change. Fiction is pleasurable at least in part because it plays with, displaces and resites these other fictions, and we need a language as critics of 'popular culture' which can politicize without abandoning the categories of entertainment. To say that everyone's art is somebody's escapism is not to underestimate the effects of a literary discourse, but to try to situate these effects across the vast spectrum of the production of meaning, of which literary texts are part. It would suggest too that it is not so much the abolition of certain literary forms which feminism necessitates as the changing of the conditions which produce them. I for one think that there will still be romance after the revolution.

If I have a soft spot for romance fiction then it is because nothing else speaks to me in the same way. It is up to us as feminists to develop a rigorous and compassionate understanding of how these fictions work in women's lives, keeping open the spaces for cultural and psychic pleasure whilst rechanneling the dissatisfactions upon which they depend. That then would seem to me to be the point of returning to Manderley.

NOTES

Alison Light is a research student at Sussex University working on a study of post-1945 British women's fiction. She also teaches on literature and Women's Studies courses in adult education.

Alison Light would like to thank Cora Kaplan for helping to clarify many of her thoughts and sentences.

1. I am referring here very briefly to the enormous body of theoretical arguments which have emerged largely from the work of the French Marxist Louis Althusser. For extended discussion of this work, and the different directions it has taken since the late 1960s see, for example, Coward and Ellis (1977), Barrett (1980). For an analysis of the historical and political relations between Marxism, feminism and psychoanalysis, see Rose 1983.
2. Barrett (1982) takes up some of these points but see also Coward (1982) and Rose (1983) for the importance of psychoanalysis as offering ways into the questions of subjectivity, representation and sexual politics.
3. In her original notebook for the novel, du Maurier put a lengthy epilogue in its proper place (du Maurier, 1981). All references to *Rebecca* are to the Pan 1975 edition.
4. *Rebecca* might also be seen – like all romances – as being about adolescence and as such a re-enactment of the choices and traumas of Oedipalization: Maxim replaces the girl's lost father (who gave her such a 'very lovely and unusual name' (27)), but is only able to become her lover once the girl has moved from identification with Rebecca's clitoral (phallic) sexuality. Mrs Danvers is important here as Rebecca's lover in an almost lesbian relationship. The girl moves to a passive 'vaginal' femininity, organized and defined by Maxim. I would argue that *Rebecca* also recognizes that moment of becoming a gendered subject as always involving a psychic division within the subject which continually resists the assumption of a coherent social and sexual identity.
5. *Mrs Miniver*, by Jan Anstruther, began as a series for *The Times* based on her own 'typically middleclass' family life. Published as a novel in 1939, it was a huge bestseller; the wartime film of the book is supposed to have helped bring the Americans into the war.

REFERENCES

Anderson, Rachel (1974) *The Purple Heart Throbs: The Sub-Literature of Love* London: Hodder and Stoughton.

Barrett, Michèle (1980) *Women's Oppression Today* London: Verso and NLB.

Barrett, Michèle (1982) 'Feminism and the Definition of Cultural Politics' in Brunt and Rowan (1982).

Batsleer, Janet (1981) 'Pulp in the Pink' *Spare Rib*, no 109.

Beauman, Nicola (1983) *A Very Great Profession: The Woman's Novel 1914–39* London: Virago.

Birmingham Feminist History Group (1979) 'Feminism as Femininity in the Nineteen-fifties?' *Feminist Review* no 3.

Brunt, Rosalind and Rowan, Caroline, eds. (1982) *Feminism, Culture and Politics* London: Lawrence and Wishart.

Coward, Rosalind and Ellis, John (1977) *Language and Materialism* London: Routledge and Kegan Paul.

Coward, Rosalind (1982) 'Sexual Politics and Psychoanalysis: Some Notes on their Relation' in Brunt and Rowan (1982).

Du Maurier, Daphne (1938) *Rebecca* London: Victor Gollancz; (1975) London: Pan.

Du Maurier, Daphne (1981) *The Rebecca Notebook and Other Memories* London: Victor Gollancz.

Euromonitor Readership Surveys

Harper, Sue (1982) 'History with Frills: Costume Fiction in World War II' *Red Letters* no 14.

Lessing, Doris (1962) *The Golden Notebook* London: Panther.

Margolies, David (1982) 'Mills and Boon – Guilt without Sex' *Red Letters* no 14.

Rhys, Jean (1966) *Wide Sargasso Sea* Harmondsworth, Penguin.

Rose, Jacqueline (1983) 'Femininity and its Discontents' *Feminist Review* no 14.

Weeks; Jeffrey (1981) *Sex, Politics and Society* Harlow: Longman.

Wilson, Elizabeth (1977) *Women and the Welfare State* London: Tavistock.

Wilson, Elizabeth (1980) *Only Halfway to Paradise: Women in Postwar Britain 1945–1968* London: Tavistock.

2

Fear of the Happy Ending: *The Color Purple*, Reading and Racism*

One of the many emotions I felt after reading this book was shame. Before I had forgotten or put aside my obligations as a woman, most of all as a black woman. Being wrapped up in myself I had forgotten the shit my sisters had to live through and even die for to put me where I am today: a Black woman able to think for myself, work for myself and plan my future.

(Review of *The Color Purple*, Gerry, *Spare Rib*, No. 135, October 1983).

NOVELS WHICH CHANGE LIVES

This piece grows out of an earlier contribution to a collective presentation entitled, 'Problems of the Progressive Text' given at the sixth Literature/ Teaching/Politics conference in 1985.[1] As lecturers in higher education we had chosen to discuss the specific delights and demands of teaching or studying those texts which appear to be overtly aligned with a left-wing politics, or whose radical reputation has gone before them, as it were. Alice Walker's *The Color Purple* (1982) seemed a good route into some of these issues since it ties together the major strands of a politics of difference – those of race, class and gender – in a contemporary bestseller by a black American feminist. Walker's story is the first-person narrative of Celie, a poor black girl in the Deep South between the wars; she relates, in a series of letters, the process of her eventual triumph over the most brutal forms of exploitation, her gradual recovery of

---

* First published in *English and Cultural Studies: Broadening the Context*, (eds.), Michael Green and Richard Hoggart (John Murray 1987).

her racial past and, via lesbianism, her claiming of an affirmatory sexuality. The novel, published here by The Women's Press, took the feminist world by storm even before it won the Pulitzer Prize in 1983. It has now been filmed by the Hollywood director, Steven Spielberg (he of *Jaws* and *E. T.* fame).

This tremendous take-off of a 'minority' text, however, not only highlights the problems of black writers being lionized by the dominant white culture; it raises also some crucial questions about the reading and reception of black writing by those of us, who, as white teachers and students, place or find such texts on the syllabus of 'English'. On the Left there has long been a deep and resourceful vein of 'countercriticism', criticism which reads 'classic' texts, the literary canon, against the grain, pointing up their complicity with dominant ideas and values and their refusal, however tortured, to admit the full range of cultural and social difference. Thus to teach a text like Walker's which speaks to and from those who are normally *absent* from the literary heritage of English, marginalized or oppressed groups, and in particular black women, sets us a different pedagogic and political agenda. *The Color Purple* is more about good subjects than bad objects; it closes with achievement and happiness, harmony and celebration – not topics which are easily accommodated by those left analyzes whose emphasis is finally upon struggle, strife and conflict.

In fact my own piece began from just such a nagging doubt about the pleasure of the text. How do we – as teachers – analyze a text which so many feminists, including myself, have felt to be about ourselves in powerfully involving and politicizing ways? Being on the side of the angels, such a novel brings forcefully home the fraught question of the influence and effect(ivity) of 'literature'. Do novels change lives, and if so, what (if any) is the job of criticism in relation to such experiences? How can the processes which the individual undergoes in reading be understood as part of that wider, collective struggle called politics? Further, what is the place of the pleasures of such a text – identification, affirmation, celebration – in political discourse and engagement?

These are some of the questions which I want to pursue here. To ask what goes on in the gap between reading and action is one way of trying to connect a cultural studies with a cultural politics, with what goes on *outside* the classroom. It is to refuse to polarize either 'culture' or 'politics' in a familiar opposition which designates the one as purely academic or aesthetic, and the other as divorced from the making of representations and their reception.[2] Instead we need to ask how the structuring of pleasures and anxieties in the practices of reading and writing help to maintain or disrupt our notions of our 'selves' in those other modes of our existence; what kinds of subjectivities are formed and offered by different texts and what are the political parameters and perimeters of our readings: what do they mean for different groups at different times in history and the culture?

Such questions take on an especially urgent form in relation to black culture when we ask them as white people in the 1980s. For how are we to understand our own 'identification' and solidarity whilst still acknowledging the political reality of difference? What indeed are we doing as white readers and white teachers when we read the black text? How are the meanings of our readings to be situated within an understanding of the history and formation of racial subjectivities? And how far do the writing and reading practices of what is revealingly called 'English' shore up and reproduce precisely, Englishness, a sense of cultural difference which depends in part on a notion of racial superiority and a history of imperial power?

The pleasures of reading and the power of racism, the connections between our supposedly private fantasies and our so-called public politics – this is an enormous area, and I shall do little more than skate across its surface. As was made clear by black delegates at the LTP conference, it is our own ignorance as white academics which has made for some pretty thin ice in places. Yet ironically, it is the passionate hopefulness of a text like *The Color Purple* which may at least help us to get our skates on. For Alice Walker's novel remains for me a profoundly inspiring and contradictory text because it is finally *utopian*: it is a fantastic success story, offering its readers an imaginary resolution of political and personal conflicts. It is the meanings and difficulties of this utopianism, how it might direct our readings and mobilize us politically, which I want to explore further.

PROBLEMS OF IDENTIFICATION

You got to fight. You got to fight. But I don't know how to fight. All I know how to do is stay alive.[3]

I co-taught *The Color Purple* recently on an adult education course, a group of about ten women, all white and mostly under thirty, although one woman was in her sixties, and of whom about half were graduates. After reading short stories (Kate Chopin, Katherine Mansfield) and extracts on 'women and writing' we chose *The Color Purple* as the only complete novel read, in the hopes that it would bring together our earlier discussions of race, class and sexual politics. Importantly, and perhaps typically, we were not looking at the text in the context of other black writing, nor even of American literature, but in the context of contemporary feminism. Nevertheless as tutors we were surprised that the discussion did not lead into the issue of racism, and at the ways in which it did not.

Our readings began instead from a position of identification rather than of difference. Many students, like myself, had found the novel deeply moving on first reading, and had been exhilarated by its ending. The opening passages of Celie's brutal treatment, in which she, as teller of her tale, is never ultimately left degraded or without dignity, and her finding of sexual pleasure or social peace – we all talked about the power and appeal of such writing in terms of recognizing, identifying with, and desiring such affirmation as women, white, working-class, middle-class, feminist or no. We felt strongly drawn into the novel because of its structure of Celie's articulation of her life. Yet it was staggering how quickly the discussion became negative when we began to 'criticize'. The shift from re-telling the pleasure of reading to analyzing its meanings was severe and dramatic. I noted down at the time that 'the book threw up the issues of its language and of Celie's development – who it was for – and of its possible romanticism. I felt people were being very heavy about the happy ending, as though it were necessarily a bad thing'.

I am still intrigued by that last comment – 'as though it were *necessarily* a bad thing'. Why were we so afraid of the happy ending and what does it mean for a group of white students to see as 'romantic' the empowering of an impoverished, beaten, raped and abused Southern black woman? Ironically, whilst we were involved in the novel's project as women, our critical terms for theorizing the questions of social and sexual conflict in a woman's life seemed to lead us into a disavowal of the importance of that process. We could only describe Celie's enrichment in a series of negative -isms: romanticism, idealism, sentimentalism, all smacked of dismissiveness. It seemed that as feminists we could never be satisfied with being satisfied; the novel's appeal to the possibility of an achievable, social and sexual transformation of your life seemed both deeply pleasurable and deeply suspect.

There were several issues at stake in this disjuncture. It might be that the problem was simply one of reading, of the strategies of English which brought with it an emphasis upon character and moral growth ('Celie's development'), and through whose distorting lens we had read the story and re-focussed it as an image of self-fulfilment and liberal humanist values, without realizing our own short-sightedness. This slippage from pleasure to displeasure could be seen as a function of English and/or Englishness – a refusal to engage with difference, all those discourses which make the text quite 'foreign' to our own culture. Alternatively, there seemed to be a special problem with the structure of the text itself, its first-person narrative which invited the mechanism of identification and needed it in order to be read. In both cases we are brought up against the complex question of politicization, either proceeding from the unifying claim to solidarity or from the fictional process of identifying, which leads us to wonder what part the formation of such 'identities' as woman, or black woman, might play in the generation of, and involvement with, any political discourse.

IS IT ENGLISH?

> The real question, however, it appears to me, is not whether poor people will adopt the middle-class mentality once they are well fed; rather, it is whether they will ever be well fed enough to be able to choose whatever mentality they think will suit them.[4]

Critics of the text, including some of my colleagues in the LTP presentation, have pointed out various reasons why *The Color Purple* is particularly vulnerable to the ravages of English. Unlike elsewhere in her work (in *Meridian* for example), Walker is not primarily concerned here with black struggle against white racism but with experience within the black community, within families and sexual relationships. This foregrounding of 'the private sphere' has made it possible for the question of difference, racial, sexual, social, to be ignored and effaced as a conflictual and political force and to be reformulated in the rhetoric of a liberal humanism (of which English is one discourse) as a repository of essential and eternal truths about a universal human condition. Celie's story in such a reading becomes a kind of latter-day 'Bildungsroman', her coming to power an embourgeoisment accompanied by the necessary modicums of moral wisdom and self-knowledge. Thus *The Washington Post*, heading the British edition, can call Walker's novel 'a fable for the modern world', reducing or transforming into myth the actuality of the social historical conditions and ideologies round which the text is constituted. Universalizing the specificity of the tale (the words 'black' and 'lesbian' do not appear on the cover of the The Women's Press edition), reproducing an invisibility to which those who are defined as 'other' are consigned by the dominant culture, such homogenizing makes the text more manageable, more marketable. Difference which is potentially alienating, frightening and challenging, is written out in favour of a transhistorical truism: as the advertising trailer for the film puts it, 'It's about life. It's about love. It's about us.'

Recent critical theories, notably within Marxism and feminism have made the exposure of this rhetoric of liberal humanism a prime target, and have revealed the ideological positions which have lurked beneath the appeal to equality, liberty and fraternity (sic). The claim of the white bourgeois male to full subjecthood has often depended historically and socially upon the relegation and exclusion of all others from just this status: the dark continent, the great unwashed, the second sex, all these others are pushed to the margins of humanity, sometimes, as in the racist theories of the nineteenth century, even denied such humanity.

But these naturalizations of the political in favour of the eternal drama of the humanist self are not the only potentially racist response. Ironically, those of us for whom this critique appears a political priority can be as much dominated by liberal humanism in our rejection of its terms as in any complicity with them. To reduce Walker's text to these discourses in order to 'criticize' it – a reading, which as white educated subjects we can well afford – is equally a way of holding on to a cultural supremacy, of denying and incorporating difference: an attempt at colonization. My own first reading, for example, saw Walker's visionary ending as akin to 'the synthetic and religiose American familialism of The Waltons'.[5] This cheap joke (which got me a laugh at the conference) betrays not just my own ignorance but a complicated travesty both of the actual history of white Americans (as opposed to the normative and conservative marketing of it on T. V.), and of the very different relation which black familialism has had to capitalism given the history of slavery and of racism itself, especially in the South. Similarly, (mis) reading the question of spirituality in the novel, wearing the cultural blinkers of English Protestantism, is to be equally ideologically blinded by our own cultural discourses; such misrecognitions can easily slide into a refusal to accept the very different meanings and possibilities which 'religion' has had for black struggle.[6]

English, then, moves in mysterious ways. At its most obvious it shores up the racist response of one student who literally could not read the text because its language was 'primitive', 'badly written': it simply wasn't English, in all senses of the word. More tricky is the colonization of the text via the naturalizing aesthetic of lit. crit. which collapses its cultural specificity into moral value, emptied of any social or political referent: a 'consummately well written novel' enthused the New York Times Book Review, whilst the US Tribune praised its 'sweetness of tone . . . the sweep and daring of its literary ambition'.[7] Both responses efface the material and political conditions within which black language emerged as a weapon against, as well as a consequence of, slavery, and as a means of creating and maintaining a separate and inviolable community for black people in the face of white oppression.[8] Yet those of us who reject the interpretation of Celie's story as yet another journey into bourgeois bliss must find ways of affirming black power and achievement; we can hardly want only fictions in which black protagonists remain powerless – we have had those for centuries. For without such acknowledgment a familiar double-bind operates whereby the black subject is robbed of history and status either by being incorporated and ignored by the dominant social order or by being made visible only

as victim, a helpless sufferer condemned to pain. Whether difference is therefore denied altogether, or whether it is (often simultaneously) insisted upon
only as lack and failure, both strategies work to subordinate black people. This
has long been part of our English inheritance, though such strategies have taken
on new historical forms since the war in our dealings with 'decolonialization'.[9]
The Color Purple is vividly at odds with the myth that 'freedom and whiteness
[are] the same destination'.[10]

Clearly, for white academics, part of the problem is that *The Color Purple* is
not about 'us' at all. Nothing is harder than for those who trade in knowledge
to admit ignorance. What is even more threatening is to feel that those outside
of 'our' dominant culture do have a knowledge and strength of their own
precisely *because* of being outside. Not only is it often the case that only those
who take privilege and comfort for granted are able to be dismissive about the
struggle to leave poverty and hardship behind; it is also such people who are
unable to learn that different lives produce their own equally important forms
of knowledge and community – knowledge, from which they are by definition excluded. Wanting *The Color Purple* (as I did) to lead into a discussion of
racism is certainly easier than seeing myself as marginal to its concerns. Thus
any real engagement with racial difference in the text (and in our politics) has
to be far more dialectical than any simple model of 'otherness' and its recupera-
tion or appropriation (embourgeoisment) within the dominant culture, might
propose. It means in part giving up the power of naming and of assuming
knowledge of someone else's struggle, accepting that there are things which
we cannot share, and intitiatives which we cannot create. Otherwise, as Stuart
Hall and Martin Jacques have argued

> our model of society is that the only things worth getting involved with
> are our things; others are not capable of creating movements and currents
> which deserve our support, enthusiasm and intervention. This is a very
> patronizing view of the world.[11]

And when white readers refuse to listen to the black voice, accusing it instead
of some kind of ventriloquism, such patronization is deeply racist.

There are many inroads to be made still into the territory of 'English', ways
of fragmenting that impulse to homogenize and thereby control the diverse
subjects and subjectivities which come within its boundaries. Cora Kaplan
has pointed to some of the strategies of re-education which the white British
reader might need in order to situate *The Color Purple* more properly in the
historical, social and textual relations from which it emerged.[12] But for this
process to be anything more than a textual encounter of the academic kind,

we have also to press hard upon our first 'naïve' readings which will tell us more about our own relation to difference, the assumptions with which we start and which structure our pleasures and anxieties as white readers. We need to return to our 'selves' not in order to wallow in guilt but because such selves are historically and socially produced. In doing so, however, it is clear that deconstructing 'English' is only part of the story since, as my own course insisted, no text can be read or written solely as addressing one form of difference; the structures of racial, sexual and class difference intersect and often contradict each other, offering a range of positions to the reader, never simply a unitary or unified one. It is to the positive possibility of these identifications which do not deny difference, but work in tandem with them, that I want now to return.

THE POLITICS OF UTOPIANISM

I'm so happy, I got love, I got work, I got money, friends and time.[13]

I have argued that *The Color Purple* appeals especially to readers of *all* kinds because it is utopian in its form: Celie gets it all at the end of the story, and through her we are offered this dream of full achievement, of a world in which all conflicts and contradictions are resolved. Whilst I have maintained that such fictions *mean* very differently for different groups in the culture, nevertheless there is a bottom level at which *The Color Purple* keys into a far more diffuse desire for personal and social changes, what Carolyn Steedman has called 'historically much older articulations – the subjective and political expressions of radicalism'.[14] The desires for a world in which all people might have love, work, friends, money and time, underpin political theories like socialism and feminism: an appeal to the possibility of amelioration, of 'progress', which is no less potent or mobilizing for being an imaginary vision, a happy ending still to come.

Yet it is the power and persuasiveness of these desires which the Left has so frequently found problematic, from the debates around Owenite socialism to the politics of the peace movement.[15] Part of the response – that fear of the happy ending – has been a definition of radical politics which sees itself as one half of a binary opposition (left as opposed to right), and conceives its job as one solely of critique from underneath the dominant culture, as it were. In this definition the day of *not* having to be on the Left never comes. This structural definition, however, offers little or insufficient insight into why people join and remain within political struggles, unless one assumes a rampant or global masochism. At its worst such a position becomes a moralistic kill-joyism which finds all pleasures in political engagement guilty ones, and indeed can see the question of pleasure itself as ideologically unsound. Running through such uneasiness is ironically a strong thread of empiricism, an insistence on the world 'out there' as separable and separate from the world 'in there' and a one-way model of determination. Such a model insists upon a divisive opposition which wrenches apart the field of 'the political' from that of personal or sub-jective space. The recalcitrant psyche, thus nominated, cannot then keep up with the revolutionary political/public Joneses and must be dismissed or deni-grated, either as outside of social or cultural change and determined by that 'outside', or as irredeemably interior – 'confessional', 'sentimental', 'romantic', 'private', 'personal' – depending on your century. Feminism alone, in its long dialogue with socialist theory, has pointed to the androcentricity implicit and produced in the making of these spheres. For clearly such demarcations of knowledge and power have political effects, working through and speaking through, for example, the meanings given to sexual difference.

Thus a novel such as *The Color Purple* can be popular with a whole range of women readers, cutting across the specificity of its black history, in its concern with family, emotionality, sexual relations and fantasy life. Walker herself has noted the operation of such collusive divisions of psychic and social existence in reproducing the inequalities of gender *and* race:

> black writing has suffered because even black critics have assumed that a book that deals with the relationships between members of a black fam-ily – or between a man and a woman – is less important than one that has white people as primary antagonists. The consequence of this is that many of our books by 'major' writers (always male) tell us little about the culture, history, or future, imagination, fantasies, and so on, of black people, and a lot about isolated (often improbable) or limited encounters with a non-specific white world.[16]

What is crucial in our understanding of the 'utopian' appeal of the text is not to reinstate subjectivity at the expense of 'the social' but to begin to dis-solve those polarities, seeing the structures and site of subjectivity as exactly (equally) social and historical, equally the site of the operations of power. Terms like 'sentimental' and 'idealistic' are not themselves transparent descrip-tions of knowledge or response. They carry with them cultural prescriptions and assumptions and have themselves to be historicized. Not coincidentally both women's and black writing have been accused of 'emotionalism'. We need to ask why this *is* an accusation. Who is calling whom sentimental, when, and with what effect?

So to call *The Color Purple* 'utopian' is the beginning of an analysis, not the end of it. Words like this signal the insistent presence of the demands of subjectivity – of how sexual and racial differences come to be lived and felt in the act of living – as being a pressure in excess of what is 'realistically' on offer in a culture. Fiction, like fantasy, is the place of this excess. It re-informs and re-imagines the scene of its production, the unconscious as well as conscious desires which social relations cannot or will not fulfil. In other words, these questions of the 'effects' of reading, of the mobilizing of desires and pleasures in the activity of reading, are questions about fictionality itself; the processes of reading and writing occupy *simultaneously* intimate and public (because lin-guistic) space, space where desire and history intersect in the subjects of those practices (writers, readers, 'characters') and where new subjectivities can be formed. Such subjectivities are shown to be constantly negotiated, constantly fragmented and contradicted by the differences (racial, sexual, class-based) which they simultaneously try to unify and encompass. These 'identities' are broken up as soon as they are forged, seeming only to remain stable at the novel's point of closure – the happy ending – but this is the point at which the disjuncture between 'fiction' and 'life' is most apparent, where you shut the book and go off to face another fragmenting day.

All fictions are utopian – though some more than others; the worry about how politically mobilizing fiction can be is a worry about the tension within the act of representation itself. Subjects, in texts as in life, are constituted and re-constituted around those cultural interpretations of, or meanings given to, difference, which always threaten to disrupt the security of defining one 'self' solely or fully as, for example, a woman, a black person. Literary texts, and pre-eminently novels, take subjectivity as their material, but to argue that any reader is either fully positioned by a novel or can ever fully resist its strategies is to underestimate the contradictory process at the heart of linguistic representa-tion: a process in which subjects, even as they gesture toward that idealized and coherent 'I' who will be marvellously coping, miraculously loving and loved, run headlong into the de-stabilizing actuality of what it means to be 'woman', 'black', 'poor' and so on, in the world.

If *The Color Purple* allows readers to speak their rage or their delight because of its appeal to a unified self, that appeal is precisely fictional, or fictitious, appealing because there is not and cannot be – other than in fictions – a safe and sealed place in which to find or be such a self. This self can be recognized both as an effect of language and of the attempt to heal the split demanded in the act of representation. It has also to be acknowledged, nevertheless, as a fiction which keeps us sane and active. For without such momentary fixings of the flux of subjectivity, the illusion of being a powerful and coherent agent in the world, how would we get out there and do things – how indeed can we have a political theory of action and responsibility? If we do not accept the force and temporary necessity of such identifications, textually and socially, are we not condemned to a theory of being which leaves us stranded in a quick-sand of discursivity, fascinated but finally immobilized by 'the play of differ-ence', fragmented always and totally, unable not just to act politically (to see and know ourselves collectively), but to act at all?

Perhaps it is not that we need to act as though we believe utopian achieve-ments are possible – that like Celie we really will get it all; rather it seems that we need to believe in such utopias in order to act, in order to survive as human beings, making our own texts and histories in the face of the divisions and conflicts in our psychic/ social existences which determine and fragment us. As Juliet Mitchell has written,

> We all live within ideology, both the general ideology of all human society and the specific ideologies of our times. It may well be the case that the humanist ideology is in itself only the liberal side of the capitalistic, free-enterprise coin – but we cannot escape it: must live ourselves (indeed, be ourselves) within its meanings while we are in such a society.[17]

To ignore the power of the fictional 'I', however much it is a figment of humanist ideology, is to risk denying the need which we have to believe that we are at the centre of our lives, a motivating need felt strongly too by those who have been oppressed by, and want to challenge the forms of this society. It is to risk robbing subjects of the chance to construct alternative histories of the world and of its power-relations, and of their politicizing visions of the future – however much we must insist on the ultimate fictionality of these accounts. For where would political struggle against oppression, against mis-ery, be without such human narratives? The narratives may be inventions, but the suffering people cause one another, and the pleasure they are capable of giving each other, exist and continue to exist.

UNHAPPY ENDING?

> It is the misfortune (but also perhaps the voluptuous pleasure) of language not to be able to authenticate itself . . . language is, by nature, fictional.[18]

Fictions are fickle and cannot alone guarantee the political directions which our identifications might take. Reading the black text as a white reader, even as a feminist or a socialist reader, does not guarantee reading as an anti-racist. On the other hand, in terms of teaching and of political solidarity there will also be readers who strongly object to having what is the moment of their politicization 'de-constructed'. The problem is how not to undermine the strategic importance of that solidarity – wherever it appears – whilst remaining open to difference, critical of any final fixing of the meanings and forms of the political. Texts like *The Color Purple* are important because they signal the tension between the necessary rhetoric of desire for identification, the importance of the imaginary unified subjectivity in the process of politicization – the tension between *that* enabling dream and the forms which such 'selves' might take in our daily lives. For fixings can all too easily become fixed, a refusal of difference and a re-instatement of new but equally authoritarian power-structures. Such absolutism is a danger for any politics. Identifying ourselves as 'woman', 'black', 'working-class' can only be staging-posts on the 'road to revolution'; they cannot be places where we want to settle indefinitely. Neither the process of politicization nor that of social change can be so simply or reassuringly 'progressive'. Stable moments of solidarity may give us the energy to move on but it is the tension between solidarity and difference which creates political urgency, and it is the dialectical relation between our knowledge and our ignorance of others which keeps a political movement moving.

Finally then, for white academics, challenging English means inevitably untacking the subjectivities in which we have dressed our selves for a long time. Many of us have indeed been made by books. It hurts to discover that so many of our investments – literally economic, as well as social and personal – are going bankrupt. For women like myself, who made the move from the working classes via a 'liberal arts' education, it is intensely painful, as well as hard, to continue to attack the positions which have only just conceded me a foothold in the dominant culture. I suspect, however, that if we cannot give up that power and those securities peaceably and in co-operation, then we will lose them in any case on much stonier ground in future struggles, when solidarity and difference will be posed as exclusive alternatives, and black and white a violently polarized opposition.

So when as critics we warn against the essentializing tendencies of humanist fictions, we need nevertheless to recognize their democratizing potential, their celebration of human agency and activity – an impulse without which both socialism and feminism are inert. Not to do that, and to dismiss the powerful optimism and the collective historical significance of a text like *The Color Purple* is to throw out the baby with the bathwater. Which is not just anti-humanist, but inhumane.

NOTES

1. LTP is a national network of teachers and students who hold an annual conference and produce a journal. The 1985 papers are available (£1.25) from Helen Taylor, Department of Humanities, Bristol Polytechnic. I would like to thank the other members of the Sussex group, and especially Rachel Bowlby, for their help with this piece.
2. See Janet Batsleer *et al.*, 'Culture and politics', in *Rewriting English* (London, 1985).
3. *The Color Purple*, (London, 1983), p. 17.
4. Alice Walker, *In Search of Our Mother's Gardens* (London, 1984), p. 126.
5. *LTP Conference Papers* (Bristol, 1985), p. 130.
6. See, for example, Alan Sinfield's discussion in the LTP 1985 papers; and Cedric J. Robinson's *Black Marxism: The Making of the Black Radical Tradition* (London, 1983).
7. Quoted on the back cover of The Women's Press 1983 edition.
8. See B. Bryan, S. Dadzie and S. Scafe, *The Heart of the Race: Black Women's Lives in Britain* (London, 1985), especially Chapter 5.
9. See Centre for Contemporary Cultural Studies analysis, *The Empire Strikes Back: Race and Racism in 70s Britain* (London, 1982).
10. Walker, *In Search*, p. 291.
11. 'People Aid', *Marxism Today*, July 1986.
12. 'Keeping the Color in *The Color Purple* (LTP Bristol 1985); see also, for further reading, the debates in *Feminist Review* no. 17 (1984), no. 20 (1985) and no. 23 (1986)
13. *The Color Purple*, p. 183.
14. *Landscape For a Good Woman* (London, 1986), p. 14.
15. See, for example, Barbara Taylor, *Eve and The New Jerusalem: Socialism and Feminism in the Nineteenth Century* (London, 1983).
16. Walker, *In Search*, p. 261.
17. *Women: The Longest Revolution* (London, 1984), p. 247.
18. Roland Barthes, *Camera Lucida* (London, 1984), p. 85.

3

Young Bess: Historical Novels and Growing Up★

THE PLACE OF READING

'What will you do when England is invaded?' he asked her. 'Will you raise a regiment and ride at the head of it? Will you be Colonel Eliza or Captain Bess?'

All her egoism was agog. What would she be? At twelve years old anything was possible. And so he seemed to think as he scanned her, and the wind flicked the wisp of hair into her eyes and made her blink.

'How can I tell what you'll be? You may become anything. Elizabeth the Enigma. . . .' (Irwin, 1944:20)

What visions of grandeur did these words conjure up for me, an eager grammar-school swot, in the early 1960s? I was introduced to Margaret Irwin's trilogy about Queen Elizabeth I by my mother on one of our many trips to the Carnegie Public Library in Fratton Road, Portsmouth: *Young Bess* (1944), *Elizabeth Captive Princess* (1948) and *Elizabeth and The Prince of Spain* (1953), all chart the fortunes of the Tudor monarch from girlhood to her coronation as England's Virgin Queen. These opening lines can still thrill me, though I'm less excited by the prospect of leading a regiment. No one in my family was a royalist – my mother and grandmother were outspoken antimonarchists – 'about time they pensioned off Mr and Mrs Windsor' was their usual attitude. Yet perhaps the fact that my middle name is Elizabeth, my birthday shared with the Queen Mother, and I too was about twelve years old when I first encountered *Young Bess*, made me more susceptible.

★ First published in *Feminist Review* 33, Autumn 1989.

This imaginary exchange between the princess and Admiral Thomas
Seymour on the flagship of her father's navy, as they watch the French fleet
approaching in the Solent, was itself not a million miles from home: my uncles
had been sailors, my father worked in the dockyard, and Portsmouth, as anyone who has ever walked along the seafront at Southsea knows, is a bulwark
of a city. From the ramparts of the Round Tower in Portsea to the line of
hill-top forts which look down over it ('Palmerston's Follies' erected during
anti-French hysteria in the 1850s), it is a place which testifies to the aggressive insularity of the English. In 1944 'Young Bess's' ardent determination to
protect war-time England and 'the long line of emerald downs' no doubt had
its own peculiar resonances; but it had reverberations too for a child who had
grown up in a blitzed town, playing on bombsites, and listening time and again
to tales from relatives of the Second World War, of entire families wiped out
in a single raid, of miraculous and courageous escapes. Perhaps we were no
more steeped in history than anybody else, but in Portsmouth the idea of a
national past was peculiarly linked to the local and to the communal.

Meeting my first boyfriend in the Duke of Buckingham opposite the place
where Charles Villiers had been murdered, and just down the road from where
the gloomy bust of his friend, Charles I, was set into the wall at Sallyport, I felt
drawn to the side of the cavaliers. They had early on provided me with the best
clothes for dressing-up games and with my first unforgettable historical novel,
also a local one: Captain Marryat's The Children of The New Forest.[1] There was,
it seemed by definition, no romance in Puritanism. Yet how do I reconcile the
idea that historical novels fed a conservative vision with the knowledge that
I was writing in those same years school projects on revolutions (American,
French and Russian)? And how did such desires flourish in a neighbourhood
where everyone like my own family was Labour?

Returning as a postgraduate student to the historical novels of my growing up is to attempt to untie several Gordian knots, all of which cluster round
the politics of reading. What could the appeal of reading such novels be? The
interweaving of different identifications which stories summon up could certainly be easily cut through with a simple accusation: weren't they merely
reactionary fictions, the light reading of discontented and aspiring poor whites,
deferentially accepting a nationalistic history which would buttress up their
prejudices and keep them in their place?

On the face of it, indeed, many of these stories have little to recommend
them to latter-day feminists. They are drenched in many of the elements dear
to the Tory imagination: high-class intrigues in the courts and the salons,
sumptuous and enviable displays of wealth, gorgeously clad females captivat-
ing the strongest and proudest of males: an appeal to old-fashioned grandeur,

whether of Tudor England, Bath Spa, or the American South, and luxuriating in myths of ancestry and traditions. History as in the novels of a Georgette Heyer or a Daphne du Maurier (neither of whom, from either political instinct or inverted snobbery were on my mother's library list), is a kind of costume drama or pageant of Merrie England, a vision of a lost past in contrast to a lack-lustre present which in turn can mobilize the most conservative views of social and national decline.

That, however, isn't the whole story. The attention to subjectivity which forms part of an analysis of the political meanings of any novel cannot be so readily contained within ideological boxes. Like many novels of the 1940s Margaret Irwin's do speak to contemporary invasion fears and unabashedly promote a staunch patriotism. But it matters too that it is a female protagonist, and a minor at that, someone weak and young, who symbolizes England's fortunes, and that the place of such novels lies well outside of approved reading and the culturally accredited notions of 'literature' which I, like everyone else, learnt at school.

In a passionate and immediate sense these novels were a popular history. Where did my knowledge of unofficial history come from if not from historical novels, film and TV? Glenda Jackson as 'Elizabeth R', *The Six Wives of Henry the Eighth*, Katherine Hepburn in *The Lion in Winter*, as well as innumerable BBC children's serials on Sunday teatime, were a staple fare. Put these against the history I was 'doing' at school, a history which was remarkably impersonal. Typically our topics – like the American War of Independence – were passionless, about remote causes and dates, legislation and policy. English history in the schoolroom was suitably bloodless, so that my keeping of a copy of Charles I's execution warrant, after a family visit to Carisbrooke Castle, felt ghoulish and excessive – not something to bring into class. Had I read *Northanger Abbey* I would, I'm sure, have concurred with Catherine Morland, Jane Austen's romantic young woman, who in the grips of Gothic fiction (chapter XIV) is left cold by 'history, real solemn history':

> I read it a little as a duty; but it tells me nothing that does not either vex or weary me. The quarrels of popes and kings, with wars or pestilences, in every page; the men all so good for nothing, and hardly any women at all, it is very tiresome.

Like Catherine Morland, I was 'in training for a heroine' and historical novels gave me a history I could appreciate.[2] The focus within them is ultimately upon individuals, but especially upon femininities, upon women's lives and loves, their families and their feelings. What the novels manage is to give the concerns of the so-called private sphere the status and interest of history, like one never-ending family saga, which indeed has become a modern view of royalty. For many people then, the historical novel *is* history, a history which is above all peopled, a history of the everyday, but an everyday, which unlike 'social' history, could also include feelings and desires: history, thoughts and all. This history could excite the twelve-year-old as well as the old-age pensioner, nor did it deal in abstract and monolithic determinations – the State, the Church, the bourgeoisie. The people in Irwin's novels are the subjects, if not always the agents of history. For those who are normally left out of history altogether such an emphasis is very welcome.

Novels like Irwin's were perhaps the ideal diet for the grammar-school appetite. Very closely researched and full of carefully chosen detail, there are careful descriptions of architecture, of fashions, changes in warfare and domestic interiors, as well as quite rigorous accounts of foreign policy, State squabbles and so on: they are usually lengthy novels and by no means always 'easy reading'. Part of their appeal was perhaps autodidactic and educative. They concern themselves with varying degrees of explicitness with the actual question of historiography, and many display some of the seriousness of the historian: Jean Plaidy's novels are typical in being all prefaced by a decent list of sources, and Irwin's *Young Bess* thanks 'Lady Helen Seymour' on the frontispiece for helping her with family papers and documents. Some, like Helen Waddell's *Peter Abelard* become historical works in their own right. Historical novels bring with them an air of learning which has more weight and cachet than mere romances: they are genuinely informative.

Reading historical novels made a bond with my mother and aunts precisely at a time when I was leaving them behind. Grammar-school homework set me apart from both my parents; it led me to 'think too much'; historical novels on the other hand were domestically unproblematic and scholastically ambivalent. As a schoolgirl answering questions on the moral character of Macbeth, I had long known how to categorize literature, and must have sensed that historical novels fell into the good bad group. In the eyes of my teachers, snobs to a woman, any library book was better than watching 'tele' and these stories provided a much needed halfway house. My own reading up until the age of eighteen continued to include *both* classics and comics: to dismiss popular fiction, now as then, would have been in some intimate and intolerable way to dismiss my own home, especially since in our family, reading was my mother's province. I still have some of her copies and writing about them as an academic is both a measure of our closeness, and of the distance between us.

My choice of reading in the late 1960s, though I didn't know it, made me part of a distinctively feminine world; historical fiction has been one of the

major forms of women's reading and writing in the second half of the twentieth century.[3] Many of these writers, like Irwin, seem to have begun writing during the twenties and thirties. Where they appear to differ from some
of the most popular Victorian or Edwardian historical romancers (Baroness
D'Orczy's *The Scarlet Pimpernel* (1905) leaps to mind) is in giving femininity, which usually has a walk-on part in the official history of our times, the
lead role in the national drama. Taken together with the historical films of
the period – Katherine Hepburn as Mary Queen of Scots, for example – as
well as the less historical and more fanciful Gainsborough melodramas, the
romance of history seems to have had a special significance for women readers
during and immediately after the war.[4] Nevertheless, many of these authors
have remained bestsellers and library favourites: fifty years after a list of 'what
England is reading now' placed Margaret Mitchell's *Gone With The Wind* and
Margaret Irwin's *The Stranger Prince* at the top (Caffrey, 1978:113), both novels
are still on W. H. Smith's most prominent shelves.

   In this piece I want to look more closely at some of the contradictory
components of the 'English femininity' I was offered in the fiction which I
read, and at the interplay of different kinds of identification which the novels
encourage: appeals made to social status, national pride and sexual longing
which interlock and even dissolve into each other in an uneasy and sometimes volatile mixture. I want to do so, not in order finally to relegate them as
morally or politically reprehensible, but to suggest that it is inside these often
ill-matched and uncomfortable identities that we all live and read books. And
that it is from the lack of their neat fit that we can find the spaces in which to
make our politics, by understanding rather than by rejecting the places from
which they so awkwardly grow.

IN TRAINING FOR A HEROINE

If, on the most obvious level, my adolescent imaginings about 'Young Bess'
were fantasies of power, my choice was certainly not a modest one. Most of
my heroines, if they were not simply fictional (like Jane Eyre and Elizabeth
Bennett) were famous women, from Joan of Arc to Marie Curie, who had
all, in some senses, been top of the class. These figures haunted my imagination and it was frequently the mistresses who were my companions in fantasy: Nell Gwynn, the Duchess of Portsmouth, upstarts all, who managed to
combine sexual adventures with social climbing. As someone caught between
home and school, girlhood and womanhood, working-class traditions and an
uncertain future, historical novels tapped in me a pool of longings. Like Caryl
Churchill's 'Top Girls', the success of the heroines was by no means wholly

laudable, and my own identifications far from innocent. I too wanted to be an achiever. Self-determination, autonomy, the will to survive through marriages, pregnancies and hardships, these novels brought together many of the consoling virtues of working-class life and the makings of a Tory feminism in which women always do it alone. It is as a unique individual, apart from the *hoi polloi* that you become a heroine.

Perhaps the attraction of the Tudor period – so often the setting for these novels – is exactly the number of women in it, a veritable plethora of queens, what with Henry's six, and the presences at one time of Mary Tudor ('Bloody Mary'), her half sister, Elizabeth, and Elizabeth's cousins, Lady Jane Grey and Mary Queen of Scots. Often in competition with each other, this excess of femininities nevertheless does function as a kind of choice for readers. All these women did actually wield power and the historical importance of their private lives is therefore unquestionable. Advancement, achievement, public power and private satisfaction: these are women who have it all, the prototypes, perhaps, of the 1980s Women of Substance.

Their power as literary transformations of feminine possibilities might best emerge when they are set against the prescriptive limitations of the female role taken as a desirable norm by many in the post-war period. The suburban housewife, gazing out across Acacia Drive, the secretary in her dingy digs, the shopkeeper's wife, the library assistant, might have found historical novels a far less tame and dutiful source for images of self when contrasted with the repressive pontifications emanating from official or public discussions of respectable femininity. We need to read a novel like *Young Bess* alongside and against the moral and moralizing messages of films like *Mrs Miniver* or *Brief Encounter*, against the subordinating representations of women offered by esteemed male writers – the lurking misogyny of an Evelyn Waugh or a George Orwell, and against the sad closures of contemporary realist novels written by other female novelists:

> 'It is all my world. . .! To make a really spongy sponge-cake my whole ambition!' When she reached home, she would despise herself and idly wondered if any others were playing the same game. (Taylor, 1951:50)

The knowing but resigned tone of Elizabeth Taylor's provincial housewives in the 1950s typically expresses a relegation of women to domesticity and inertia which echoes repeatedly down the corridors of the realist novel from the 1920s to the present day. Laura Temple, the restless wife of E. M. Delafield's ironic *The Way Things Are*, consigns herself to respectability with these chilling sentiments that must have spoken – and still speak – for many:

Only by envisaging and accepting her own limitations, could she endure the limitations of her surroundings. (Delafield, 1988:336)

From the hilarious but equally circumscribed celibacy of a Barbara Pym heroine, to the cool and sardonic self-immolation of Anita Brookner's, or the witty martyrdom of Margaret Drabble's, the twentieth-century woman's novelist has frequently viewed the constraints of marriage and motherhood with a self-deprecating and ultimately self-defeating worldly wisdom. After suffocating beneath their antiromantic insistence upon the immovable obstacles of everyday life, the weight of the moral or personal failure of individual women to avoid the prisons of their sex, historical novels come as a breath of fresh air, with their fantasies of emancipation and of a life untethered.

Compare the statement of Delafield's heroine, tied to the life of her caste:

The children, her marriage vow, the house, the ordering of the meals, the servants, the making of a laundry list every Monday – in a word, the things of respectability – kept one respectable (Delafield, 1988:336);

to the declaration of autonomy which Helen Waddell gives to the fourteenth-century Heloise in 1933, a Heloise who feels that she would be lowered by marriage to Peter Abelard. She wants:

no bond but your love only. I am not ashamed to be called your harlot. I would be ashamed to be called your wife. (Crosland, 1981:159)

It is in this context of cross-reading, that we might begin to talk about the expressive scope of historical novels, their keeping open the potential for wayward subjectivities outside of the norms on offer – or differently shaped within them. At best, they speak to the hope which many readers must have shared, that life might have more to offer the woman of the mid twentieth century than the conventional expectations of marriage and motherhood.

The shamelessness of historical novels is surprising; even du Maurier's *Frenchman's Creek* (1942), which ends with the bleakest advocacy of the heroine's return to her boring husband after an illicit affair with a foreign pirate, provoked the *Sunday Times* critic into a half-joking nervous admonition against her 'questionable behaviour'. He was surely sensitive to the fact that it is the *escape*, rather than the return, which these novels warm to. For whilst it is the private sphere of marriage and relationships which dominates, in the context of the fourteenth or the fifteenth century, these take place with a frequency and a carelessness as to make contemporary bourgeois beliefs in loyalty and monogamy ideal only by their absence.

Marriage is often depicted as inadequate and oppressive, the realm of violence (including wife-beating and wife-murder), and of bad or nonexistent sex. These novels (like 1980s soap operas) are about broken families, 'broken homes', disrupted, unhappy partnerships, and absent, often impotent (as well as boorish and ignorant) men. Margaret Irwin's description of the young Elizabeth's upbringing emphasizes this disorder:

> Family life was a difficult affair with a father who had repudiated two of his six wives, beheaded two others and bastardized both his daughters. (Irwin, 1944:8)

Hardly the nuclear family.

Similarly, motherhood is far from idealized. Childbirth and childdeath happen with almost heartless frequency and arouse very few passages of sentimental reflection. Katherine Swynford is left to give birth in horrifying circumstances, surrounded by disease and rebellion, alone in a deserted house. Her child grows up to hate her, though they are eventually reconciled in the closing scene of the six hundred pages. Family relations, including 'the maternal instinct' are shown to be less than loving and reliable. Equally importantly, these mothers move on to their next lover, or their next adventure: childbirth is not ultimately a confinement. Most of the women have several marriages, several lovers, do not get tied down by motherhood, are socially mobile, make the best of absent men and wartime, and even get the top jobs! In a fourteenth-century context there is no question of their being stigmatized as 'career women' either. They can have full public and full private lives.

Certainly the past is sexier, however much desire heaves within rather than actually bursts the seams of the heroine's bodices. Kathleen Windsor's *Forever Amber*, whose heroine survives plague and fire and several lovers in the steamy atmosphere of the Restoration, was the first book I read for its erotic content, guiltily sneaking it from my mother's shelf. Sexual desire, on the part of women, is not taboo, nor does its fulfilment lead automatically to incarceration within the home or the family. Being a queen or a wench means side-stepping the rules of respectable behaviour:

> She laid a hand, which had begun to tremble, on his shoulder. She moved closer to him. Her body was crying out for him. She wished in that moment that she were not the Queen surrounded by courtiers. She longed to be alone with him, to say: 'I love you. We will marry one day, but for

the moment we may be lovers. . . .' She turned away, dizzy with desire.
(Plaidy, 1967:278)

Mary Stuart, in Plaidy's novel of 1955 does – a few pages later – throw herself
into Darnley's arms and command him to be her lover. As it turns out, Darnley
is more than willing but there is no question here of self-denial for the sake of
being a good woman.

Whilst it is almost entirely heterosexual – with the key exception of Mary
Renault's sequence of novels about Ancient Greece – it is still a far more plural
and perverse model of desire than one would associate with the years of Dr
Spock and *Readers Digest*. Irwin's trilogy begins with Elizabeth I's alleged love
affair with her uncle: she is twelve years old. Catherine Howard in Plaidy's *The
Sixth Wife* (1953) is twelve when she has her first lover, whilst Anya Seton's
Katherine (1954) is fifteen when she is forced into sexual experience. Indeed
most of the queens and princesses have lovers, are married and divorced often
before the age of twenty-five. This is certainly not the ideal bourgeois pattern. When the absence in the 1940s of magazines for young women is taken
into account, the appeal of these novels is even more understandable. And it
is striking that the notion of adolescent sexuality is rarely seen as the object
of outrage and disgust as it is elsewhere in post-war discussions which take
'youth' as one of its central anxieties.

Instead it is as the place of 'about to be' – inchoate with sexual as well as
social promise – that Irwin, like many authors, takes girlhood as her starting
point. When Tom Seymour in that opening scene is inspecting the scrawny,
undeveloped Elizabeth, it is for signs of sexual as well as intellectual maturity.
He asks, 'Will you be beautiful? Will you be plain?'. To which Bess (whom
the reader knows to turn out a white-faced, carrot-haired queen) replies ada-
mantly, 'I *will* be beautiful, I *will!*' At twelve, the state of your face is as important as the state of the nation and becoming accustomed to male scrutiny can
be deeply traumatizing. Here it is legitimized by Elizabeth's royalty, but more
satisfying in Irwin's account, erotic interest is both excited and fulfilled with
impunity. Seymour all but becomes her lover, and Elizabeth gets only pleasure
from it. What would be fraught with fear and guilt in actuality, is made pain-
less in fiction.

The reversal of roles which these powerful women embody – their 'masculine' licence and independence – calls into question many of the values usually
attached to the sexual division both of labour and of love. The dilemma, for
example, between selfless public duty and hampering private pleasure which
we are used to as an heroic choice in which the male decides to love 'em and
leave 'em, is thrown out of kilter. The usual dismissal of love and sexuality

as lesser, more trivial pursuits is problematic given that these novels uphold a view of femininity as being naturally more caring and emotionally more alert. What frequently happens instead is a momentary tremor when the inadequacy of cultural assumptions about gender is revealed. Such troublings may be brief but they are often explicit.

Consider the force of a passage like this where Philip of Spain is trying to persuade the young Elizabeth to a night of passion with marriage looming on the horizon:

> 'Can you never leave politics and become human? . . . I must have you in the end, – but why not now, this night? We shall never be younger. What are you? Not woman only. Not man –'
> 'God forbid! Do you make me out an hermaphrodite?'
> 'God forbid again. Yet there is something in you that is of either sex, and of something beyond sex, – a goddess maybe – but not holy.'
> 'No. I am that Other Woman that husbands love to worship in secret. A wedding ring is a yoke ring.'
> 'Not if it were with you.'
> 'But *I* might find it so.' (Irwin, 1953: 198)

Fighting talk in 1953. Elizabeth is able to reject the wedding ring without incurring the usual loss of status that contemporary bourgeois heroines in realist novels might undergo. She refuses also simply to become a mistress in the acceptable competitive alternative to being a wife. If she is the Other Woman, then her sexual charms are not at the beck and call of her powerful lover. It is she, in this scene, who calls the tune. Irwin leaves the tension between public power and private desire inevitably unresolved: impossibly, Elizabeth is neither unfeminine nor destined for motherhood and wifedom. She is a masterless woman whom we are asked to respect and admire.

The historical representation of Elizabeth which Irwin offers does circle around mid-twentieth-century, rather than sixteenth-century feminine dilemmas, even though she is drawing upon the anxieties within Renaissance treatment of the Virgin Queen and the rhetorical play Elizabeth herself made with her anomalous position.[5] What is unexpected, however, is the vehemence and self-consciousness with which many fictions discuss the limitations of normative views of women. Admittedly Elizabeth, in Irwin's account, doesn't transcend the options (she goes without sex in order to avoid pregnancy) but she does suggest that they are pretty paltry. Her regal autonomy is seen as powerfully celebratory in the final volume in 1953. Her choice of spinsterdom (not usually a radical choice) appears to leave her with the best of all possible worlds. Irwin must, of course, end with the coronation, thus avoiding the potential problems of actually being a virgin queen.

The transposition into a historical past is necessarily double-edged. On the one hand, contemporary mores can be differently placed and explored: these heroines are able to take up what would usually be seen as the masculine reins of public power and sexual autonomy; on the other hand, precisely because they are not 'ordinary' women, and this is not realism, such figures are self-proclaimed as 'escapist': as romantic fantasies, they are compensating registers of profound discontent, whilst remaining mediated and distorted expressions of it. They are not feminist novels, though there is a proto-feminist feel to some of the passages. It is typical, however, that the historical transformation of the contemporary feminine choices is imagined upwards (as it were) into the aristocratic or royal setting – these are rags-to-riches novels in many cases. The expansive and dynamic existences of a Young Bess or a Mary Stuart are a magical compromise with the anguish of a feminine subjectivity; they cannot literally be contemporary models, which is at once their attraction and their fault.

NATIONAL FICTIONS

The class politics of many of these novels are often difficult to tease out. Even if we wanted to, they cannot merely be read off from content, not least because many of the settings deliberately pre-date modern class references or terminology and are thereby mystified. Katherine Swynford, in Seton's novel, for example, is the daughter of a herald – calling her 'petit-bourgeois' seems limp, to say the least. More importantly, however, what it means to be working or middle class are not themselves historical constants, any more than are political ideologies or expressions of nationalistic sentiment: the conservatism of the 1930s is as different from the 1950s as from our own. It is clear, though, that the royal and aristocratic milieux can serve the most depressing and deferential kinds of Tory atavism. What is more disturbing is that this can be evoked in the same novels whose depiction of feminine struggle is in many ways progressive.

Daphne du Maurier's saga, *The King's General* (1946), for example, is a bitter but moving account of one woman's experience of the English civil war. Her heroine, Honor Harris, is a royalist who is violently crippled in the first chapter, but whose disability does not prevent her from being a resourceful and desirable heroine. It is possible to read in her image an intensified and displaced version of the experience of being a helpless civilian, of being a woman on the Home Front, which must have struck many chords. Suffering appalling losses and physical deprivations, the break-up of her home and her family, and the continuous absence of the man she loves, Honor Harris manages, despite her sense of uselessness and her growing depression, to cope and to survive. Even so, her retrospective account bears a distinctly political message, since she blames the dashing of all her dreams and hopes on the philistine and plebian New Model Army who have destroyed the old order and set up a brutal, totalitarian state. Du Maurier's account has actually much in common with Waugh's *Brideshead Revisited*, also published just after the war, apparently sharing his fears that Britain might come under 'enemy occupation', not from foreign tyranny, but from the working class as the levelling effects of increased social democracy made the post-war world their oyster. Du Maurier's description of the 'grey world' of the Puritans is fuelled by a Tory revulsion at egalitarianism:

> And what a world! Long faces and worsted garments, bad harvests and sinking trade, everywhere men poorer than they were before, and the people miserable. The happy aftermath of war. . . . Manners are rough, courtesy a forgotten quality. We are each of us suspicious of our neighbour. Oh, brave new world! (Du Maurier, 1974: 12)

Not surprisingly, when the roundheads arrive, they all look the same (and remarkably like Nazis with their cropped hair and brownshirts), and speak like Cockney barrow-boys.

By the same token we might find a different kind of modern conservatism in the 1987 winner of the Georgette Heyer Award, *I Am England* by Patricia Wright. It is subtitled an epic 'of the life, the drama, the passions of a great nation' but its biography of the State is a long way from du Maurier's high Toryism. Centring around the Weald of Kent, and stretching back into its primeval mists, it relies upon the power of notions of the land, an almost mystical vision of Englishness residing in the folk and the soil, which is closer to more fascistic strains but also, ironically, likely to appeal to an ecologically aware 1980s readership. Above all, its Elizabethan woodsmen are given us as our true fathers, forging the national destiny in their smithies, setting up local industries as forerunners of an enterprise culture with the Home Counties coming close to resembling a well-run Youth Training Programme.

In spite of her royalism, Irwin's fiction, on the other hand, may have been compatible with, and even shaped by, a Labour imagination, one which believed in social mobility and which could indeed find expression in the ethos of the grammar school, and a belief in giving people their 'chance'. Irwin's is an open society, an equal opportunity State whose confident and optimistic tone captures something of the buoyant mood in which Labour won the 1945 election. Elizabeth's rise to fame is seen as somehow outside of and able to ignore class limitations. She is 'some say, not a Lady at all' – a:

> young woman, begotten of God knows whom, of the son of a Welsh adventurer who made himself king, some say, of a strolling base-born musician, say others, . . . posing as, – a Virgin queen. (Irwin, 1953: 240)

Such an image needs to be set against those in common circulation in the 1950s which celebrated the young Elizabeth II and her coronation, the coming of a new Elizabethan age. As the archetypal young mother, *her* sexuality was all but nonexistent and her gentility strictly consonant with conventional norms.

The elevation to royalty, for all its Tory potential, can also be read as a means by which the assumption that all women might be longing for middle-class status can be set aside and the logic of *embourgeoisement* marvellously forgotten. The desire for the adventurous expansion of ambitions in these fictions does not always lead to the baby clinic or the New World cooker. And it is certainly far more exciting than passing the eleven plus. For those women whose lives had been disrupted and upset (as well as broadened) by wartime work, historical novels might have seemed more sustaining than many of the more 'serious' kind: in seeing women's upward mobility as an answer to the nation's problems, such fictions weren't to be scoffed at, especially when the path upwards was through action and autonomy, rather than increased consumerism and home-ownership.

Being England's queen does have other, less equivocal, meanings. However much it wrestles with contemporary class and gender limitations, Irwin's account of Elizabeth's growing up gives us a careful and thoroughly ideological pre-history of the English state. England also begins the trilogy as an unruly, restless being full of waging elements and desires which must learn to be controlled. Young Bess's adolescence is especially suspenseful since upon her teen-age years rests the security of England, and its futurity is bound up with hers. In Irwin's novels the emotional crises of Elizabeth's sexual development are also national crises; the last volume charts the exigencies of her sexual interest in the Catholic Philip of Spain, precisely because it conflicts with her need to 'unite' the English people under Protestantism.

The secure and unquestioned position offered to readers in these novels – the safe narrative haven which can resolve all the readers' worries and the heroine's fraught choices – lies in the appeal to an unexamined notion of the supremacy of the English. The making of a national identity is implicit in the strengthening of Elizabeth's ego: her maturity is equivalent to that of the body politic as a whole. Thus in the coronation scene which closes the work, the sneers at Elizabeth's bastardy and impudence come directly from the devious Spanish ambassador, peevishly watching from the sidelines as the new queen is cheered and balladed by 'true hearts' and 'lusty throats'. Protecting the realm against heathens and Catholics, religious and political fanatics, Elizabeth's reign is taken as the beginning of the establishment of law and order: the point at which the real England begins. Irwin relies upon a sense of Englishness which sees England as always about to be internally riven, religiously divided and threatened by foreigners from outside, and in need, therefore, of a strong leadership. It is a deferential, even fearful mentality, which had its particular forms in the late 1940s, but which has continued to find its exponents. It is one which assumes the superiority of the English as well as enumerating a catalogue of outsiders, excluded from both Englishness and democracy. Elizabeth, in this account, is the great unifier of her people and the forerunner of that toleration which comes to be seen as one of their most sterling qualities. Irwin successfully mythologizes a queen, and her government, whose brutalities included the burning of Catholics and the execution of gypsies, and whose colonial expansion contributed to the enslavement of millions. And it suggests that England is and has been one people and one history, where it has been many, different and conflicting peoples and pasts.

There is little here to disturb the most conservative of historians, and much to seduce the reader, flatter her into Englishness. Reading again that ending makes me wince, but Young Bess's story makes no sense without it. As an outsider in my family, and at school, perhaps I too was grateful to transcend growing feelings of exile and find comfort in a make-believe sense of national unity. As a child waiting for *Listen With Mother* on the afternoon wireless, I knew by heart that magical incantation of the shipping forecast which mapped a whole country in coastline words, like the edges of a puzzle, and I also knew that when the announcer finally got to 'Wight', somehow he meant me, my family and all our friends; the sea-shanties that we sang from infants' school onwards ('Farewell and adieu to you Spanish ladies . . . From Ushant to Scilly is thirty-five leagues'), and the local pubs with their sea-faring memorabilia and namesakes: the Still and West, the Lord Nelson, the Captain's Table – it would take another essay to prise loose the powerful threads of a nationalism which tied my sense of self umbilically to Englishness. If historical novels excited me into adolescent sexuality, and stirred a social discontent which only leaving home would answer, then they washed over me too with a groundswell of patriotic feeling, murky waters, whose currents I have only just begun to chart.

The study of popular fictions will always founder on the rock of ideological purity, clung to in political desperation. Not least because the identifications which all literary texts offer are multiple and conflictual, even irreconciliable. The problem with all novels is always the one thing which is pleasurable about them: their fictitiousness. Though they give us a semblance of reality, they draw too upon feelings, upon unspoken assumptions and unknown desires. Ultimately no one can legislate for when we wander the twilight world of reading, laying down in advance what we might wish to encounter, and which bits we'll simply ignore. What's clear is that the capacity to fantasize which novels encourage, is notoriously unbiddable, and that for those of us who judge novels by their messages, moral, social or political this has always been a mixed blessing.

At best popular historical novels may have helped open up a space within which different groups of women have started to perceive how marginal their needs and concerns have usually been taken to be. They offer a number of new perspectives on the past, which sit less easily alongside text-book history; the working-class sagas of a Catherine Cookson, the Jewish family sagas of a Maisie Mosco or a Clare Rayner, have enabled other voices to speak out from history, other readers to claim a past. But any attention to subjectivity in historical novels needs itself to be historical: such a reading should remind us of the different positions which can be simultaneously felt and experienced in reading, and that how we learn our sense of our selves is a differential and a differentiating process. To see yourself as Young Bess may be a radical act for the working-class refugee; it may also, and at the same time, be a reactionary one. The grammar-school girl is always top of her class at somebody else's expense.

NOTES

Alison Light is a member of the *Feminist Review* collective and teaches in the Humanities department at Brighton Polytechnic. Her study of British women's writing and the conservative imagination, *The Feminine Nation*, will be published by Routledge in 1990.

I would like to thank the staff and students on the Cultural Studies MA programme at Middlesex Polytechnic for violently arguing me into rewriting and rethinking much of this paper – I hope they will improve upon it further; Jean Radford, for refusing to be seduced by the romance of history, and Raphael Samuel for having faith in the first draft.

1. Anna Davin's interesting account of historical fiction for children (Davin, 1976) is a rare and early attempt on the Left to take such literature seriously, and one which makes a good antidote to my own piece: most of the

novels I refer to would definitely fall into her category of bad history – 'a poor unbalanced diet' which offers 'illusions, not reality'. Carolyn Steedman, on the other hand, is drawn to reflect on why it might be precisely the most conservative of illusions which appeal to young children in school. (Steedman, 1989).

2. For another discussion of historical romance, which refers especially to Jane Austen and Georgette Heyer, and to the gendering of literary and historical categories, see Robinson (1978).

3. Anyone with any doubts about this should consult Mussell (1982).

4. Sue Harper's accounts (1983 and 1987) of Gainsborough films and their exotic and erotic pleasures are helpful. She also provides a brief sortie into a Mass Observation directive of 1943 which goes some way towards a sociology of readership. Whilst she makes the point that it was mostly 'middle-class women in jobs' who read 'costume fiction', it is beyond her brief to distinguish the different forms of such fiction (Georgette Heyer and Margaret Irwin are poles apart), and we cannot assume that a 'middle-class' readership in the 1940s or 1950s (and one which includes library assistants, secretaries and teachers is already a very broad class definition) does not rule out working-class readers in later years, nor even the possibility of black readers. Public (as opposed to circulating) library borrowing and cheap paperbacks have greatly widened the market for such fiction. In any case, sociological information about readership, however illuminating, does not fully answer the question of how people read, and the place of reading in their lives. For a unique attempt to understand the different readerships and the historical meanings of one historical romance in depth, see Helen Taylor's work on *Gone With The Wind* (Taylor, 1989).

5. Queen Elizabeth I's sixteenth-century dilemmas as token woman and honorary male are discussed in Heisch (1980).

REFERENCES

Caffrey, Kate (1978) *1937–1939: A Last Look Round* London: Gordon & Cremonesi.

Crosland, Margaret (1981) *Beyond the Lighthouse: English Women Novelists in the Twentieth Century* London: Constable.

Davin, Anna (1976) 'Historical Novels for Children' *History Workshop Journal* No. 1, pp. 154–65.

Delafield, E. M. (1988) *The Way Things Are* London: Virago; first published 1927, London: Hutchinson.

Du Maurier, Daphne (1974) *The King's General* London: Pan books; first published 1946, London: Gollancz.

Gledhill, Christine (1987) editor *Home Is Where The Heart Is: Studies in Melodrama And The Woman's Film* London: BFI Publications.

Harper, Sue (1983) 'History With Frills: The "Costume" Novel in World War Two', *Red Letters*, No. 14, pp. 14–22.

Harper, Sue 'Historical Pleasures: Gainsborough Costume Melodrama', in GLEDHILL (1987).

Heisch, Alison (1980) 'Queen Elizabeth I and the persistence of Patriarchy', *Feminist Review* No. 4, pp. 45–55.

Irwin, Margaret (1944) *Young Bess* London: Chatto & Windus.

Irwin, Margaret (1948) *Elizabeth, Captive Princess* London: Chatto & Windus.

Irwin, Margaret (1953) *Elizabeth and The Prince of Spain* London: Chatto & Windus.

Mussell, Kate (1982) editor *Twentieth Century Romance and Gothic Writers* London: Macmillan.

Plaidy, Jean (1967) *Royal Road to Fotheringay* Pan books; first published 1955, London: Robert Hale.

Robinson, Lillian S. (1978) *Sex, Class and Culture* New York: Methuen.

Samuel, Raphael (1989) editor *Patriotism: The Making and Unmaking of British National Identity* London: Routledge.

Steedman, Carolyn (1989) 'True Romances' in SAMUEL (1989).

Taylor, Elizabeth (1951) *A Game of Hide and Seek* London: Peter Davies.

Taylor, Helen (1989) *Scarlett's Women: Gone With The Wind and its Female Fans* London: Virago.

4

Outside History? Stevie Smith, Women Poets and the National Voice*

In recent debates about Englishness and the part played by English literature in creating and sustaining national feeling or images of the nation, scholars and critics, if they are men, have concerned themselves almost exclusively with male writers.[1] I was especially struck, during the fuss made over the publication of Philip Larkin's letters and Andrew Motion's biography of Larkin, by how difficult it seemed to be to extend the arguments about a peculiarly English mentality or poetic appeal to the ways in which women might be addressed, both as readers and writers. Is there any particularly different relationship to nation and to its invention that could be traced amongst women writers? Were women to be considered free of the taint of more explicit nationalist feeling (something I could hardly credit)? What then had their different contributions been? And how might this change (perhaps even revolutionise) our concepts both of nation and of its history? In addition to the unwillingness – or refusal – of male critics to take on the other half of the nation, it seemed that feminist literary scholarship had also, on the whole, concentrated far more upon fiction and found it much harder to historicise poetry or know how to include the poetic in its politics.[2] And yet poetry, in earlier centuries at least (or so the argument ran), had been the dominant literary form for the creating of a national consciousness.

This piece represents a first attempt to wrestle with some of these questions. It was shaped within a very specific teaching and institutional context. Moving to a post in one of the older universities, and returning to teaching poetry as a large part of course work within a traditional English degree, I found myself disheartened by the numbers of first year students who either

---

* First published in *English*, Vol.43, no. 177, Autumn 1994.

insisted that they'd never read any poetry or that they hated it and were intimi-
dated by it; and by colleagues who raised their hands in horror to proclaim that
these same students did not know what *terza rima* was.[3] I found myself having
to struggle to keep a similar sense of inadequacy from creeping over me: that
poetry was somehow irredeemably highbrow and specialist, needed a battery
of technical terms which were in themselves particularly complex, and which
mere amateurs could not hope to master. If, as Tom Paulin has put it, 'there
is a common ambition to make the aesthetic unapproachably difficult', this is
nowhere more so than in some university teaching of poetry.[4] The first task
as a teacher seemed to be to grapple with the cultural highjacking of poetry
which had produced these feelings. I had to remind myself (and the students)
over and over again of the absolute centrality of poetry, not just to certain
phases of social history or certain spokesmen for the public culture, but to all
forms of articulacy, all kinds of people.

Schoolteachers are in a position to understand much better than university
dons that far from being remote and mandarin, poetry is one of the first and
most familiar forms of encountering language. Indeed we learn the language
by playing with it – an impulse at least as primary, and one which comes earlier, than learning to narrate. As babies and children we rapidly discover the
pleasure that comes from repeating sounds, rhyming or stressing words and
syllables, inventing new words and inverting others; we pick up and imitate in
vernacular phrases as well as in the more formal experience of song, nursery
rhyme and storytelling, the powerful tug and sway of rhythm, the anticipation
or satisfaction that can lie in a silent or a missed beat, in the proverbial or the
ritual saying. It can't be too strongly emphasised that poetry, even in its most
highly sophisticated, self-consciously literary forms, is simply an elaboration of
activities which are ordinary and intimate. Who hasn't tried to make a poem
at some point in their lives?

The first aim, then, seemed to be to establish that far from being the territory of the few, poetry could claim to be the most common form of expression
amongst every variety of human culture. Those same students, who maintained that poetry had nothing to do with them, of course spent hours listening
to pop-lyrics, knew, without knowing, plenty about metre and stress, from
advertising, from their favourite stand-up comedians, but also from their own
conversations. In any case I began to wonder whether it was true that the public role of poetry in English culture had been eclipsed. It seemed to depend,
in part, on what counted as literature. As recently as my own childhood in the
1960s verse recitation and public-speaking competitions were frequent school
and church pursuits; relatives would recite poems or favourite lines at parties
or do's, comic monologues regaled us from the wireless, newspapers carried

local verse just as gravestones did. Part of the problem in teaching, and in the available histories of poetry, was the dissevering of these local, apparently more private or domestic uses of poetry from more formal and culturally-invested ideas of the poetic. I hoped that turning to poetry by women would queer this pitch: that it might call in question any easy opposition between public and private notions of the poetic, make it harder to champion either a simply elite (and therefore reactionary) or simply popular (and therefore radical) version of verse-making, and make us reconsider too the places where the nation might find itself, where Englishness might be lived.

STEVIE SMITH, PHILIP LARKIN AND ENGLISHNESS

> Miss Pauncefoot sang at the top of her voice
> (Sing tirry-lirry down the lane)
> And nobody knew what she sang about
> (Sing tirry-lirry all the same).
> ('The Songster')

Though it is short and sweet, 'The Songster' is typical of Stevie Smith's poetry. With their mixture of whimsy and buried melancholy, of archness and sadness ('Lamb dead, dead Lamb,/ He was, I am'), her constant use of parody and pastiche, together with the mimic's magpie gift of collecting and savouring odd snatches of social idioms ('Oh there hasn't been much change/At the Grange'), her verses are as likely to irritate as to amuse. Their rhyming (or more usually halfrhyming) is laconic and deceptively casual, and they have the feel of the nursery or the bedtime story. And yet their throwaway humour and singsong quality sit uneasily with Smith's subject matter and a frequent preoccupation with death and illness, desolation and abandonment:

> She said as she tumbled the baby in:
> There, little baby, go sink or swim,
> I brought you into the world, what more should I do?
> Do you expect me to be responsible for you?

Moving without authorial comment from the banal to the highminded, the poetry's tone, as Hermione Lee has suggested,[5] is 'at once alarming and domesticated', whilst Smith's imagination might seem freakish or morbid:

> Do take Muriel out
> She is looking so glum

Do take Muriel out
All her friends are gone. . . .

Do take Muriel out
Although your name is Death
She will not complain
When you dance her over the blasted heath.

As the note of self-deprecation warns us, Smith, like Miss Pauncefoot, is not an obvious candidate for the role of bard. Beginning her writing career with the monologic *Novel on Yellow Paper* (1936) and publishing her last volume of verse posthumously in 1972, Smith's collected works have received a mixed press. Her poetry seems both too prolific and too slight; too piecemeal and too samey, eminently quotable and eminently forgettable. This is in part due to that same oral quality which Seamus Heaney has called 'memorable voice'[6] and which demands a kind of party piece performance for each poem (the sort of popular turn which Smith gave hilariously in her own readings in the 'sixties and which Glenda Jackson impersonated so convincingly in the film *Stevie*). As Philip Larkin observed, she might seem – at first glance – to lie somewhere 'between children's and humorous'[7]; there is something of Edward Lear and Walter de la Mare about her and both are the kiss of death as far as inclusion in any canon of poetic endeavour is concerned. (The English may love nonsense or light verse but they don't like to be found reading it.) To make matters worse, there are the reams of dotty drawings which Smith doodled in the margins of her work, and, as though to dispense finally with her claims to serious attention, there is her devotion to cats, a passion which, Larkin suggests, 'casts a shadow over even the most illustrious name'.

Faced with such overwhelming evidence of her feyness, Smith, like Miss Pauncefoot, has readily been relegated, even by those who admire her most, to an idiosyncratic world of one, somewhere between the loveable and the obscure. This is ultimately the effect of Larkin's affectionate discussion of her work, for although he tries to argue against her being seen as a mere 'light-hearted purveyor of bizarrerie', he nevertheless calls her 'an almost unclassifiable poet' and judges that the poems do not belong to any particular epoch or decade. Smith emerges as a curiosity, outside history, shunted into one of the sidings of literature. Oddly, this is also the effect of the poet Seamus Heaney's view of the poetry, despite his ostensibly taking a very different approach. For him, Smith's poems are too dated: too heavily saturated with their place and time, with the local idioms and accents of her class and region. Whilst appreciating the accuracy of Smith's satire, her clever ventriloquy of the accents of 'disenchanted gentility', he concludes that she evokes only a 'peculiar emotional weather'. In the end, her poems lack, he says, 'that larger orchestration that they encourage us to listen for'; they 'retreat from reso-nance' and remain 'eccentric'.

There is something fishy going on here. How is it that Smith's poetry can be placed outside time and place and yet so clearly articulate, in Heaney's words, the registers of 'educated middle class English speech'? Surely it is not only her gallery of characters and voices, 'Miss Pauncefoot', Reginald, Muriel, Major Hawkaby Cole Macroo, Lady Susan Smart, Mr Sholto Peach Harrison, Miss Cheeseman, etc., or the numbers of poems made from a mosaic of their linguistic tics ('Emily writes such a good letter', 'I could let Tom go – but what about the children?'), but more intimately the patterns of feeling within the poetry which conjure up a particular and distinctive Englishness. Even in so brief a burst as 'The Songster', Smith evokes that sense of the kind of Pyrrhic victory over feeling which is only one, but one of the most powerful, of the underlying emotional themes of her verse. If the poem is ostensibly cheerful, then like so many of Smith's it puts its best foot forward only to keep demor-alisation at bay ('Away melancholy, away'). The Englishness which resonates through Smith's poems is often brisk and sometimes brittle; it keeps up appear-ances and spirits at all costs, and being matter of fact, its pathos often lies in what reticence represses:

'Happiness is like England, and will not state a case'.

Here are some of the characteristic grace-notes of an Englishness at once antiro-mantic and confidently small-minded – 'Now Agnes, pull yourself together' – conservative with a small 'c', self-disparaging and quiescent, an Englishness founded upon the virtues of private life: how can this not be heard, in its own way, as a national voice?

We might want to say that the kind of Englishness Smith speaks to and from – superannuated, parochial, often bored with itself and its conventions, but convinced of the virtues of ordinariness – is the kind of suburban English-ness more frequently vilified than recognised as one of the heartlands of national feeling and identity. Certainly in the nineteenth century, as John Lucas has argued, whilst the English became an increasingly suburban nation, they were at the same time imagining the Englishness of England to reside beyond the town, in an idealised Nature, a rural retreat.[8] But the picture becomes more complicated, I think, after the First World War when many of the rhetorics of national address became gradually more and more unpalatable, their secu-rity undermined. Rather than a nation of warriors and missionaries, one might argue that the English are re-imagined as a primarily domesticated, essentially private people, modest and unassuming rather than expansionist or aggressive.[9] It is this Englishness of the interwar years that a poet like Betjeman both pillories and celebrates (of course, for him it is always the suburbs of the past – the Victorian era – rather than the present – which embody the best of England). And it is as much this vision of the nation that takes them into the Second World War: in the years of national crisis and in Britain's 'finest hour' of 1940, Englishness seemed best represented by the Home Front, the cup of tea and the bit of back garden, the red pillar boxes and Sunday joints eulogised by Orwell, or the kind of little men and sterling housewives who make up Noel Coward's 'happy breed'.

After all, it is something of this Englishness, tempered with a feeling for England's postwar losses, which many critics have identified as part of the characteristic idiom of Philip Larkin. Larkin is frequently seen as spokesman for the defeated and wry Englishman of the postwar era, the urbane voice of the essentially private citizen. Yet why is Larkin's clearly a national voice and Smith's not? In the first place, I would say that Smith is much more on the inside of private life than Larkin would ever want to be. Where Larkin's poetry characteristically incorporates a distance from the England under observation, Smith's remains immersed, and this sense of being meshed in the rhythms of a private life is linked to the question of gender. The masculinity of Larkin's poetry may be diffident, apparently needing a great deal of privacy, and to some extent critical of its own sexual proclivities, but it is still founded on a profound distrust of the domestic, a distance from home life. Larkin's bachelordom may seem sad but even the saddest bachelor life has a certain kind of dignity and cultural approval. In Larkin's 'I remember, I remember', we encounter a symptomatic reflex: the man proclaiming his ordinariness – 'the forgotten boredom' – of a suburban childhood, whilst firmly putting a distance between himself and his past. For all his insistence on the unromantic character of his growing up, the speaker in the poem is nevertheless looking out of the window of a train – 'Coming up England by a different line' – in the antiheroic pose of the man on the move. This stance, which has a long cultural history, took particularly vivid new shape in the 1950s and 60s (from the Movement poets to Salinger, the 'Angries' to Bob Dylan). At its heart is a view of social mobility which involves a masculine disavowal of, and disdain for, domestic 'ties'. When men see themselves as rolling stones, you can guess what the moss is.

Smith cannot make a forgotten boredom of a suburban childhood, since she is, like many women, identified with the patterns of domestic life. There is more continuity than discontinuity between the past and present; more sense of circular journeys – to and from home – than of moving on, moving away. She continues, like so many women, to speak from inside the fabric of what Larkin sees as a humdrum existence. There is an indoors quality to the verse, which can be both claustrophobic and comforting – a tension which Smith's verse frequently projects on to domestic objects like the fireside cat, homely and cooped-up, or like the exotically named gas fire – 'the Persian' – that becomes the focus of a displaced loneliness and mounting hysteria, only to be fiercely headed off before it threatens to overwhelm the speaker:

> The gas fire
> Seemed quite like a friend
> Such a funny little humming noise it made
> And it had a name, too, carved on it you know,
> 'The Persian'. The Persian!
> Ha ha ha; ha ha.
> Now, Agnes, pull yourself together.
> You and your friends.

As in 'The Persian', where we are plunged into an echo-chamber of voices, with a blurring of speakers and agencies, Smith rarely allows the reader the kind of distance from which it is possible to strike an attitude towards what we hear: rather we are left in the midst of emotional contradiction and the reader is often uncomfortably implicated in the emotional mêlée beneath the irony and the tight severity of the lines. We do not progress.

As many critics have observed, Larkin's tentative and reluctant persona can be another kind of authority; Smith's facetiousness cannot. This is most visible (or audible) in her refusal of a guiding poet's persona in the verse: she gives us all voice and no ego, or rather a series of strategies for fending off the sonority of that superego who is always threatening to come into Larkin's poetry and shift us from a querulous 'I' to a confident 'we': the voice at the end of 'Church Going', for example. Though Smith is always speaking in other people's voices, she makes few moves to speak for them; rather her ventriloquy of their attitudes often disconcerts their authority, as is made clearer than usual in this poem, 'Advice to Young Children':

> 'Children who paddle where the ocean bed shelves steeply
> Must take great care they do not
> Paddle too deeply'.
>
> Thus spake the awful ageing couple
> Whose hearts the years had turned to rubble.

But the little children, to save any bother,
Let it in at one ear and out at the other.

Indeed many of her poems expose the illusory nature of the authority, that of
the parent or husband or religious dogma, the precariousness of commonsense,
but in ways which do not allow the reader to settle into the luxury of superiority. We search in vain for that consistent and coherent ego in Smith's poetry,
an authorial fiction which makes possible, however attenuated, however qual-
ified, the bardic address from one representative man to another.

Smith's poetry evinces the same kind of uneasy relationship to the land-
marks of a national literature: she draws quite self-consciously on the poetry of
the past but in ways which remind us deliberately of their status as anthology
pieces, the well-known snippets and boiled down bones of the poetry learnt
in the classroom, the half-remembered (often misremembered) fragments and
poetic debris which floats to the surface of most people's education; she takes
the national literature of her generation, the Bible, mediaeval romances, Milton, Blake, Wordsworth, Byron and Tennyson, but as it has been filtered
through the school assembly, the recitation pieces, and the tattered copy of
Palgrave's Golden Treasury or Quiller-Couch's *Oxford Book Of Verse* and dissolved in the private memory of the individual. Hers is a national literature at
once enshrined and debunked as an unthinking part of consciousness; dero-
manticised and yet personalised; a central point of public reference and yet
privatised. Poetry's lofty processes of inspiration are at once travestied and
familiarised in 'Thoughts about the Person from Porlock' in which the mysterious figure who interrupted Coleridge's writing of 'Kubla Khan' is gradually
transformed into a member of the middle classes with suburban leanings just
like herself:

He wasn't much in the social sense
Though his grandmother was a Warlock,
One of the Rutlandshire ones I fancy
And nothing to do with Porlock.

And he lived at the bottom of the hill as I said
And had a cat named Flo,
And had a cat named Flo.

Smith seems to be able to speak from right inside an emotional economy,
which keeps her captive even as she mocks and mimics it. Both the radicalism and the potential conservatism of her verse can be seen to dwell in the
refusal to separate the internal spaces of fantasy, the often bizarre imagery and

dreamlike visions which make up much of the ambivalent psychic drama of
the poetry, and what is usually called the 'real world', placed externally and
believed to be separate from that inner world. It is as though that Englishness so given to asserting no-nonsense attitudes, to a ruthlessly empirical and
down-to-earth view of experience, is also haunted by its opposite. Smith gives
us many of the pleasures of 'nonsense verse', in which grotesque impossibili-
ties and surreal scenes which seem arbitrarily to upset the cheerful tenor of
the verse, emerge from the most domesticated and homely landscapes: like
those of images of a wildness tamed which frequent the poems in the shape
of a tigerish cat or the ape swinging all night outside the terraced house,
whose contented movements Smith sets to the plangent and wistful (and haut-
English) tune of 'Greensleeves':

> Outside the house
> The swinging ape
> Swung to and fro,
> Swung to and fro,
> And when the midnight shone so clear
> He was still swinging there.
>
> Oh ho the swinging ape,
> The happy peaceful animal
> Oh ho the swinging ape.
> I love to see him gambol.

If this is not the Englishness of Grantchester or Adlestrop or the Whitsun
weddings, it is the Englishness of the girl from a good school who doesn't
go to university, of the thriving unconscious of the shopping parade and the
outpatients department, of the linguistic reaches of respectable English home
life and the enormously rich reservoir of repression which the small empire of
home can create: the jungle' which is always on the edges of Avondale Road
or Palmers Green, a place into which one longs to escape and where one goes
at one's peril.

    If Smith's verse is, as Heaney says, more inward-looking, and more con-
servative in its social address, then it is also more radical in its modernism, in
its refusal to offer a convenient attitude or summation; in its parody of the
past, in its sending-up of the very Englishness it evokes, in its insistence upon
drawing our attention to the psychic and emotional repertoires of an Englishness which begins at home, as equally played out in fantasy, as it is lived
in 'the real world'. Smith's poetry would make an uneasy addition to the

national literature because it reminds us that if – to use another of Heaney's phrases[10] – England is always an England of the mind – it is an England whose boundaries are never clearly delineated between the private and the public. The inner life of an individual can never be kept magically apart from what is designated social and historical. For Heaney to say that we miss 'the kind of large orchestration that [the poems] are always tempting us to listen for', is to miss the point. Isn't the kind of 'resonance' he mourns as a lack precisely the bogus claim to generality and inclusion, the generating of mistaken authority, and the forging of mythological homogeneity that has made the appeal to the nation actually so excluding?

WOMEN AND POETRY

Some Englishness is more English than others, or rather, it is possible to be recognised as English and yet not to be part of a national identity or tradition. Whether she be deliberating cocking a snook at the Bard, or offering an Englishness simply lived in a different – though connected – linguistic and emotional space, either way, the woman's voice, it seems, is not a convincing voice of generality. The bloke in his bicycle clips wandering into Church can represent the nation, but not the spinster, or the school mistress. If we wonder why Smith isn't heard as part of a national voice every bit as recognisable as her male contemporaries, then we have to imagine that it is because the nation is conceived of in particular ways both by critics and partisans. Nor is it simply a matter of the language of nation being founded only on a notion of Englishness framed in the public realm: for it seems that even when national identity is recognised as resting on the valorisation of particular collective forms of private life, the woman's voice is still felt to be a marginal one. Clearly it is one thing to dote on adorable tennis girls' knees, quite another when Miss Joan Hunter Dunn starts writing poetry herself.

In other words, both the conservatism of Smith's verse and its experimentalism take on a different complexion when they are read not as 'wholly individual', 'weird' or idiosyncratic'[11] but as sharing in that long history of the fraught relationship which women writing poetry have had to its place as high art, to the forms of poetic verse, and to the reception of their verse. As the loftiest and least lucrative of the arts, with its priestly associations and its insistence on the imitation of classical models and knowledge of Greek and Latin, poetry has long claimed the most hallowed ground for itself amongst the arts: one thinks of the ancient Greek notion that when the lyric poet utters, 'it is a god that speaks'.[12] For many centuries, European literati have found something incongruous about the very idea of the woman poet approaching such a citadel: the 'woman poet' must be a contradiction in terms. Divine 'afflatus' or inspiration may be happy to come in the female shape of the Muse, but only if the expired breath is suitably male. For many critics and, of course, most notably male poets, there seemed an affront in the woman aspiring to the role of rhymster, let alone prophet or soothsayer (as witnessed by the contempt which Pope heaps upon 'poetesses' in *The Dunciad*). And even when the classical models were somewhat more democratised, the poet, in the famous words of the Preface to the *Lyrical Ballads* was still 'a man speaking to men'. Wordsworth might feel himself estranged from the decorative and mannered verse of polite circles in the late eighteenth century but he nevertheless imagined himself the inheritor of a patrimony bequeathed by his elders – Milton and Shakespeare – as from 'father to son'.

Some feminist critics have argued that even in the nineteenth century, when many bourgeois women found a new and successful identity for themselves as writers, it seems to have been far more difficult for the woman to be a poet than a novelist. Perhaps because the claim to self-legitimation which poetry invites was considered too bold and open (a woman might be forgiven scribbling novels if it were to support her family); perhaps because prose allows an author to hide behind its apparent objectivity; or simply because to be taken seriously as a poet has usually meant having a classical, and at least a university, education, private means of support, or both – no doubt all of these factors might have made writing poetry a difficult pursuit for women.[13] Whilst many aspiring young men must have felt the want of means and influence, they were less likely to be afraid of the sound of their own voices or to have their sexual propriety impugned for wanting to be heard in public. When Poet Laureate Robert Southey, in that famous dismissal which can still bear quotation, rejected the young Charlotte Bronte's offerings with the words: 'Literature cannot be the business of a woman's life, and it ought not to be', she had just sent him her verse.

The idea of the poet, let alone of any distinctly feminine relation to that idea (and there is never just one class or group of 'woman') clearly has many and complex histories, and it would be foolish to generalise too far. But if we were to take in passing only one element of the notion of a 'Romantic' revolution – the celebration of the childlike – we can sense immediately what different resonances the Wordsworthian quest for innocence might have for the different sexes. The woman writing poetry was already infantilised, not only under the law where she had no more rights than a child, but, ironically, as part of the idealisation of femininity as a purer, more spiritualised state. Norma Clarke, in *Ambitious Heights*, gives us a poignant account of the pressures suffered by Felicia Hemans, whose work rivalled Byron's in popularity and who was looked on as a kind of sacrosanct model and eulogized by other women poets in the nineteenth century.[14] Equally beloved by male critics, she nurtured their respect by projecting in public all her life the expected image of feminine helplessness. In private she brought up a family of five sons without a husband to lean on and efficiently managed an immensely successful literary career. In 1836 her memorialist, H. F. Chorley, went to great lengths to free her verse from any hint of self-advertisement, rather she was 'self-distrustful, open, with a child-like gratitude, to words of kindness and encouragement – seeking rather sympathy than praise'.[15]

The other side of this idealisation was, of course, the view of women as creatures of caprice, lacking rational self-control, a view which was as likely to produce misogynist contempt as adoration. As the place where subjectivity could be asserted and shaped, the lyric, in particular, has offered double-edged possibilities for a sex at once seen as too readily prone to feeling and yet crucially lacking in enlightened selfhood. One way of answering the charge of unwomanly self-assertion which writing poetry might seem to invite, has been for critics to stress the 'artlessness' of feminine compositions, as though they were a kind of spontaneous overflow of feeling but without the recollection in tranquility which is the mark of the rational man: 'Mrs Hemans's poems are strictly effusions, in fine keeping with the sex of the writer'.[16] C. H. Sisson introduces a recent selection of Christina Rossetti's work for Carcenet Press with an endorsement of her 'simplicity' and 'directness', quoting with approval Ford Madox Ford's comment that Rossetti 'dealt hardly at all in ideas: nearly every one of her poems was an instance, was an illustration of an emotion' (and this despite the fact that very few people feel in octets and sestets).[17] Sisson reinforces the idea of her as an innocent and childlike being by calling her 'Christina' throughout, feebly excusing this familiarity as a way of distinguishing her from her brother, but since Dante Gabriel is not discussed in this introduction, the confusion can hardly arise, and it never strikes Sisson that, had he had a tribe of more famous sisters, one would never dream of calling Tennyson Alfred or Wordsworth Bill.

Feminists are used to these lapses. It is still the case that poetry by women is subject to the kind of *ad feminam* readings (as Elaine Showalter has called them[18]), which reads the work as thinly veiled sexual biography, either celebrating what the reader believes femininity to be, or praising the poet for avoiding its 'pitfalls': just as one reviewer could praise Felicia Hemans for never leaving the path of womanhood, so Al Alvarez could appreciate Plath's first book for gainsaying it: 'She steers clear of feminine charm, deliciousness, gentility, supersensitivity, and the act of being a poetess'.[19] The notion that 'the woman is the style'[20] reproduces that double bind of femininity whereby womanliness is either a kind of handicap or a specialism in the way that being masculine is not. The masculine is the universal, mysteriously unsexed, whilst the feminine is weighed down with its sexual trappings, like some poor albatross. As Eavan Boland has observed, poetry about motherhood is 'women's poetry' but poetry about war is just poetry.[21] No-one seems to fear that writing endlessly about father figures – whether they be literary influences or an old man digging potatoes, will limit or ghettoise the poetry.

Unless we can recognise this very different climate in which women have written, and the gendered meanings which attach to the different forms of poetry, we cannot begin to understand many of the strategies which women writing poetry have employed. Given the tendency to read lyrics by women as purely expressive of their femininity, and femininity itself as a kind of emotional outpouring, we can better understand the kinds of protective camouflage which enabled poets to defeat the reader's expectation of feminine revelation. Far from being 'simple and direct', the poetry of Rossetti, for example, like that of her contemporary, Emily Dickinson, is often deliberately elliptical and cryptic, dependent on the use of particular modes of metonymy, and on the displacements and condensations similar to those of dream. The effect, as Cora Kaplan has argued, is firmly to resist the transparency of the lyric and its identification with any easy 'confession' on the part of the author. Poems like Rossetti's 'My Secret' and 'The Dream', and notoriously 'Goblin Market', work, as do many of Dickinson's abbreviated and concertinaed lyrics, to fling the desire for interpretation back in the face of the reader, and might better be read as a kind of 'antilyric'.[22]

We might wish to read a kind of resistance in the use made by many women poets – including Stevie Smith – of alternative modes of collective address: the folk tale, the nursery rhyme and children's game, the alternative linguistic spaces of the vernacular. Tom Paulin has recently argued that Rossetti and Dickinson should be read as fighting a rearguard action against the high style of the Bard (feminist criticism, notably Adrienne Rich's essay on Dickinson, put similar arguments many years before).[23] It is tempting to see these writers as conducting a kind of guerrilla warfare against the Parnassian rhetoric and vatic authority of a poetry claiming the nation's cultural and moral high ground, planting their small bombs set to explode the masculine hubris of that tradition in its more bombastic forms. Given the imperialist and expansionist implications of the bardic, did the woman poet not resist that authority from a finer sense of its aggressive and sanguinary implications? Yet between Philip Larkin's view of Emily Dickinson as a Big Victim,[24] a repressed and dotty spinster (a Miss Pouncefoot for him, if ever there was one), and Tom Paulin's heroicisation of her, there is less to choose than we might at first think:

both risk leaving the woman in the private sphere, back indoors, a creature outside history; or rather of refusing to see history as in any way a psychic, internal as well as external space.

Feminist criticism has long had a strong sense of why it is difficult to offer any kind of reading of poetry by women as simply a protest or resistance. In the first place, to be 'shut out' (the title of one of Rossetti's poems), to be relegated to the lowest room, to be marginal, is never just oppositional, it is also heartbreaking and demoralising, and we do not pay these poets the respect of their suffering if we insist only on their courage, reading the repeated images of containment and exclusion, of emotional exile in the poetry as achieved states of resistance rather than the fragile psychic management of deeply fragmenting pressures. For if there are tones of intransigence and rebellion in the poetry, the split figures and divided subjectivities of the verse give us equally images of selfwounding hatred and despair – enactments of what has been called 'the aesthetics of renunciation' in nineteenth century verse, or what we might see as the complex projection and dramatisation of how women have internalised what being 'feminine' has meant.[25] Emily Dickinson may have been volcanic in her writing but if we are to say that she was 'forced' to risk her poems lying dormant indefinitely, the problem for the feminist lies in the complex admission that those forces lay also on the inside of the female psyche – Dickinson's own limits – as externally in any patriarchal world. Dickinson's famous likening of publication to prostitution suggests as much her internalisation of the limits of female respectability – a lady does not solicit attention in public – as it does the dream of an inner autonomy where we can 'reduce no human spirit to disgrace of price'.

As Cora Kaplan has suggested, reading poetry by women cannot easily be reconciled to that search for a liberated, fully achieving selfhood, breaking free of the bonds of patriarchal oppression, which some feminists have seemed to need. Rather it can mean looking full in the face some of the most recalcitrant and even unpalatable aspects of being designated woman: in Rossetti's verse, for example, we cannot register the paralysing limits of English womanliness in the Victorian years – something Rossetti clearly understands as a class sexuality in 'Enrica' where she contrasts the bourgeois English woman with her Italian contemporary – we cannot measure that internal struggle against such numbing ascriptions of the feminine, unless we also measure Rossetti's strenuous attempts to subdue and contain herself within those limits. A full account must take on board the more conservative longings of the devotional and religious poetry, themselves fraught with contradiction, and the many women poets who found solace for a sense of their internal exile in the church, and in a language of religious discourse which could speak powerfully to the question of what a woman was or desired.

Rather than search either for heroines or victims it may be more helpful, as Jacqueline Rose has proposed, to begin by considering that poetry is,
'among other things, one of the places where what has not been lived can be
explored'.[26] Outside the demands of narrative and of being 'shut up in prose'
as Dickinson saw it, poetry can be read as dealing in the shifting scenarios of
fantasy, in the most unmanageable, utopian and perverse desires, in the rapid
exchange of gendered position and possibility which can be figured without
the need for recuperating the contradictions they contain. From this perspective, the desire to find the comfort of a fully coherent poetic ego, one which
would celebrate and affirm a feminist politics, or a fully oppositional relation to
the nation or the state, is as romantic in its own way as the more conservative
visions of womanhood which feminists and progressives would decry. This
is not to say that what goes in the psychic interiority of so-called private life
is remote from politics or public life; quite the reverse, it is to insist on their
interdependency.

POETRY AND NATION

Any historical account worth its salt will have to look across the whole panoply
of possible relations which women and men writing have had to the idea of a
national voice. In so doing it will insist that the nation begins as much at home
as abroad; that it is lived as much in the dreams and imaginings of the apparently private individual as it is in the overtly public and political languages of
the State. Rather than imagine that any poet could occupy a purely other kind
of domestic space, we need to see that both the apparently private forms of
verse, like the lyric, and the ostensibly public, are bound up with the meanings given to sexual difference and that these meanings in turn contribute to
the ways in which the nation might be imagined and addressed. Poets like
Laetitia Landon and Felicia Hemans in the late eighteenth and early nineteenth
century might be read as part of a domestication of English national feeling
which begins to celebrate the nation in terms of the virtues and sentiments of
home life or the family circle. Hemans's most famous poem – much antholo-
gised and, until quite recently, lisped in English junior schools, 'Casabianca'
with its frequently parodied opening, 'the boy stood on the burning deck', is
a case in point. It takes a public sea battle as its setting but its message is that
of eulogising filial loyalty and domestic virtue (the boy waits for permission to
leave from his father who has already perished). Hemans's comments to her
friend Maria Jane Jewsbury, on reading Wordsworth's poetry, are suggestive of
the powerfully domestic ways in which the nation could be conceived: 'This
author', she wrote, 'is the true Poet of Home', and of all lofty feelings which

have their root in the soil of home affections'.[27] For readers in the early nineteenth century the nation and home were already indissolubly linked.

We certainly slew our history of women's poetry if we refuse to admit those writers who were in fact far from reluctant to address the nation directly. In these cases, too, what is at stake is the sense of the centrality of gender to the claiming of literary authority and to literary value itself, as well as the particular problems of reception and reading which women writers are subject to once they are seen as taking up a 'masculine' position. In her decision to be 'unscrupulously epic' in the writing of her 'novel-poem', *Aurora Leigh*, Elizabeth Barrett Browning was consciously transferring the masculine epic virtues which are appropriate to the making of a nation, 'courage, daring, unappeasable anger',[28] to the making of the woman poet, her theme. *Aurora Leigh*, with its secular vision of a New Jerusalem formed in the new dawn of more equal relations between women and men, makes a reply not only to Milton's *Paradise Lost* but also, with its insistence on the forming of a woman's subjectivity to Wordsworth's *Prelude*, as well as engaging in more contemporary debates with Tennyson and Clough on the issues of female emancipation and social reform.[29] As many feminist critics have noted, Barrett Browning's employment of iambic pentameters was a deliberate claim to critical seriousness, putting herself on a par with the men; perhaps equally important, was her sense that the historical account of the interior life of her heroine was worthy of political and public understanding and further, that political changes which took no account of how 'life develops from within' would be deeply inadequate.

We need another history of Englishness which can include its domestic history and the history of its domestication (or perhaps privatisation or interiorisation). Such a history is bound to suggest that we look in other places for the shaping of the collective life of the nation, apart from the usual sites of academic or scholarly research, breaking down the usual literary apartheid between so-called high and low forms: from the poetry of provincial newspapers to the history of recitation, of verse-speaking competitions, Sunday schools, home journals, of funeral verses (the dirge seems to have been very much a woman's form) and albums, the anthologies and popular collections. What of all the unofficial laureates from Eliza Cook to Jean Ingelow, Patience Strong to Pam Ayres, who are part of the context in which the more well known poets wrote and against whom they need to be read? One thinks of those lady versifiers whom Dickinson despised and yet borrowed from; those grandmothers whom Elizabeth Barrett Browning, given her own form of highbrown partiality, would not have cared to claim, and yet who also set the limits of her aspirations, and gave meaning to the high culture she was herself a part of.[30]

Whilst there are many reasons, then, for wishing to argue that the relationship between women and poetry has its own special histories, we should
not make the mistake of assuming that it is a necessarily progressive one. It is
within this history of relationships, however, that Smith's so-called 'bizarrerie'
might get a better hearing and her 'retreat from resonance' begin to appear
as a different kind of 'English line', one which runs from Rossetti through
Charlotte Mew and Anna Wickham, as powerfully as it does through Betjeman and Larkin. Within this history we can also see her frustrating forms of
feminine resistance as representative rather than eccentric. When Smith coyly
names her essays and sketches *Me Again*, one can hear in the note of feminine
self-disparagement a whole history of the woman's relation to being a poet:
think of the young Alice Meynell grudgingly writing in her journal, 'whatever
I write will be melancholy and selfconscious as are all women's poems'.[31] But
Smith also evinces a thoroughly modern selfconsciousness about that history
even as she evokes it, and a desire to send up those 'damp Victorian troubles'
so 'richly, compostly, loamishly sad'.[32] It is her ironic use of feminine selfdis-
paragement, her satirical relation to the family and to sexual desire, her comic
shifting of gendered voice, of agency and positioning in the poetry, and her
modern mockery of the gush and tosh of an earlier feminine style, which can
feel at times like feminism. Above all, her capacity to playact, as she did on
stage at her readings, in ankle socks and hairslide, has its own air of defiance.
Making such a performance of her English girlishness or 'playing the part of
the spinster' could be seen as Smith's ambiguous spotlighting of how much
being female is always a matter of histrionics, an act.[33]

If being a woman and a poet has not necessarily produced a radical politics,
it always produces a radical disturbance to dominant ideas of the poetic, to
how we usually conceive of history, to how we recognise national identity. It
is hard for those critics who are used to formulating their idea of nation in
terms of the State, citizenship and rights to recognise that inside the house
there is also a historical and social space, one that is never cut off from the
street or the town, the apparently larger world beyond its threshold. Yet
it is precisely the proliferation and fertility of these oppositions, the setting
up of internal as well as external boundaries to what the nation means and
where it lives its sense of itself, that are central to what gives Englishness its
resonances, its peculiar emotional and linguistic economies. If – as many critics have argued – nationality and masculinity cannot be separated (and the
masculinity of a Pope is clearly different from that of a Clare), if Englishness
is, amongst other things, a matter of fabricating an image of 'the real man in
the real place', then what defines masculinity if not the feminine – that which
masculinity sees as other to itself?

If it is true that whatever the woman does she risks being placed, in Eavan Boland's phrase, outside history, we should not mistake that for meaning that she is.[34] We cannot rest content with that verdict, however, sympathetically intended, which leads John Lucas to write of Rossetti that whilst she was 'one of the finest poets of the period', she was simply 'disadvantaged', or to conclude that women have had no part to play in the making of Englishness because they were not 'empowered'.[35] On the contrary, I would argue that there has never been a human being without power, even in the most degraded and abject conditions, and even where what is wielded can only be the most perverse and dangerous compensation for other forms of helplessness: only the dead have no weapons. Rather, I think we should insist on the presence of the other half of the nation in the making of its history.

The difficulty is that if Englishness is lived in the most everyday actions and domestic attitudes, it equally can be lived most proudly and patriotically by those people whom the public discourse of the nation appears not to address: the ideas of nation and of national history which do not seem to recognise and include the needs of half of its constituency, can nevertheless continue to inform their consciousness. As women, we know that it is possible to feel oneself strongly English or Irish or Serbian whilst also knowing that the public language and rhetoric of the nation is in some crucial ways excluding. Yet if ideas of nationality are to be fully acknowledged as part of subjectivity, then women have clearly been as capable of founding their own sense of themselves upon notions of national or racial difference even when their actual political power has been minimal. The 1990s have already given us plenty of painful examples of how often those peoples struggling for nationhood depend upon the demonisation of others, and how much this is a part of feminine as well as masculine response. On a more local level, the recent row over the Field Day anthology of Irish verse which saw feminist protest at the almost exclusively masculine selection of poets included, will be ill served by countering that father-ridden tradition of Irishness with the figure of the washerwoman or Cork peasant, as though she were miraculously free of national prejudices or chauvinist blemish, and were not also haunted by the folk devils of a national imagination.

The big question remains, and it is one which women are well placed to ask if not to answer: what would it mean to get beyond nationality and is it possible to imagine a world in which a sense of belonging and a defence of territory – geographical, psychic, domestic – could be separate? I realise that the desire for an existence beyond nationality is more easily felt when one's nation has been powerful, colonising and controlling. I have always distrusted, though admired, Virginia Woolf's rhetorical assertion in the late 1930s that 'as a woman, I have no country. As a woman I want no country. As a woman my country is the whole world'.[36] Distrusted it because it came as much from powerlessness as power (Englishwomen only became citizens a few years before Woolf wrote this), and it effaced the complex mix of English upper- middle-class privilege and of feminine exclusion from the political sphere which were part of Woolf's own contradictory attachment to Englishness. It is perhaps best read in the light of growing fascism in Europe as a wish rather than a description. (For it is easy to forget that behind it lay a sense of how deeply attractive to many English women – especially of Woolf's own class – the fascist programme was). The first demand for women in national struggles is for the same human and legal rights as their male peers – to become citizens of their own country – before they can afford to become citizens of the world. But surely in the end, nationalities can only be temporary dwelling places and not permanent homes; structures of interest and passion, but not obsession or finality. We cannot live by nationality alone.

If we are to discuss such grand themes as poetry and Englishness, let us begin, then, not only with 'The Charge of the Light Brigade' or 'The White Man's Burden', but with a silly woman singing cheerily and nonsensically all to herself in the middle of nowhere. I have argued that one way to break down the divisions upon which the fictions of nation and of Englishness have been built is to insist that women have always been there, inside history, and that none of these terms – nation, Englishness, poetry – can hope to have a meaningful reach without working out how the relation between the private and public has been constituted, in its most intimate as well as most publicised forms. But Miss Pauncefoot's problem is as much with her listeners as with her song, and whether they be writers about poetry or the nation, or both, there are plenty who show every sign of continuing to be cloth-eared when it comes to hearing the alternative strains in history. I suspect that many male critics, including those on the Left, are deeply attached to the very notion of nation which they say they wish to dismantle.

How tempting it is, after all, for the female critic and poet alike to shrug one's metaphorical shoulders and leave the men to it! The bardic voice is exhausting to listen to whether it be in the pages of Tennyson or the literary critics of the *Times Lit. Supp.*, or in all its lesser and more familiar forms, at departmental meetings, over the supper table: they do go on, these men, and one can forgive the desire to chuck verbal graffiti, spray-paint them with deliberate facetiousness, or for the sake of enjoying life, simply refuse to join in – in Wendy Cope's words 'men's boring arguments'?[37] Sing tirry lirry all the same. Hasn't Smith achieved a kind of sublime sanity when she writes, 'All Poetry has to do is to make a strong communication. All the poet has to do is listen. The poet is not an important fellow. There will always be another poet'?[38] And why resuscitate the idea of a woman poet when it always brings with it, like some bad penny turning up, its diminutive shadow, the 'poetess'?

Part of me would like to be able to leave Miss Pauncefoot burbling merrily away on the margins of society – to leave her without comment and without judgement, as Smith herself does. I would like to be able to say – in the manner perhaps of some recent French exponents of 'ecriture feminine' – that poetry by women belongs honourably to the periphery, to the land of pure song, beyond interpretation, and floating free from the weighty draperies of the Bard. But if Miss Pauncefoot belongs to Poesy, Stevie Smith did not: she was a real woman in a real place and I am loathe to place her poetry outside history at a time when the need to be heard is as urgent for women as it ever was. And how can we be sure, unless we are prepared to risk the inadequacies and moral intrusiveness of interpretation, that those far-out gestures mean a person waving, and not drowning? Until such time that women and the concerns which they have represented are recognised as having always been inside history, I don't think we can afford to keep our songs to ourselves. Perhaps we must first have a woman Poet Laureate before we can be rid of Laureates altogether.

NOTES AND REFERENCES

1. See, for example, John Lucas, *England and Englishness* (Hogarth Press: 1990); John Powell Ward, *The English Line: Poetry of the Unpoetic from Wordsworth to Larkin* (Macmillan, 1991) and most recently, and least forgiveably, David Gervais, *Literary Englands: Versions of 'Englishness' in Modern Writing* (Cambridge University Press: 1993). Robert Colls and Philip Dodd (eds.), *Englishness: Politics and Culture 1880–1920* (Croom Helm: 1986) does have a chapter on women but tends to assume elsewhere, as do these other writers, that 'women' will just be added in at a later date to analyses of Englishness without completely transforming the basis of that discussion.

2. As the footnotes below will reveal, this situation is now changing and what I imagined, when I started this work, to be a lonely project, now turns out (as might have been expected) to reflect the *Zeitgeist* in feminist research. Feminist criticism of *fiction* has developed a large body of work on gender and empire and on issues of gender in relation to nationalism, though it has largely concentrated on the nineteenth or early twentieth century. For a more specific example of work on twentieth century Englishness, see Gillian Beer's essay, 'The island and the aeroplane: the case of Virginia Woolf' in Homi Bhabha (ed.), *Nation and Narration* (Routledge, 1990).

3. *Terza rima* (Italian – third rhyme) is a poetic measure (adopted by Dante for his *Divina Commedia*)) which consists of a series of interlocking 'tercets' (or groups of three lines) in which the second line of each one rhymes with the first and third lines of the one succeeding, in the pattern aba bcb cdc etc.

4. Tom Paulin, *Minotaur: Poetry and the Nation State* (Faber, 1992), p. 10.

5. Hermione Lee, (ed.) *Stevie Smith: A Selection* (Faber, 1983).

6. Seamus Heaney, *Preoccupations: Selected Prose 1968–1978* (Faber, 1980).

7. Philip Larkin, 'Frivolous and Vulnerable', in *Required Writing: Miscellaneous Pieces 1955–1982* (Faber, 1983).

8. Lucas, *op. cit.*

9. I have developed this argument in *Forever England: Literature, Femininity and Conservatism between the Wars* (Routledge, 1991).

10. 'Englands of the Mind' in Heaney, *op. cit.*

11. Quotations taken from the back cover of *The Collected Poems of Stevie Smith* (Penguin, 1985).

12. See Seamus Heaney's title essay in *The Government of the Tongue* (Faber, 1988).

13. See the introduction to Sandra M. Gilbert and Susan Gubar (eds.), *Shakespeare's Sisters: Feminist Essays on Women Poets* (Indiana University Press, 1979). More sense of the history of the reception of women's poetry, especially in the eighteenth century and women writers' relation to Romantic ideas, is beginning to emerge. Roger Lonsdale, for example, in his very acute introduction to *Eighteenth Century Women Poets: An Oxford Anthology* (Oxford University Press, 1989) points out that the eighteenth century actually saw a substantial growth in the number of women publishing and that there is no simple story of male prejudice and literary condescension to be told – though both of these existed, of course. He also suggests that fear of a literary takeover by women, and a desire to *reclaim* the territory of poetry, might lie behind the inflation of the poet and of poetry which we associate with Romanticism. Amongst the burgeoning numbers of editions and studies of women poets see R. E. Pritchard, *Poetry by English Women: Elizabethan to Victorian* (Carcanet, 1990); Donna Landry, *The Muses of Resistance: Labouring-class women's Poetry in Britain 1739–1796* (Cambridge, 1990); Jennifer Breen (ed.), *Women Romantic Poets 1785–1832* (Everyman, 1992); Richard Greene, *Mary Leapor: A Study in Eighteenth Century Women's Poetry* (Clarendon, 1993); J. R. de J. Jackson, *Romantic Poetry by Women: A Bibliography 1770–1835* (Clarendon, 1993).

14. Norma Clarke, *Ambitious Heights: Writing, Friendship, Love* (Routledge, 1990); see also Anne K. Mellor, *Romanticism and Gender* (Routledge, 1993).

15. Clarke, p. 33.
16. *Ibid.*
17. C. H. Sisson (ed.), *Christina Rossetti: Selected Poems* (Carcanet, 1984), p. 10.
18. Gilbert and Gubar, *op. cit.*, p.xvi.
19. Cited by Jeni Couzyn, *The Bloodaxe Book of Contemporary Women Poets* (Bloodaxe, 1985), p. xv.
20. Sisson, *op. cit.*, p. 19.
21. Eavan Boland, Lecture at the Voicebox, Royal Festival Hall, London, April 1992.
22. Cora Kaplan, 'The Indefinite Disclosed: Christina Rossetti and Emily Dickinson' in Mary Jacobus (ed.), *Women Writing and Writing About Women* (Croom Helm, 1979). See also Jan Montefiore, *Feminism and Poetry: Language, Experience and Identity in Women's Writing* (Pandora, 1987) and Angela Leighton, *Victorian Women Poets: Writing Against the Heart* (Harvester, 1992); Isobel Armstrong, *Victorian Poetry: Poetry, Poetics and Politics* (Routledge, 1993).
23. Paulin, *op. cit.*; Adrienne Rich, 'Vesuvius at Home: the Power of Emily Dickinson' in *On Lies, Secrets, and Silence* (Virago, 1980).
24. Larkin, *op. cit.*, pp. 191–7.
25. See the chapter on Christina Rossetti in Sandra M. Gilbert and Susan Gubar, *The Madwoman in the Attic* (Yale, 1979). One remembers too that the young Rossetti had wanted to join Florence Nightingale on the expedition to Scutari in the Crimea (she was turned down as too young) and that the poet she most admired was Barrett Browning, the most embarrassingly public of female voices.
26. Jacqueline Rose, *The Haunting of Sylvia Plath* (Virago, 1991).
27. Henry F. Chorley, *Memorials of Mrs. Hemans*, volume 1, (Saunders and Otley, 1837), p. 172.
28. Lucas, *op. cit.*, p. 16.
29. See Cora Kaplan's introduction to Barrett Browning's *Aurora Leigh* (The Women's Press, 1978).
30. 'England has had many learned women. . .and yet where are the poetesses? I look everywhere for grandmothers, and see none'. *The Letters of Elizabeth Barrett Browning*, edited Frederick G. Kenyon, (Macmillan, 1899), 1230–32.
31. June Badeni, *The Slender Tree: A Life of Alice Meynell* (Tabb House: 1981), p. 29.
32. Stevie Smith, *Novel on Yellow Paper* (Virago, 1980), p. 13.
33. Jeni Couzyn argues that Smith 'played the part of the eccentric nervous spinster because it gave her a form in which to be courageous', *The Bloodaxe Book of Contemporary Women Poets* (Bloodaxe, 1985) p. 35.

34. Eavan Boland, *Outside History* (Carcanet, 1990); see also her pamphlet *A Kind of Scar: The Woman Poet in a National Tradition* (Attic Press, 1989).
35. Lucas, *op. cit.*, p. 200.
36. Virginia Woolf, *Three Guineas* (Penguin, 1977), p. 125.
37. Wendy Cope, *Serious Concerns* (Faber, 1992), p. 66.
38. Stevie Smith, 'My Muse' in Couzyn, *op. cit.*, p. 42.

PART II
SHORT CUTS

5

The Vampire and the Dog:
Caryl Churchill's *Mad Forest**

A lonely vampire, recently come down to the city from his Transylvanian castle, encounters a starving mongrel in an empty church. The dog is desperate for a master and they strike up a pact: although the fastidious ghoul finds canine slavishness distasteful, it will at least be company, so he agrees to vampirize the dog. They go off to feed together on the human *mêlée* of easy victims in Romania's post-Ceauşescu chaos.

This gruesome coupling, played as dark comedy, was one of the most forceful and surprising moments in *Mad Forest*, a play by the British dramatist Caryl Churchill, which was written during the trip that she and a company of student-actors made to Romania, and in discussion with students of the Caragiale Institute of Theatre and Cinema and other citizens of Bucharest, in the spring of 1990. It was performed in London at the Royal Court Theatre (home of much innovative and radical theatre) later that same year, and so clearly was produced at white heat while political events were themselves rushing forward. Yet despite the speed of its production and its focus upon the events of December 1989, the overriding concerns of *Mad Forest* went far beyond the topical and are not likely to date: like the image of the vampire and the dog which has stayed with me over the months, as an allegory for some of the darker forces of social revolutions, the play as a whole went beyond the occasion of its writing: it asked us to consider the nature of political change itself and the different kind of theatres in which it takes place, the dramas which are enacted in the theatres of the mind and of the emotions, as well as on a more public stage.

Churchill's achievement in *Mad Forest* was to represent the collapse of communism as in part a kind of derepression: political transformation seen

* First published in *Feminist Review* 39, Autumn 1991.

not just as the overthrow of oppressive regimes and tyrannical hierarchies, but as turning the psychic world upside down, launching a landslide of emotional securities, opening up the internal floodgates. This state of flux and fragmentation produced a volatility both potentially emancipating and undermining. Churchill's characters were dislocated people experiencing a kind of inner meltdown, finding that the taken-for-granted truths of their lives had come away from their moorings; the goal posts, as we might say, had been moved. Rather than the crude Cold War image of a regime run by cynical functionaries who had long since stopped believing in the system, Churchill gave us the much more disturbing portraits of those 'ordinary people' who had, despite all the odds, really wanted to believe, who had tried to make their lives work in this belief, however threadbare, and who now felt a kind of bereavement: the schoolteacher who is about to be dismissed for having been a propagandist and whose professional and home life is now breaking up, 'Twenty years marching in the wrong direction . . . Twenty year's experience and I'm a beginner.' As her son turns against her and her husband, sneering at their use of Party jargon and furious at their having toed the correct line, we see her left with a vacuum where once was self-affirmation and a sense of pride in her work, hollowed out by change and paralyzed by it.

Exhilaration but also puzzlement, relief but also apathy and fear, all these were represented as the different and simultaneous responses to violent changes, changes which, even when they improve upon the quality of life, involve a sense of loss. At one point a young woman expresses her increasing sense of anger at what she sees as the blood-thirsty heroic posturing of her male friends and their fomenting of hatred and division, by saying that she feels oddly bereft: 'I miss him', she says of the dictator whose downfall she also welcomed. And in a scene where the newly liberated young Romanians visit their elders in the country, utopian fantasies and the vicious pathologizing of others go hand in hand. As they lie on the ground in the sun, they let their wishes spiral, imagining for themselves a new life in which they can have everything from Toblerone to immortality. Meanwhile, their peasant grandmother abuses the local gypsies and warns them off Hungarians as murderous people.

Both the emergence of suppressed racial prejudices and of impossible and romantic desires appear in the play as a kind of speaking out of what had formerly been silenced. Atavistic demons, like the vampire and the dog, and unbounded appetites, in excess of the socially possible or acceptable, seem to have been loosed upon the world by the crumbling of the old structures of repression and control. It is as though the events of December had set in motion an unstoppable train of psychic as well as social and economic demands, and throughout Churchill's play we hear the insistent clamour of these unmet needs, which, like masterless dogs, wander in the ruins of the state, threatening to feed upon their fellows.

But such desires and fears, however wildly individualist they seem and however uniquely they are experienced, are always within an historical context, a time and a place; they are part of a common history and a shared life. This relationship between different levels of change – psychic, cultural, economic – is what *Mad Forest* asked us to contemplate, and indeed it is what has long made Caryl Churchill's work of especial interest to feminists. Instead of giving us a history written from 'the top down', as it were, charting the effects of state policies, the machinations of military-economic complexes, or the doings and failures of great men, *Mad Forest* began from inside the different responses of two very different families – the one professional and university-educated; the other 'blue collar' – resisting any easy division between what is usually called 'the private and the public', and suggesting just how much that division obscures. Further than this, we were asked to acknowledge too the dreams and nightmares of those living through such changes. Not in order to see them as simple reflections of political events but in order to recognize how often they are out of kilter with them: a psychic life not simply determined by public activities but also shaping and limiting, and often contradicting them. Churchill's point seemed to me to be that we have to make this kind of imaginative leap into these other interiors if we are to make sense of political change. A historical record which can offer no account of subjectivity, and which makes no attempt to understand the cultural shaping and containment of unconscious as well as conscious needs is no history at all.

Churchill's play also worked hard to remind its London audience that there are limits to how far those who were trying to understand another people's struggle in translation, as it were, could 'identify' with the action they were watching. Flagging each scene with Romanian phrases and putting us in the position of pupils learning a language, our authority, as observers who could pass judgement on what we saw, was called in question. As the programme notes told us, where Bucharest now stands there used to be a large forest, especially impenetrable to foreigners who did not know the paths through it and had always to go round: to them it was 'Teleorman' or 'Mad Forest'. In this sense Churchill's play was taking us round the events and the aftermath of December 1989 and not aiming to cut a clear swathe of meaning through them. Those who wanted the surety of arriving at a definitive or authorized version of historical or political truth would have been disappointed.

Churchill's technique, which was increasingly to destabilize our assumptions and ready formulations as the play progressed, gained force as it took us further inside the unfinished material from which, in fact, we make history and make sense of events. This impulse to go beyond the apparent meaning of what was being said on the stage was reflected very simply in the form of the play which divided into three very different and yet closely connected acts, each of which effectively commented upon the others and upon the different kinds of knowledge they produced. This was why the play moved between apparently realist or documentary scenes of family life or public events, to hallucinatory and bizarre moments of the fantastic and the folkloric like that in which the vampire and the dog made their entrance.

The first act of the play was a kind of prologue to the events of December. It gave us a sequence of almost silent tableaux in which we saw not the dramatic or sensational horrors of state torture and police brutality but the routine pressures upon expression and language in everyday life which had become the common culture and history of Romanians. It stressed the actual mental and physical effort involved in living even in the most humdrum ways in an atmosphere of constant anxiety and suspicion: friends turning up the radio to blaring pitch in order to speak in whispers to one another; a father asked to report on the activities of his daughter's friends in order that the other members of the family keep their jobs; a doctor going through the motions of preaching on the crime of abortion as he accepts money to perform the operation. Where the only loud speeches are the official ones, private communication is at its most expressive when it says least: the moment when, for example, a woman as a matter of course scrapes up a broken egg from the floor in order to save it. And this despite it having come as a gift from a sister's American boyfriend whose impending marriage is making the family the object of official displeasure and leaving them shunned by neighbours and friends. Throughout these scenes we caught glimpses too of the contradictory buried thoughts and feelings beneath the quiet surface of their lives, the frustration and anger which made its way into jokes, the sad internal monologue of a woman who talks to her dead grandmother in order to hold on to a lost past; the confused and agonized priest who communes with an angel in the hopes of quieting his conscience.

Where the first act hushed its audience into listening hard to what was not being said, the second was entirely a polyphony of voices, eager to speak and tell us what happened during the last weeks of December, from the reverberations of the shootings and demonstrations in Timisoara to the execution of the Ceauşescus and the setting up of the National Salvation Front. After the cramped sentences of the first act the audience was overpowered by a medley of different eyewitnesses all offering their accounts from a variety of viewpoints: the student, the doctor, the soldier, the housewife, the painter, the bulldozer driver, reliving again what the rest of us saw on our TV screens during those Christmas holidays. As an oral history it was at once very moving and engrossing. One immediately assumed these testimonies were based upon interviews with 'real' people and that this was the kind of reportage that could form a reliable history of shared public events. It was only in the final act that we heard how many questions remained unanswered about the events themselves ('How many people were killed at Timisoara? Where are the bodies? Who was shooting whom on the 22nd? Why did no one turn off the power at the TV station?'), and how fractured and dissonant this apparently collective experience was.

There is no easy fit between the languages of public activity and events and the people who make them and are made by them. Even that most material and determinate of events – the execution of the Ceauşescus – was understood in the play as producing a backwash of panic and guilt even in those who supported their shooting. That event took on terrifying proportions not by being realistically staged but in the recurring nightmare of violence taking place in one woman's head: we saw her dreaming of herself as Elena, trying desperately to escape, being seized and captured, giving up her money and few remaining favours, and then, appallingly, her hands and feet, until only her torso was left. A soldier opens and shuts her mouth: it blurts out like a ventriloquist's dummy the sound of the jubilant crowds. Ceauşescu and his wife appeared in the play, not as 'real people' but indeed, as they were to the majority of their subjects, as representations: the figures that other people had painted on posters and walls, and carried in their minds as symbols of belief and of authority. Later a group of highspirited students out on a binge make street theatre of the execution as a drunken charade; its horror is a kind of personal and national trauma which needs to be acted out over and over again in order to be exorcized. We are impressed by a sense of the enduring violence done to human sensibility by this act, whatever its justice: the idea that the Ceauşescus were not removed by their execution; on the contrary, their power as disturbers of psychic peace, as internalized objects of hatred and fear, envy and ambition, may have expanded.

Churchill's play was clearly deconstructive in tendency; itself a remarkable piece of ensemble playing and collective work, it tried to capture the moment in which territories shift, the moment of the dissolution of collective beliefs and systems. As such it was under no obligation to offer grand strategems or to cast political horoscopes and predict the future; in any case the assurance with which we might rely on older forms of political narrative has itself been undermined by the crisis of socialism, making older vocabularies, at the very least, inadequate. Rather, *Mad Forest* concentrated upon the mess of actuality and the improvised nature of human activity which our interpretations then harden into consistency or fact. Whilst what we call history may have now moved on, the psychic terrain remains in uproar and turmoil.

It seems to me that the politics of the play lay in its capacity to bring those who were outside it to ask questions with respect; to hold off from pronouncements and assumptions, to hang fire and to listen, and where we can, and as far as we are able, to understand the complexities of a cultural history which is a history of human emotion as well as one of legislation or economic organization. There seems to be more than a strong case for this kind of listening and watching. As we recognize with dismay the rearing up of violent nationalisms in the wake of collapsing authoritarian orders, the pathologizing and hounding of other racial groups, the attacks upon alternative sexualities (to name but a few of the unleashed Furies of the last year or so), we are obliged to ask questions not only about the economic and social structures of those countries, but also about what it means to lose one's national identity, the scaffold of collective belonging which, although it may have been rigid and even punitive, was nevertheless a firm framework of support. The play brought us to the point where we could begin to understand the shocking reversal of feeling and expectation which might bring a Romanian to say of the last twenty years, 'I felt free then. I don't now.'

Mad Forest ended with a wedding between the two families in which carnival exuberance teetered on the edge of violence – a common feature of family life – but also a correlative for the state of the country as a whole. Throughout the play the creative energies released, the coming together of different groups and the possibility of new alliances always remained hedged about by fear of others and of oneself; was always likely to be capsized. Churchill's play, beginning with the singing of a Romanian socialist anthem, necessarily attached more emotional force to the travesties of communism than to its earlier idealism, and this was one of its inevitable historical and dramatic limitations. For those of us of a younger generation than Churchill, who grew up on the Cold War, on Orwell, Koestler and Solzhenitsyn, but also James Bond and le Carré, and who may have relatively little experience of any kind of political organization, there is so much one also needs to hear, not about corruption and the bankruptcy of beliefs, but about belief itself. It is perhaps relatively easy, especially for us in the West, to understand that what were once communism's shared ideals became structures of repression; less easy to reverse the process and free up what is now frozen into rigidity, seeing how it might once have been the much-desired way of giving form to the contingencies of social existence. It is relatively easy to condemn aggressive nationalisms; much harder to understand the ways in which they have also been progressive forces; it is relatively easy to attack the role of religion, much harder to see the moments when it provided a platform for rebellion against other authorities.

Mad Forest left me wanting to see more of those other prologues to the drama that we watched on stage – some tapping of those other wellsprings of the action which took place in the 1920s and 1930s, or even earlier. These accounts can perhaps only be written by insiders but they would give those of us who have been neither believers nor belongers more ways of understanding the appeal and the excitement, the collective drive and commitment that had created and sustained those now crumbling regimes. Without a sense of the achievements and the pleasures of those idealisms how else can we fathom their present-day perversions or seek to channel those incorrigible desires and fears anew?

For even the vampire and the dog were lovable once. They are distortions of humane possibility: the dog's mindless obedience to his master is the twisted image of the need to devote oneself to something bigger than the individual, to find something to love that is beyond oneself, something to make larger sense of one's own small life. And seen through another lens, the vampire feeding on his fellows is a metaphor, though a sinister one, for how much we all must take our nourishment from other people if we are to be a truly social species. Both are tokens of human interdependency, refusals of the increasingly privatized and defended world-of-one which might sometimes seem to be capitalism's ultimate goal.

6

Women Writers and Conservative Sensibilities

MURDER IN SUBURBIA*

The centenary celebrations of Agatha Christie's birth seem unlikely to challenge the well-worn assumptions about our favourite literary aunt and her work: that her settings are backward-looking, her social attitudes simply snobbish and her imaginary milieux idealised pictures of the English upper middle class in the Home Counties.

Christie is usually patronised as an old-fashioned Tory whose only considerable talent was for producing puzzles rather than crime stories, palpably unrealistic when compared to the American hardboiled school or today's more psychologically feisty writers. As the theatre programme to *The Mousetrap* informs us, Agatha Christie has now been raised to the status of a national institution – 'as English as Buckingham Palace, the House of Commons and the Tower of London.' Consequently, it's harder than ever to look critically at a writer who has become, after Shakespeare and the Bible, the world's biggest publishing phenomenon.

Certainly, television viewers watching the recent re-runs of some of her *Miss Marple* stories could be forgiven for assuming that Christie was the high priestess of nostalgia rather than the Queen of Crime. *Nemesis*, for example, took place in the BBC's best 1950s never-never land: gleaming vintage cars, faded floral prints and glistening permanent waves, all the unobtrusive detail of a well-varnished period look. *Nemesis* seemed to revolve around the restoration of a misjudged heir to his stately home in the country, a rags-to-riches

---

* 'Murder in Suburbia: Agatha Christie'. First published in *New Statesman*, 14 September 1990.

fantasy calculated to warm the cockles of any Tory heart. In the final scenes, a chamber orchestra broke into muted and reverent chords as the camera wafted us up a noble drive toward a miniature Blenheim. Miss Marple, deferentially twittering, was all but curtseying among the venerable columns.

Yet much of this razzamatazz was dreamed up by the producers. The original novel (published in the seventies, not the fifties) barely mentions the country house which they made so central. And the wronged hero in the novel turns out to be a 'jailbird' who assaults women. Inspector Slack (the wideboy-cum-policeman who frequently crosses swords with the genteel sleuth on TV) is nonexistent. His character, marginal in the novels, has been largely worked up by the series as the main televisual evidence of Christie's snobbery. Neither is the reader treated to any descriptions of England's lost grandeur; the second murder, which the series used as an excuse for showing us round an 18th-century library, takes place in the original on a blowy clifftop. Whatever the nature of Christie's conservatism it is not of the English heritage variety.

In fact it is easy to forget that Christie was essentially a modern. She began writing after the Great War and made her reputation in the 1930s, not the fifties (Miss Marple is the creature of her own late middle age). Her appeal depended on Poirot, a displaced person spanning both the Edwardian past and a new commercial present of cheap flats, cocktails, the wireless and burgeoning tourism. Her cast lists include typists, dentists, salesmen (like the anti-hero of *The ABC Murders* which excels in Graham Greeneish seediness), receptionists, shopgirls, as well as the comfortably well off. Her stories are as likely to take us into the tudorbethan villas of the stockbroker belt, the bungalow and the boarding house as the library or billiards room.

It is the respectably ordinary that intrigues her most. Compared to many of her fellow-scribblers, Christie is seldom given to the kind of writerly self-aggrandisement which disfigures English letters in the period. Unlike Dorothy L Sayers (with whom she is frequently yoked), she is not in love with a Lord and is far less interested in aping the aristocracy than in identifying the mood of a new middlebrow readership. Her characters express a cheerful and relaxed philistinism, voicing their insular prejudices while she maintains a strict autho-rial neutrality. Not surprisingly, contemporary fans like Herbert Read and Sergei Eisenstein enjoyed her dispassionate formalism.

Far from being sealed in aspic, even her rural settings are disturbed by the figures of change: weekenders, newcomers and refugees from the city. The inhabitants of King's Abbot in *The Murder of Roger Ackroyd*, her first major success in 1926, were up to date in being primarily tenants, like the retired colo-nel who 'had never been in the Shanghai club in his life'. (*The Mousetrap*, still pulling them in with its image of English traditionalism, is set among strangers in a guest house.) These are villages in which no one's lineage is reliable. Her much-maligned 'pasteboard types' – the dyspeptic squire, the acidulated spinster, the mild-mannered family doctor – are indeed theatrical, since even the most innocent-seeming in such a demobilised world is potentially acting a part. More than any other writer, Agatha Christie found a form that successfully played upon the distrust circulating within an expanding middle class between the wars. She made entertainment out of the anxiety about each other's standing that is at the heart of English class feeling.

As for being the most English of writers, that too depends upon a paradox. Christie's affection for middle-class England was one which, like many of us, she was best able to feel at a distance. Though she was a passionate home-maker, she was also a dedicated traveller and wrote many of her best-known novels – *Murder on the Orient Express, Appointment with Death* and *The ABC Murders* among them – on the hoof. This most proper of English ladies recovered from a breakdown when her first husband left her, by travelling alone in the Middle East, shocked her friends by marrying again at 40 a man 15 years her junior, and regularly spent several months in the year roughing it on archaeological digs in Syria. Plotting murder in the vicarage as she sat writing inside a hot tent in the desert, her England was always imagined as a façade, an appearance, which, like that of social position, one tries to keep up no matter how many times it is exposed as a sham.

If this is a conservative message then it is an ambiguous one. It made her as eager to relish the present as to conjure up the pathos of the past. Even Miss Marple, in one of Christie's late efforts, *At Bertram's Hotel*, solves a crime by recognising that nostalgia is a species of cover-up: 'One should not ever try to go back . . . the essence of life is going forward. Life is really a one-way street, isn't it?'

THREE ENGLANDS: DOROTHY L. SAYERS[*]

Woman of Parts: Dorothy L. Sayers: Her Life and Soul by
Barbara Reynolds (Hodder And Stoughton)

If England is always a country of the mind, there are always at least three
mental landscapes which dominate the life and work of Dorothy L. Sayers.
Most familiar is the imaginary England of Lord Peter Wimsey, Sayers's silly-
ass sleuth – 'all nerve and nose' – who brayed his way through her twelve
detective novels between the wars. His England is a retrospective recasting of
Sayers's Edwardian childhood, a place of settled customs and local pieties, of
deferential or surly rustics, ignorant policemen and superior gentry. It is epito-
mised by the church in *The Nine Tailors* where the mild Anglican rector in the
Fens (reminiscent of Sayers's own father and her childhood home) becomes
an unlikely leader and saves the community from drowning in a flood. By the
late 1930s this England seemed to be more and more engulfed by the tide of
democracy, the new civilisation whose 'jungle', as Lord Peter puts it, threatens
his ancestral home. And under the impress of war, Sayers became a forceful
spokeswoman for high church views, arguing for the national reconstruction
of England's moral and social order.

This England was the vision, however, of a woman who, in private life
at least, seems to have done her best to shed the trappings of her Edwardian
upbringing. The England that Sayers got to know in the Wimsey years was
a far cry from the patrician. She was more at home drinking beer in Fleet
Street than with debutantes or Debrett's. Her milieu was amongst the flotsam
and jetsam of new commercial times, car-salesmen, motor-racing fiends and
demobbed officers turned journalists, like the whisky-drinking crime reporter
she eventually married.

A permanent job at Benson's, the most modern and progressive of advertising agencies, where she was one of the first female copywriters, gave her the
chance to develop Lord Peter and finally to shake him off. And if Peter, as a
fawning fantasy was her ideal man, her own romances were shockingly unre-
spectable: a sexually tormented affair with a Russian Jew, and a purely physical
fling with a motor-mechanic, who took her to the Hammersmith Palais and
finally left her pregnant. She rarely went home to the rectory, except on the
back of a motorbike. For even at her most reactionary, Sayers was always in
tune with the times.

---

[*] First published in the *Guardian*, 17 April, 1993.

This was the Sayers who could lecture with gusto on 'The Importance of Being Vulgar' and write racy, down-to-earth prose on some of the most high-flown subjects. When she took up the cudgels for the church in the 1940s, her talents lay in popularising its dogma. She clearly understood the art of broadcasting as well as advertising and her mammoth religious drama for the BBC, *The Man Born to be King*, provoked outraged headlines when the disciples were heard using Cockney slang. Her capacity to entertain and her common touch gained her friends on both sides of the ecclesiastical fence (the Labour-supporting Archbishop William Temple was a keen admirer), though her bull-in-a-china-shop manner could easily alienate.

Sayers's third mental kingdom, and perhaps the most lasting place in her imagination, was Oxford. For her, it was both ancient and modern. Despite her academic predilections for the medieval past, Sayers insisted that her Oxford was not backward-looking but emancipating. She was among the first generation of women to receive degrees; Oxford gave her an intellectual confidence and lifelong collaborative friendships with women. But Oxford also represented an ideal of timelessness. The life of the mind was at once engaged and removed, rising above history and above one's sex. When Harriet Vane, the independent woman, scholar and writer of fiction, upstages and then falls for Peter Wimsey in *Gaudy Night*, the union of the modern blue-stocking and the feudal past can only take place in Oxford.

A search for order, for the rigorous and universal pattern – be it in detection or church doctrine, her theories of creativity or the mathematical formulae of bellringing (whose intricate complexities she mastered for *The Nine Tailors*) – was the emotional bedrock of her conservatism. Of her group of Anglo-Catholic apologists, which included her friends Charles Williams and C.S. Lewis, she is closest to T.S. Eliot, whom she was most in awe of. They would have made strange bedfellows, him pale and proper and her flamboyant and loud. Yet *The Four Quartets* is equally intent on cerebral control, keeping at bay an emotional flood of doubt.

Her last project, a translation of Dante's *Divine Comedy*, returned her to her Oxford skills, though typically she wanted to modernise the *terza rima*. Her Dante was not the *altissimo poeta* of Catholicism, but a live Italian, feeling his beliefs on the pulse and voicing his visions in a dramatic vernacular. She got twenty cantos into the *Paradiso* before she died in 1957 and, appropriately, passed the work on to a young woman scholar, the author of this new biography.

Where others might have looked for the conflict between these worlds, Barbara Reynolds looks only for their consonance, imposing her own kind of protective pattern on what was a messy past. Sayers maintained an extraordinary reticence about her emotions, making a secret for life of her illegitimate son, and almost concealing her unpresentable husband. But Reynolds is even more withholding. She puts Sayers into soft focus, countering earlier biographical impressions of her (as sexual deviant, bad mother, heartless wife) simply by asserting what a good and kind friend she was. Instead of the exuberant, rude and fat eccentric, dramatizing herself and bullying others, she gives us a dreamy young woman, practising a Mona Lisa smile.

Barbara Reynolds is chairman of the Dorothy L. Sayers society, and this biography is part of its centenary celebrations. She was also, though she doesn't say so, Sayers's god-daughter (from an adult baptism). There is an irony about all this. For as the Victorians knew, the writing of the 'great life' was also a way of giving it decent public burial. And I found myself wondering whether the burden of living so long with Sayers as mentor and almost-mother might not have become a little wearying. Perhaps this biography has been as much a working free (however unintentional) from that association as an enshrining of it. In any case the relation between biographer and subject is never simply sunny. Hagiography must first kill in order to canonise.

A DREAM OF THREE CONTINENTS:
THE FILMS OF MERCHANT IVORY*

For many of today's cinemagoers the name Merchant Ivory means period films. Loose talk (not least in this magazine – see *Sight and Sound* June 1991) has identified the company's recent adaptations of E. M. Forster's *Room with a View* and *Maurice* in particular with a conservative evocation of Englishness, in which the Edwardian era figures as a more civilised lost age, filmed as elegant costume drama. And now we have their version of *Howards End*.

Yet far from being insular, Merchant Ivory are essentially cosmopolitan. Their other recent work includes a documentary on street musicians in Bombay, a feature about Thomas Jefferson's sexual liaison with a woman slave, and a film of Anita Desai's *In Custody*, the story of a poor teacher's attachment to Urdu poetry. Whatever the nature of Merchant Ivory's romance with the past, Robert Emmet Long's new book reminds us that it is part and parcel of an extraordinary crosscultural project.

For thirty years Merchant Ivory have depended on an international collaboration (the longest-running in the industry) between producer Ismail Merchant, a Bombay Indian who grew up during the violent years of Partition as well as the heyday of India's commercial movies, director James Ivory, an American from the mid-west, and Ruth Prawer Jhabvala, born in Cologne to Jewish parents of Polish-Russian extraction. A respected novelist and script-writer of fifteen Merchant Ivory productions. Jhabvala's marriage took her to India, where she lived for twenty-four years.

Influenced by the work of Satyajit Ray, Merchant Ivory were pioneers in representing Indian life to western audiences. *The Householder* (1963), *Shakespeare Wallah* (1965), *The Guru* (1968) and *Bombay Talkie* (1970) explored contradictions in the lives of westernised Indians and the inability of westerners to come to terms with post-independence India. Emmet Long does not comment on the films' racial politics, but part of their originality lies in their unashamed preoccupation with the romance of another culture; with cultural diversity as the source of desire and pleasure as well as fear. Their unembarrassed treatment of mixed race love affairs suggests how much Merchant Ivory's films owe to an older politics, formed before 1968, both more internationalist and more liberal than today's 'identity politics'.

---

* 'A Dream of Three Continents: Merchant Ivory Productions' first published in *Sight and Sound*, March 1992.

The idea of conflict within and between cultures has consistently marked their films – the clash between European romanticism and New England puritanism in *The Europeans*, between northern feminism and southern chauvinism in *The Bostonians*, and homosexual love between the classes in *Maurice*. But these oppositions are usually offset by a longing to transcend differences and find a secure place for oneself, an identity and a home. Emmet Long points out the centrality given to particular buildings in Ivory's locations, the white frame houses of New England, the deserted palaces of the Raj, ambivalent symbols of settlement. Sometimes Ivory's over-lyrical stylishness can drown Prawer Jhabvala's irony: in *Quartet*, his loving recreation of Parisian cafés worked against the realisation of Jean Rhys' sense of placelessness.

Merchant Ivory are an anomaly: an independent company making 'quality' films about awkward subjects for an increasingly mainstream audience. They straddle the boundary between art film and Hollywood without belonging to either. Emmet Long is certainly less comfortable with the company's 'oddball movies' like *Wild Party* or *Slaves of New York* and his lavishly produced volume reinforces their image as 'literary film-makers'. His book radiates culture, but of the sort that makes many want to reach for a gun.

Whereas Merchant Ivory's films have treated both the art market and the film industry ironically, they seem to believe in literature as a purely civilising art. In fact, Jhabvala's scripts have edited out some of the snobberies and cruelties of the liberal tradition: *Room with a View* was a far more genial celebration than Forster's own picture of the English middle classes; her *Bostonians* substituted a feminist triumph for Henry James' vicious climax. How can the limits of these novels and their milieux be exposed if their 'realism' is taken at face value? I am less sanguine than Emmet Long at the prospect of Merchant Ivory 'finding their forbears in literature'. Better to remain rootless.

Merchant Ivory's films offer us a dream of three continents (the title of one of Jhabvala's most ambitious novels); a never-never world like that of *Roseland*, their film set in the New York dance palace, where differences may turn sour but where romance can offer temporary resolutions. The company itself seems admirably to have represented humanistic ideals of cooperation and reconciliation. For some tastes this liberalism will always smack too much of faery tale; but faced with increasingly virulent forms of conservatism and radical sectarianism, we might feel like raising at least two cheers for their dream.

SENSE AND SENSITIVITY: ANITA BROOKNER AND JOANNA TROLLOPE*

On the surface they couldn't be more different. Brookner is melancholy, cosmopolitan, her heroines the denizens of heavily-carpeted mansion flats and prosperous London suburbs, well-heeled and well-turned out but ultimately life's losers and its natural solitaries. Trollope, on the other hand, is cheerful and mildly Anglican, her territory the shires and cathedral towns, crowded married lives with boisterous families of growing children, with her middle-aged heroines going in for successful 'late flowering'.

Different generations, too. Anita Brookner, the child of Polish parents, grew up in the 1930s and her novels (even when set, like *A Family Romance*, in the present) return inexorably to the long summer of conservatism (roughly 1930–1956) when life was supposedly simpler and more austere. A good 20 years her junior, Joanna Trollope seasons her tales of the provinces with a strong helping of the contemporary. *A Spanish Lover* captures, among other things, the aspirations of a couple for whom setting up an art gallery, getting an Aga and Edwardian brass beds are their wildest dreams in Mrs Thatcher's 1980s.

Yet despite these real differences, their writing is of a piece. Though Trollope is more chattily downmarket and has little of the aphoristic formality that won Brookner the Booker prize in 1984 for *Hotel du Lac*, they share an investment in an emotional economy. Respectability and its limits fascinates both; the traumas of the quiet life, and the longings of those comfortable people who feel themselves deprived. For if there is such a thing as the bourgeois psyche, it is as much at home in Shepton Mallett as in Vienna.

Women writers have long been well placed to record what George Eliot called the unhistoric acts woven into the fabric of most people's history: the small change of everyday life – caring for relatives or running a home – that can cost an enormous expenditure of spirit and energy. The novel developed as a place where the middle-class woman could explore her identification with the interior life of private feeling: with what, in fact, being middle class meant. In their emotional struggles, 19th-century heroines test out the limits of their communities. Cramped by social laws, desiring to break free, a Maggie Tulliver or a Jane Eyre learned to reconcile private needs with public demands. Their self-awareness was given such a moral charge that it could make readers forget the need for more sweeping change.

---

* 'Sense and Sensitivity: Anita Brookner and Joanna Trollope' first published in *New Statesman*, 9 July 1993.

Brookner and Trollope might seem to follow in these footsteps. Like Rosamund Lehmann, Elizabeth Taylor and Barbara Pym in our own century, they too make women the guardians and the victims of respectability. And they rehearse the inevitable bourgeois question: can you have both passion and position? Such writers set great store by social and emotional order. They relish and fear whatever disrupts its calm surface. This usually means sex, which even in the Cotswolds or in Maida Vale is the great destroyer.

A Family Romance sets up a familiar Brookner opposition between the appeal of the self-seeking life and the virtuous but mousey one. The same polarities, between desire and its repression, sensibility and sense, play themselves out in *A Spanish Lover*, where the English puritan heroine falls in love with a married Catholic foreigner. You can be sure she won't be allowed to eat her cake and have it. Pleasure has always to be paid for.

Why do readers keep on going back for more? Because the compensation for self-control, as Freud believed, is to think yourself more civilised. Brookner and Trollope offer their readers a training in character as restraining as those 18th-century conduct manuals designed to supplant the aristocracy with a new moral class. Always keep your voice low; never shed a public tear; avoid embarrassment; always be well-groomed. And however much they leaven their advice with self-mockery, they assume their female fans, like their heroines, will want to be ladies. Readers are flattered into thinking themselves rather clever and a bit superior: if they can't be happy and successful, they can at least be *sensitive*.

The real fear in the heroines' lives is not to be found loveless but tasteless. Caste rather than class feeling animates them. Brookner and Trollope, belonging to different *couches* of the middle-class, remind us how much the respectable thrive on self-division.

Both are obsessed by money while continuously denying its importance. The materialists are always *other* people; the vagaries of the vulgar are displayed in order to distance the heroines from them. Trollope's chosen few are definitely not the ones who modernise their cottages with Laura Ashley wallpapers and Marks & Spencer curtains. Rather, they are makeshift bohemians like the rector's wife. They wear trailing skirts with gaily-coloured scarves tied round their waists and live in a muddle of cats and quarry-tiling. Always keen to put down others as the dupes of consumerism, they don't see that their own style is as much a creature of the times.

Like many middle-class children of both left and right, they find their own class endlessly absorbing. They don't bother much with the working classes, though both can manage those tough warm-hearted types who belong to a better, more deferential past. Brookner's 'helps' and taxi drivers are the usual spirited Cockneys, while Trollope's village locals never rise above the level of Hodge. Such people, like the upper classes, hardly have an inner life at all.

Yes, this is *Cranford* and *Middlemarch* revisited. But what's missing is what took Gaskell and Eliot beyond the boundaries of their own small selves. Their vision of renunciation was in aid, not of being special, but of belonging to the world beyond their windows. That engagement with the unknown – the Manchester poor or the Jewish community of *Daniel Deronda* – wrenched the plots out of frame and made for violent or unconvincing endings. They took real risks as authors, and as women, in trying to imagine a society in which their needs were tempered not just by family and friends but by the genuinely unfamiliar.

Brookner and Trollope always play it safe. They have nothing bigger to offer women than themselves. The lonely pleasures of individualism take over where the idealisms of romance and politics fail. It's true that insisting on your individuality is emancipating for those brought up to subordinate their needs. But emotional independence is only a halfway house towards a better kind of dependency. Seeing yourself as special is only the first step toward seeing all others as equally so. Gaskell and Eliot knew there was no such thing as just individuals and their families, but such a thing as a society: that great web of responsibility that connects us all.

7

Against Empathy[*]

The season of sixth-form interviews has come round again: one of the few official times in the teaching year when colleges and schools get some glimpse of each other's work. This year I have been struck by the sounding of a new note in the applications. Asked why they want to spend the next three years doing a degree in English, candidates frequently reply: 'because it is about people'. 'I am fascinated', wrote one sixth-former feelingly on her UCAS form, 'by ordinary human beings'. Why do I find this so dismaying? Isn't such evidence of fellow-feeling in anyone, let alone a 17-year old, a Good Thing?

ORDINARY HUMAN BEINGS?

Well yes and no. On a simple level one might wonder why a degree in English studies should be seen as more 'about people' than history or geography. It is certainly far less directly so than social work, management studies, nursing, and many other vocational courses. Pressed to say more, interviewees reveal that the kind of reading they most enjoy is where they can identify with the characters and share their feelings. Reading is about empathising; by identifying with others, literature can also be a process of self-discovery. Thus despite Jane Austen's Emma being a young lady living in 1815, she seems to make mistakes just like any headstrong adolescent of this day and age.

The trouble is that what seems the most generous of claims for literature can become the most narrow-minded. The accent on empathy which appears to be about the toleration of difference and the explanation of sensibility

---

[*] First published in *The English Review*, Vol.5, Issue 2, November 1994.

and sensitivity, can work in reverse. At the worst, the emotional and moral certainty of those who want literature to underwrite their own experience – 'I like it because it is about me' – can harden into a fundamentalism quite immune to argument; at best it can severely hamper, rather than prepare students, for the scope and demands of literary studies.

THE LANGUAGE BARRIER

In the first place, encouraging empathy as a primary literary response is historically inappropriate and downright obstructive as a way of exploring vast stretches of literary territory. Students are likely to be baffled by literary cultures which do not deal in the currency of self-expression or put relationships between individuals as the highest good. A vocabulary of characterisation and a romantic view of authorship is unable to cope with writing which values literary imitation, repetition and ritual, be it medieval or high modernist. Placing a premium on personal feeling does not get you very far with an Elizabethan sonnet, except perhaps to bemoan the poet's failure to be 'original'. If it is not a lyric which can be constructed to be about the self, then how is it to be read? Epic verse, ballads, satire, court poetry: the stress on empathy puts obstacles in the way of making sense of such writing. Not surprisingly, students come to feel that they can only read novels.

Underpinning empathy is the idea that literature primarily tells us what individual writers feel about their world. Language is seen as a purely expressive instrument, reflecting the world back to us. Earlier forms of language are seen as obscure and needing translation. This may be why interviewees talk cheerfully about getting through the 'language barrier' of earlier times, as though the aim is simply to make the language transparent, to look through it and discover that despite differences in religion, speech, concepts of love, honour, family, sexual relations and so on, in the end there are people just like ourselves in the pages of Chaucer or Shakespeare or Thomas Hardy.

Such students are likely to resent the notion that writing is artificial; that much literature is about itself (not a trendy postmodern idea but an ancient one); that our responses are not natural but are elicited as effects of writing; that far from being an unmediated reflection of the world, novels, poetry and all forms of writing help to shape and construct the world. With so much stress placed on feeling, it can seem a bit of a come-down for literary critics to concern themselves with the materials and the mechanics of writing – how it is done in words – rather than just going with the flow. It may be that students studying A-level language will come to be more sympathetically prepared than those studying literature.

THE CONSTRUCTION OF EMPATHY

I was not reassured by sixth-form tutors at a recent conference held at my college, who insisted that empathy could only be the first stage of reading, the foundation upon which other, more critical skills are built. This division, presented as a choice between primary response and literary analysis, is surely a misleading one. Empathy is itself a form of literary analysis and it is not only encouraged by the choice of reading matter (hence Chaucer's 'Prologue' with all those nice characters makes a suitable A-level text, but not 'The Book of the Duchess' or 'The Parliament of Fowls'), but is also naturalised as a way of responding to literary texts by the kinds of questions asked in class, titles to essays and assignments, and the moral and social assumptions of teachers.

That it is neither neutral nor natural is clear from the way that empathy can easily mask a nervous moral agenda. Analysing 'relationships' between characters tends toward moral judgments of them, judgments which are inevitably parti-san. Do we ask students to identify with Iago or Bill Sykes? (Though it would be worth asking why Dickens and his readers found the murder of Nancy in *Oliver Twist* such compulsively thrilling reading.) Alternatively, literary texts are anxiously searched for stable 'role models'. Teachers might rightly feel uneasy about inviting impressionable 16-year olds to share in Sylvia Plath's feelings ('the poem is the poet'), let alone Dostoyevsky's or Edgar Allen Poe's. The apparent liberalism of letting pupils *feel* is always tempered by bourgeois restraint.

Empathy is closely tied to the notion of learning moral truths from read-ing and to the ideas of self-development and moral scrutiny. In other words, it tends to treat all literature as a species of realism and therefore makes it all the harder to recognise that realism is a species of writing, historically limited, morally pointed and socially situated. It makes it easy to forget that the tech-niques of the realist novel which seem to us to be so much about the individual life, were part of an attempt to get beyond individuals and their worlds of one, to link them in what George Eliot saw as the great seamless web of society, and to escape the confines of a socially-divided world by making other kinds of bonds. Reading realist novels historically is to read the history of the idea of individuality and the dissatisfactions, as well as the ambitions, of a culture which has set so much store by this idea.

HISTORY AND CULTURAL DIFFERENCE

Empathy, on the other hand, only pays lip service to history: it is relentlessly modernising in outlook. History may be there in the form of carriages and crinolines and the class system, like so much furniture cluttering up the pages, but the people remain the same. What is disheartening is that every picture ends up telling the same story: human nature, universal in its needs and ideals, is seen learning or failing to learn the moral truths of existence. Whether it be King Lear struggling on the heath, Marlowe in *Heart of Darkness* up the Congo without a paddle, or the weary heroine of *Hotel du Lac* coming to terms with romance, all are translated into moral homilies which might just as well have been written in the same year.

Yet nothing could be more historical than our ideas of ourselves, our social, moral and personal values, our subjectivity, our waking thoughts and even our dreams. Beatrice and Benedick are not twentieth-century persons in a costume drama, with the values and choices of the contemporary person. And, in any case, if Emma's emotional universe is simply your own in drag, why bother with it? If people read the literature of the past looking for themselves, they can surely find contemporary sentiment and feeling much better represented in contemporary forms like television, film and pop music.

The idea that the literature of the past is a hall of mirrors endlessly reflecting back one's own face, ought to be an appalling one. It is much more intellectually exciting and challenging to recognise our distance from the past, its strangeness rather than its familiarity. Acknowledging rather than sliding over historical and social differences is part of the effort of learning. If literature must be seen as being about people (and there are other better reasons why it should be), there is more intellectual mileage in comparing its study to that of anthropology than psychology. If we are happy to introduce children to 'the people of Borneo and their customs', why not encourage the same attitude when approaching the writings of earlier times and different cultures? Any fellow-feeling worth its name is learnt through the appreciation of difference, not sameness. What's more, empathy tends to homogenise and to play down the differences between readers as well as texts. It assumes that all children will automatically share the same structure of feeling and the same cultural outlook.

THE USES OF PLEASURE

Finally, the strongest argument against empathy is that it sells short the many different pleasures of reading. In fact we know from childhood that literature is the 'land of faery' where we may encounter worlds way beyond ourselves; worlds we have never known and are not likely to know – except in books. There is at least as strong a case for saying that reading even the most realist of novels is as much about self-forgetfulness as self-discovery, the abandonment of our small individual lives in some larger dream; that all art is a kind of anarchy, whatever order it might finally impose; that it demands a temporary suspension of our knowledge of ourselves and others, a reaching out to our limits rather than merely a reassurance that we are eternally what we are.

So much of the pleasure of reading and writing is a flight into the fantastic, the imaginable but unmanageable, the socially inoperable but desirable, what Coleridge called 'the vast' ('I never regarded my senses in any way as the criteria of my belief'). The fascination of repulsion which inspires so many literary creations from Gargantua to Fagin reminds us that writing and reading are as much about the buried conflicts and longings within societies, as the conscious intentions of either writer or reader. Jane Austen's head may have preferred Fanny Price's decorum but her heart is ineluctably drawn towards Maria Crawford. 'Identification' is itself a complex and unpredictable process. There is no easy fit between reader and what is read: no reason why readers, if they do identify, should do so only with the same sex or age, or race. Empathy dubiously implies that we can control and channel our responses but readers frequently read against the grain of the messages they are offered.

Literature is larger than life: this is both its strength and its weakness. So much is lost by seeing Miss Havisham, Raskolnikov or Othello as people like ourselves and by reducing literature to life. When Dickens wrote that as a boy he lay 'reading as if for life' he did not mean, in that instance, in order to understand its exigencies but to escape from them. But it is not only fairy stories or fables which are 'escapist' – so too are the consoling moral fictions of Jane Austen and George Eliot and, of course, Dickens himself. Like the impossible inheritances and coincidences of the realist novel, their moral visions could magically reassure readers that the divisive workings of modern industrial society could be humanised and understood. In a society where class was not felt as 'a hurt without a name', there would be no way of understanding Pip's great expectations or the moral consolation with which Dickens hopes to dissolve their pain.

To say that literature compensates for life's damages is not to underestimate its importance. One of the reasons why we need literature is because we make such a mess of our social relations. When 18-year olds say they want to read in order to understand people, they are commenting upon the inadequacies of the present as much as the literatures of the past. Behind their desire must surely lie another question as to why humanity has needed so many stories to see them through the night. It was Dickens too who wrote (in sentiments still-appropriate for the 1990s): 'in a utilitarian age, of all other times, it is a matter of grave importance that Faery tales should be respected.'

8

The Mighty Mongrel: on Biography*

I remember the illustration: a souwestered Grace Darling in her father's life-boat, storm-tossed on a high sea, coming to the aid of half-drowned sailors. Perhaps her bravery meant something special to me, living in a coastal city. But like the other heroines in my *Wonder Book for Girls*, she was mainly fodder for those day-dreams in which I was saving the school from fire (to resounding cheers from the Upper Sixth) or rescuing puppy dogs from freezing brooks (no mean feat in our terraced streets). Although the exemplary life was a far-off fantasy, the feelings it inspired came from closer to home: the need to know your actions mattered, that you hadn't just landed a bit-part in history. You too could be centre-stage.

The search for *example* – for a pattern, in the sense used by religion and dressmaking – is one of the deepest and earliest impulses of biography. And it is an impulse that survives even when the subject invites mixed feelings rather than any simple admiration. In fact, the present boom in biography suggests that the appetite for the exemplary is even more voracious in a secular society than in a strictly religious one.

For it's wrong, of course, to assume that the revelation of the sordid or the scurrilous can rob a life of its status. The discovery that our idols have feet of clay may make them more, not less, fascinating. And it's just as likely to provoke the moral or the moralising response. We may no longer imitate Christ, but the urge to scrutinise the exceptional, put ourselves in their shoes and learn from their lives, is one way of understanding the contemporary cult of personality, be the icons Virginia Woolf or Tina Turner. The exemplary can be a warning as well as a model.

---

* First published in the *New Statesman*, 17/31 December 1993.

And nothing can make a pattern of our days like biography. At least as sig-nificant as the nature of the life is biography's confidence that it *can* be told as a story, a story that makes sense. Nothing seems more innocent or artless than the form of biography; every life must run from the cradle to the grave and chrono-logical progress goes firmly hand in hand with psychological development.

Through the labyrinth of the most unstable or obscure events, biography guides us with its steady thread of narrative. The poor old subject may never arrive at enlightenment, but the reader, leaning on biography's rod and staff, makes a safe pilgrimage through the wilderness of the world.

No wonder biography appeals. As Richard Holmes writes in *Footsteps* (his exemplary history of romantic individualism), biography can be the most pro-foundly hopeful of literary forms. The emphasis may fall differently on the outer or the inner life – the life of a politician, say, as opposed to the life of an artist – but biography convinces us that a discernible continuity between the public and the private can be found.

It asserts the integrity of character (that a person's actions and words do constitute a meaningful whole) and it affirms a faith in individual agency. Most persuasively, it can reassure us that human identity is ultimately knowable and reachable in all its variations: an emotional geography that can be mapped and plotted whatever its peaks and troughs.

That's why learning about Roald Dahl's homophobia or anti-Semitism (via leaks from Jeremy Treglown's forthcoming life) need not disturb the essential romance of biography, its celebration of the self. On the contrary, our own age of popular Freudianism would expect to find this journey to the centre of the psyche getting muddier and muddier. In this topography, the unconscious is both an inner sanctum and the innermost circle of hell inhab-ited by shadowy, perverse creatures. The nastier it is, the more convincing the account may seem.

If the real person is the inner person, it's hard, especially these days, not to conflate privacy with sexuality, and make the sexual the most authentic part of the self. The closet (or the lumber-room) becomes the first place to look. Andrew Motion's discovery of Philip Larkin's porn library was thus a red-letter day for the biography. Here at last was the key to the man. So too, Mar-garet Forster's unveiling of Daphne du Maurier's 'Venetian tendencies' was intended not as a slur but as the missing piece of the puzzle, a fitting together of the life and works.

Maybe that's why Richard Ellmann's *Oscar Wilde*, which heralded the new biographical goldrush, was such a spectacular bestseller. No other figure could have presaged so painfully the century's obsession with sexual identity. No one could have been a greater tease about its significance.

At its worst, the psycho-biography reduces the outer life until it is almost an encumbrance or an irrelevance. All that matters are the psychic needs and unspoken longings that the biographer analyses. It moves us as readers from a straightforward (occasionally supine) admiration, through the halfway house of compassionate distance (what Dr Johnson called 'complicated virtue'), to a proprietorial knowingness, a smug, sometimes embarrassing collusion with the writer.

Not content with the written leftovers of a life or even others' testimony, 'psycho-plagiarists', as Nabokov called them, forge (in both senses) a version of your psyche too. Such borrowings have taken a new, even sinister, turn with the emergence of 'bionovels' such as David Leavitt's *While England Sleeps*, which Stephen Spender has accused of swiping his life.

But if the psycho-biography sequesters the self, mewing it up in a room of its own, a close attention to the inner life can foster more democratic feelings. That same claim to intimacy that curdles the stomach can, in a different vein, be the biographer's attempt to write a history of the everyday, to capture the rough and tumble of the past. Biographers, after all, are a species of oral historian, listeners for whom no testimony is too lowly. Life-stories are just as able to unsettle ideas of rank and privilege as to promote them. Biography can be a kind of people's history – written not from below, but from inside.

Biography's focus on the personal has led the more muscular disciplines to suspect it of triviality and self-indulgence. In academic circles, biography has been largely patronised; it isn't *proper* scholarship. The professionalisation of literary studies was certainly quick to give it short shrift. Chatter about Shelley smacked of the kind of velvetty *belle-lettrism* (and ladies' amateur classes) spurned by serious, virile graduates. Long before Roland Barthes proclaimed the death of the author, university English in this country had (via practical criticism and 'close reading') depersonalised the writing of books. Continental structuralism helped stiffen the sinews of many a man who had always feared he was teaching a sissy subject

Antidotes to infatuation with the individual involve a strong dose of the historical. Making more than a vague gesture toward 'the age', such biographies will look for typicality and insist on the common structures of private feeling. At the other extreme from the psycho-biography lies the collective or the cultural biography. But if the former risks shrinking the social world to the psyche, the latter is in danger of reducing people to 'mere symptoms of the past'. Lytton Strachey, like other modernists, implies history is an illness.

The faith in individual agency alone – that people simply make history – is a romantic fantasy. But a social fabric wiped clean of the mess of humanity, manufactured only by impersonal forces, is equally wishful thinking. Should

we diagnose the current fever for biography as a morbid sign, putting its popularity down to a privatising response?

The recourse to biographical stories of social change, in a world where
political movements and programmes no longer convince, might seem a last-
ditch affair. Worse still, it could be of a piece withthe aggressive individualism
that passes for much government policy. I wonder. The opposite view seems
just as plausible. In the clamour for biography, the bio-pic, the TV mini-
series, isn't there an echo of more sociable desires, a longing to enter the lives
of strangers? As the spaces available for such chance encounters become ever
tenser, biography is one way of getting beyond your own neck of the woods.

The best biography manages to give a meaning to the relationship between
the life and the times. And the history of biography (which has still to be written) would chart the various religious, moral or political interpretations of that
relationship. For the forms in which we make connections between our own
interests and practices and those of groups much bigger, and sometimes quite
other, than ourselves are also subject to change. They need constant reap-
praisal, new vocabularies, new ways of seeing.

In the late 20th century, this is especially true of biography's usual framework, 'the private and the public'. What might once have been a useful tool
for analysing the patterns of social life and how it felt to inhabit them – the
separation of home and work, for example – could well belong to the past.
How much purchase do these terms have on the way we live now? And how
much does this opposition belong to European histories, suggesting organisations of social and psychic life out of synch with other cultures?

Biography's hope for the future may lie in its hybridity. Neither fact nor
fiction, neither record nor hearsay, neither highbrow nor low, it has long
been a literary cross-dresser with an ambiguous position. If it is to get beyond
those convenient shorthands – 'inner and outer', 'individual and society', 'life
and times' – this great mongrel among pedigree narratives will have to go on
mixing it.

9

Hitchcock's *Rebecca*: A Woman's Film?*

It's not just that Hitchcock's *Rebecca* wasn't exactly Daphne du Maurier's; it wasn't entirely Hitchcock's either. Arriving in Hollywood in 1939, Hitchcock's first American feature was overshadowed by David O. Selznick, the producer who had bought him and who liked to run things his way. 'Selznick's *Rebecca*' (as the publicity had it, relegating the director to the position of a 'mentor' who had 'collaborated' with Selznick) was to be 'the most glamorous picture ever made'. Made in 1940, it was heralded as the successor to *Gone With the Wind*, the film which in fact absorbed nearly all Selznick's energies during the actual shooting of *Rebecca*, though he reserved the last edit to himself and laid in the corny Franz Waxman score.

But it was the feminine angle of *Rebecca* that caused ructions. Or rather which Selznick defended in injured tones, rejecting as 'distorted and vulgarised' Hitchcock's first treatment of the novel, and insisting that the picture respect 'the little feminine things which are so recognisable and which make every woman say, "I know just how she feels. I know just what she's going through." ' And this meant sticking to the story.

Selznick was renowned for his filming of literary classics (*Little Lord Fauntleroy, The Prisoner of Zenda*). He revered the capacity of film to bring books and their characters to life. The promotion of *Rebecca* concentrated on book tie-ins. From lending-library stands in cinema foyers to illustrated bookmarks, advance screening for 'book experts' and 'thorough school coverage', the literariness, and thereby the borrowed cultural cachet, of the film was enhanced. Tributes to 'the importance of the du Maurier family in English letters and the stage' mingled with shameless exhortations to the English distributors to 'cash

---

* First published in *Sight and Sound*, May 1996.

in on the appeal of Your Famous Bestseller'. A letter competition invited local girls to discuss such nervous topics as 'Should A Girl Marry Outside Her Social Class?' or 'Would You Marry A Man You Knew Little About?' (though not, it should be noted, 'Why Marry A Man Old Enough To Be Your Father?').

There was every kind of tension between Selznick and Hitchcock. Hitchcock was impatient with the idea of movie-making as 'picturisation'. But he also in later years disowned the film as catering too much for the female audience Selznick clearly had in mind. 'It's not a Hitchcock picture,' he told François Truffaut. 'It's a novelette really. The story is old-fashioned; there was a whole school of feminine literature at the period, and though I'm not against it, the fact is that the story is lacking in humour.' (Two of the scenes which Selznick had cut from the script were of vomiting: hearty male jokes, presumably.) The taint of the novelettish lingered: 'Boots library in its level of appeal,' sneered Lindsay Anderson in 1972, with public-school hauteur and far more cultural snobbery than 'Hitch', who wanted to make films that could be both experimental and popular.

Slavishness to the literary and, even worse, to the woman's novel of the 1930s, was compounded by the kind of romantic glamorisation of settings and of actors that offended Hitchcock's more democratic sensibilities and documentary leanings. Where Selznick was drawn to the past, the gorgeous and the patrician, Hitchcock wrote articles in the thirties championing 'the only genuine life and drama' in Britain, that of 'ordinary everyday citizens'. He proclaimed himself a believer in the 'little man', loathing 'dress shirts, cocktails, and Oxford accents', the bottled-up stiff breeding of the English upper classes and the stagey actors who mimicked them. Like Laurence Olivier playing Maxim de Winter, du Maurier's suave but tormented hero.

It is easy to see *Rebecca* as a transitional, settling-in kind of film: Hitchcock's debut in Hollywood, his compromise with the producer-director system, his trial run of the superior resources that the American film industry had to offer. In the *auteur* theory, which charts the director's progress as the inevitable development of his genius (followed usually by the sad decline of the old man: enter his young disciples), *Rebecca* is an 'immature' film which nevertheless shows 'the Master' emerging from his apprenticeship. In their now classic account of Hitchcock, Eric Rohmer and Claude Chabrol did their best to blame du Maurier for any of the film's faults, curiously arguing that while Hitchcock absolutely faithfully adapted the 'gossipy and somewhat affected novel', he turned it into something quite different – a 'modern and disquieting' thriller.

Did they read the book? Fans of du Maurier's original might well argue that far from Hitchcock saving her novel, *Rebecca* provided him with the kind of material that brought out his strengths. *Rebecca* was in fact a long way from the Edwardian novelette or the standard fare of interwar romance, which is why it survived when so many titles faded into oblivion. (Who now reads Berta Ruck?) Transporting the gauche heroine to the aristocratic Manderley, the novel kicks off where most romances end, with life after marriage. None of du Maurier's novels close to the sound of wedding bells: rueful, violent, frequently gloomy, *Rebecca* is the most introspective of the lot. A post-romantic novel, it suggested that at the heart of every marriage is a crime.

More about hate than love, du Maurier insisted, *Rebecca* is above all a study in jealousy. The girl's first-person narration, her incessant imaginings about the dead Rebecca and her projections of her (and Rebecca's) life back and forth into past and future, crosses precisely that unstable psychological territory of fantasy and obsession, of guilty memory and fearful innocence, which were to become Hitchcock's hallmark. Herself a shy and lonely young wife, du Maurier wrote as the second Mrs de Winter. Her own romance with Frederick Browning, the strong, silent man who had swept her off her feet, was rapidly wearing thin. 'Tommy' or 'Boy' Browning, a war hero of the First World War, still suffered from nightmares and depressions: the family nickname for him became 'Moper' (though he became better known as one of the generals in the disastrous command of Arnhem through Dirk Bogarde's portrayal of him in Attenborough's *A Bridge Too Far*). Billeted abroad, Daphne dreaded regimental functions and found herself haunted by fears of her husband's passion for his ex-fiancée, Jan Ricardo, darkhaired, beautiful and exotic.

Part of the struggle over the film was between Selznick's love of the lavish, of expensive costumes and big houses, and Hitchcock's desire for surface realism and the carefully observed detail of the everyday. *Rebecca* begins as a love story and advances as a thriller. Manderley (like Tara in *Gone With the Wind*), with its loyal retainers and sumptuous breakfasts, represents a conservative longing; it bespeaks another kind of England (the sort that went down very well in Hollywood), frozen in the aspic of tradition. Manderley is the England Hitchcock must have felt well shot of, inhabited by stuffed shirts with cut-glass accents, as closed to him as to the nameless, and thereby average, girl. The film works hard to deglamorise it.

The first prospect of Manderley is not a view at all. Obscured in the pouring rain, it is reflected like a miniature paperweight model in the misty windscreen of the car (one of the many shots that seem to prefigure *Citizen Kane*, which came out the following year). We are never asked to marvel at sweeping shots of the grounds. Very little is made of the romance of Cornwall. The retinue of servants, who might be expected to stir up the viewers' envy and admiration, merely underline the girl's nervousness. Mrs Danvers, in particular, Rebecca's sinister housekeeper, appears suddenly and soundlessly, reminding us that servants make intimacy and ease impossible. In the film, as in the novel, Manderley, as Rebecca's home, is ultimately repudiated as excessive (like a good bourgeois, the girl is shocked by the leftovers), false and corrupt. It must be – and is – destroyed in the cleansing fire at the closure of both.

Hitchcock enjoys gently debunking the upper classes, making mild fun of the barmy upper-class relatives, using George Sanders, in a wonderfully camp performance (as Jack Favell), to expose their snobbery and complacency. The orphaned heroine may be Cinderella but she is also, in her shabby cardigans and sensible skirts, clutching her handbag, Miss Ordinary of 1938 (the kind of 'thoroughly nice girl' Hitchcock wrote so warmly of). Hitchcock brings the romance down to earth by means of contemporary idiom: 'toodle-oo,' 'right you are,' or the pipe-smoking Maxim, a brusque father-figure, telling his schoolgirl wife to stop biting her nails and eat up her breakfast: ' "There's a good child." '

The topography of the Gothic – both its literal and emotional geography – is where Hitchcock really meets du Maurier. Combining the extravagant with psychological realism, it had room for Selznick too. The crenellated towers of remote Manderley, the long corridors down which the child-bride is compulsively drawn toward the secret atrocities of the hero-villain's past, the hint of deviant sexuality and the eroticism of death, *Rebecca* recasts many of those elements of the Gothic which had for centuries provided a pre-Freudian vocabulary for what we would call repressed desires. Hitchcock's camera works constantly to capture the vulnerability and insignificance of the girl dwarfed and isolated in draughty baronial halls or shrinking on oversize plush sofas alongside cabinets of treasures (Susan in Kane's Xanadu comes to mind again). As curiosity impels her – 'What was Rebecca really like?' – we watch her framed against vast oaken doors, reaching up like a prying child to turn the handle and enter the forbidden chamber, drawing back the curtains and veils in which Rebecca, and all she stands for, is shrouded. Alice in Wonderland (Joan Fontaine wears a velvet Alice band and Olivier calls her 'Alice', to reinforce the point) wandering in Bluebeard's Castle.

A home-movies scene, in which the anxious and insecure girl silently watches images of her own past happiness ('only four months ago,' so quickly does romance wither), is one of many brilliant improvisations for visualising the breakdown of her identity as she disappears into her fantasies of Rebecca. But unlike du Maurier, Hitchcock and Selznick, whatever their intentions, cannot really identify with the girl's point of view. The hindsight of the voice-over in the first five minutes is never resumed. They only give us half of the story of female identification and projection.

Joan Fontaine's tremulous expression in close-up always emphasises passive dissolution: what the film cannot show is her pleasure in imagining Rebecca, the active component of longing which could take the girl beyond her dullness, her orthodox femininity. The famous scene in Rebecca's bedroom, where Mrs Danvers seductively invites the girl to take Rebecca's place, shows Joan Fontaine's humiliation, disgust and nausea at being situated as voyeur. It conveys little of the voyeur's satisfactions. The novel, on the other hand, is as much *attracted* to Rebecca, her thrilling independence and sexual assertiveness, as repulsed by her: 'She had all the courage and spirit of a boy [. . .] She did what she liked, she lived as she liked. She had the strength of a little lion too.' Hitchcock and Selznick's script tries to limit this kind of damage: they don't want their female viewers believing that being Rebecca, and acting like a man, might be a great deal more fun than marriage to boring old Max.

HOSTILITY WHITEWASHED

However loyal its makers thought they were being, the film is crucially unfaithful. Not least in its treatment of Olivier. Though he first appears as a remotely elegant romantic hero (in an immaculate suit, tie and trilby, brooding on a dizzying drop outside Monte Carlo), his mysterious dark moods are never quite sinister. Good-mannered, kind and quietly amused, he is hardly a hunted creature, the Maxim who (according to du Maurier) 'was not normal, not altogether sane'. And in the film version he turns out not to be a murderer at all, merely covering up the accidental death that Rebecca had brought on herself. (Du Maurier's Maxim, on the other hand, remorselessly insists, 'I'm glad I killed Rebecca. I shall never have any remorse for that, never, never.') It may have protected Olivier's image (just as Cary Grant's was in *Suspicion*), but this whitewashing is of a piece with the inability of the film to deal with female hostility toward men and marriage, the bedrock of du Maurier's novel, and the flipside too of her delight in Rebecca.

The masculine point of view runs away with the film, finally leaving the heroine literally behind as the men all go up to London to discover the truth about Rebecca. In the novel she takes on Rebecca-like confidence, managing the now wounded and helpless Max. (Hitchcock limits this to dressing Fontaine 'maturely' in a dark wool costume and putting her hair up.) Worst of all is the sentimental ending which leaves her a potential victim of the conflagration. And poor 'Danny', to boot, made more demented than devoted; the part is pure Grand Guignol. Not only responsible for the blaze but burnt to a cinder in it, she is the madwoman in the attic, proxy for Rebecca. This is the producer-directors' own kind of overkill, going one further than du Maurier in obliterating (they hope) all trace of errant or 'perverse' female desires. At least du Maurier involves Rebecca's incestuous cousin in the arson, and lets Mrs Danvers disappear.

Hitchcock liked his actresses to be docile and compliant, 'the kind of girl I can mould into the heroine of my imagination'. The latest 'discovery', twenty-three-year-old Joan Fontaine, got used to his well-known teasing, which bordered on erotic cruelty: 'Hitchcock kept me off balance, much to his own delight . . . He would constantly tell me that no one thought I was very good except himself.' Of course 'the girl' couldn't actually be mousy and dull (though du Maurier's heroine really is): no amount of twin-sets and pearls, hunched shoulders or clumsiness can mar those idealising portrait shots where the breeze ruffles Fontaine's hair and she is radiant, wide-eyed and malleable. As a director who hated 'sex appeal', 'fake glamour' and 'the lady pose', Hitchcock had his own reasons to give Rebecca, the bold aristocrat with her see-through negligée and chiffon boudoir, a violent comeuppance. 'Modesty,' Frank Crawley, Maxim's aptly named agent, tells the girl in a pregnant moment, 'means more than all the wit and beauty in the world.'

So what seems like a woman's film turns out to be a man's after all. We might have guessed. Had we looked closely there was one stable point of view, following the path of the director, that might have led us through the film's apparent labyrinths. It is that of Jasper, the cocker spaniel, who is one paw ahead of the viewer. At first he signifies the lingering dominance of Rebecca: he leaves a room when the girl enters it; he sleeps like Cerberus at the entrance to Rebecca's apartments; he drags Mrs de Winter down to Rebecca's fateful beachhouse. But his allegiances shift and when we see him finally curled up at his new mistress's feet, we know Rebecca has been exorcised, and that we too must relinquish our attachment to her. Not only a marvellous part for a canine actor, Jasper is the film's unsung hero, since he is last seen, his head in the girl's lap, scenting danger in Mrs Danvers's ominously flickering candle. We must assume he saved the heroine. A pity he doesn't feature in the film's final clinch.

Du Maurier's ending is quite different. In fact it comes at the beginning of the novel, steeping it in retrospection. Beached up abroad in expat loneliness, the de Winters are a sad couple of relics, maundering about in hotels, reading *Country Life* and listening to the BBC World Service. They absolutely can't, whatever the film implies, start life afresh. 'We can never go back,' du Maurier keeps telling us. And yet in this circular novel, which ends up where it began, they do nothing else. On the final page the second Mrs de Winter is still imagining herself as Rebecca, only this time murdering Max.

ELEGY FOR LOST GIRLHOOD

It was in Alexandria, in stifling August heat, that du Maurier conjured up Rebecca's Cornwall, an artificial landscape redolent of a more glamorous past, but also of a bolder, more autonomous life, where she might even let out her 'Jack-in-the-box', as she called it, her desires for other women. The novel feels like a swansong, an elegy for lost girlhood and a lament on the way marriage might move you from one state of anonymity to another. Her England is far more nostalgic than Hitchcock's, but then maybe she had more to lose. In fact she was thrilled and relieved by the film (unlike her reaction to Hitchcock's earlier travesty of her *Jamaica Inn*); despite the changes, she felt it had caught 'the atmosphere'.

For the film has its own central mournfulness, its pervasive sense of guilt. All the trouble starts because Maxim is a widower whose 'grief' can't be discussed; reticence is always muddled in the English middle classes with decency and respectability. Which is why it remains a trap. Despite its gleeful fire (and much of England was to go up in flames very soon), melancholy haunts Hitchcock's film like the mists around Manderley. Perhaps he too had a sense of the dangers of revealing oneself to one's partner, in what Angela Carter called 'the unguessable country of marriage'. Years later he wrote of his wife Alma, only half in jest, as 'The Woman Who Knows Too Much'.

Perhaps the English between the wars were especially stuck in mourning, traumatically reliving their memories, unable to let go of the past or make their peace with it. The Englishness of *Rebecca* lies not only in its overt references to the charismatic and intimidating power of class, but in its chafing against the so-called virtue of 'reserve'. It is one version of that model of a tight emotional economy, barely holding out against what it most dreads and desires, whose phobias and paranoias so fascinated Hitchcock. Though he shrugged off the paraphernalia of the Gothic and found more vernacular American subjects, he too returned obsessively to the pathology of repression.

Rebecca, coming back over and again, unscathed through water and fire, has given her audiences and critics a good run for their money. Reckless, decadent aristocrat: the woman who knew too much and the woman we longed to be; acting out lesbian desires, the female Oedipal drama or Hitchcock's tabooed femininity; the return of the repressed or just popular Freudianism itself; she is one of those larger-than-life figures who tempts us to inhabit her world and her feelings at the risk of losing our own. Just like going to the movies.

10

Re-reading *Great Expectations**

Do children still worry about becoming snobs? At 13 I was terrified of putting on airs and graces and of looking down on where I came from. 'It is a miserable thing to be ashamed of home,' Pip, the hero of *Great Expectations* , tells us, and I was amazed to read a book in which such secret, agonising sentiments were displayed. Dickens's story of the blacksmith's boy taken from his sphere by a mysterious benefactor to be made into a gentleman made me squirm. As the adult Pip looks back on his obnoxious younger self, watching himself grow into a fully-fledged snob, he shares the most embarrassing, guilt-ridden confidences with the reader. I'd never read a book before that turned me into an accomplice.

Around this time, my second year at grammar school, I was being bullied. I was a noisy, bouncy, chatterbox of a girl who loved putting her hand up in class, and I convinced myself that the problem was not just being brainy but also being 'common'. My schoolmates certainly did their utmost to take me down a peg or two. They ripped up my belongings (a treasured George Best poster torn from inside my desklid, I recall), flushed my school-hat down the toilet, poked and elbowed me at random, and, with rather more originality, formed an anti-Alison club whose members sported home-made 'AA' badges. My unpopularity went on for years. And like many a working-class child, the better I did at school, the further it seemed to take me from home.

There are pages in *Great Expectations* I still read with my heart in my mouth. No other novel I've encountered makes the connection between bullying and deference in English society so unflinchingly. It is an intimate account of

---

* First published in *The Guardian*, 21 September 2002

learning your place, of class as a feeling but also as character formation, something that goes on inside. Dickens calls it the 'metaphysics' of ill-treatment, what comes of being made to feel inferior.

'Why, he's a common labouring boy!' exclaims Estella, the little girl up at the big house, when Pip is sent to play with her, mocking his clumsiness and the way he speaks. Pip is changed for ever by this new vulnerability – 'I had never thought of being ashamed of my hands before'. The woundedness Pip feels goes beyond words: it is 'the smart without a name'. Pip is 'humiliated, hurt, spurned, offended, angry, sorry' but nothing can describe the damage done to his self-esteem. It's an extraordinary analysis of the pathology of class. He becomes more, not less, deferential, angry not with his 'betters' but with his guardian, Joe the blacksmith, for not being genteel.

A timid little boy, cowed by his sister's beatings and as undersized as his name, Pip starts telling tall stories about his experiences, inflating his sense of self-importance. When he comes unexpectedly into money, he seizes this social elevation as his right. How could he not be a conformist? He is only doing unto others what's been done to him. In this novel you are either a victim or a bully. Like Pip, Magwitch, his convict benefactor, is another abused child: 'I've been done everything to, pretty well – except hanged,' he says.

The English novel is full of warnings to upstarts and mockery of their pretensions. At 13, I was learning that if you want to go up in the world you must do so without rocking the boat. I read *Great Expectations* as a moral fable and I wanted Pip to get his come-uppance. But Pip isn't blamed for having aspirations; his 'poor dreams' are not in themselves a crime. What Dickens condemns is his selfishness, the heartless individualism of a society that encourages people to better themselves by disowning others. Only when he realises his 'fellow feeling' for Magwitch, and shares his good fortune, can Pip be redeemed.

Dickens, of course, was not from the working classes, but as the century's most successful novelist, he had come an awfully long way. *Great Expectations* makes an uneasy peace with his social advancement. It transposes that earlier, more ebullient version of his autobiography, *David Copperfield*, into a minor key. Shaw remarked that by reappearing as a blacksmith's boy, Dickens apologised for the disgust and shame he'd felt in boyhood working alongside street urchins in a blacking factory while his father was in debtor's prison. Unlike David Copperfield, Pip becomes not a writer but a hardworking businessman, a cog in the wheel of Empire, the respectable member of the lower middle class that Dickens ought to have been.

I first read *Great Expectations* as a novel about the misery of moving on. But it's also, as disturbingly, about the misery of staying put. Behind Pip is his shadow, the slouching Orlick, who smashes things up for pleasure and meets any attempt at government with rage. Orlick is a prospective member of the 'mob', but he is also created by envy and exclusion and injustice (Pip gets him sacked from his job). When Pip dines with Jaggers, his London lawyer, he is asked to admire the caged strength in the housekeeper's hands. What would happen, we're made to wonder, if the underclasses really flexed their muscles?

In *Great Expectations*, as throughout his work, Dickens hankers after that place where nothing ever hurts. It is what he means by home. But again and again homes are revealed as places where husbands and wives fight for supremacy and where parents are cold and cruel. Dickens, like so many of us, wanted to believe that indoors might be a sanctuary, outside history and sheltered from the world, but his imagination knew better. For every Pip who leaves home there's an Orlick; for every Biddy who is content not to see the world and to marry the honest blacksmith, there's his first wife, the furious, unbiddable Mrs Joe, finally bludgeoned into docility. With its ironic title, the book suggests that in an unequal society, you always thrive at the expense of others. Nobody is innocent or immune – least of all the children. Or to put it differently, class feeling, like charity, begins at home.

Great Expectations, my Penguin backcover tells me pompously, is 'a mature and serious' novel. But in fact the book is wonderfully puerile, full of high spirits and silliness. There's a lot of gallows humour (it begins with a convict threatening to cut a child's throat) and it can come very close to the bone. Yet it's also a comedy of forgiveness towards one's younger self. The little boy squeezed into the corner of the table and offered the meanest portions – 'those obscure corners of pork of which the pig, when living, had had the least reason to be vain' – is free, at least, in his imagination, to enjoy the lion's share. Dickens's famously unruly humour is part of his firm belief in wishful thinking, in our capacity for poor dreams and fabrications, and the obstinate hope that there might be places where the long arm of rank and distinction cannot reach. What larks, as Joe says, what larks.

In 1860, when he began this novel, Dickens was becoming depressed by the society around him. He was nearing 50 but he seems never to have lost his capacity, as he put it, for 'accumulating young feelings in short pauses'. However sobering his portrait of his middle-aged narrator, however darkened by loss and loneliness, the book is a rejuvenating read. Dickens was often accused of being a show-off but there are times when it's right to be full of yourself. It is not the story of a boy who got too big for his boots, but of a child who, like all children, was perfectly entitled to begin life with great expectations.

11

The Figure of the Servant[*]

Down ill-lit corridors the servant scurries, disappearing into darkened chambers, hurrying back to the kitchens or the courtyards, a blur on the edge of vision. Servants form the greatest part of that already silent majority – the labouring poor – who have for so long lived in the twilight zone of historical record. In the servant's case, though, anonymity often went with the job.

In mid-to-late 19th-century Britain, when live-in service was at a peak, servants' labour was meant to be as unobtrusive as possible. Relegated to the basements and the attics, using separate entrances and staircases (their activities muffled and hidden behind the famous 'green baize door'), they lived a parallel existence, shadowing the family members and anticipating their needs – meals appeared on the table, fires were found miraculously lit, beds warmed and covers turned back by an invisible hand.

In the grander households the lower servants were often unknown 'above stairs'. The writer Vita Sackville-West recalled that at Knole her mother was supplied with a list of first names from the housekeeper before she doled out seasonal gifts. More conveniently, servants were often hailed by their work titles such as 'Cook' or 'Boots', or, if their own names were considered too fancy, given more 'suitable' ones: 'Abigail', 'Betty', 'Mary Jane' were all in vogue at one time. Deportment and body language, the bowed head, the neatly folded hands, all prevented servants from 'putting themselves forward', though few employers were like the Duke of Portland at Welbeck, who expected his staff to turn their faces to the wall if they encountered the family.

Few, that is, except for the royal family, some of whose archaic practices were revealed last week by Paul Burrell in his book *A Royal Duty* (including

---

[*] First published in *The Guardian*, 8 November 2003

the Sunday task of ironing a £5 note for the Queen's church collection). Royal servants have long been a source of fascination because of their proximity to rulers who were otherwise remote. Such relationships often caused friction at court, as when Queen Victoria allowed her Hindustani teacher, or Munshi, the 24-year-old Abdul Karim, to take his meals with the royal household. The Windsors may expect a feudal level of fealty from their staff and, as the self-styled 'keeper of Diana's secrets', Burrell is one in a long line of upstarts who has overstepped the mark. Yet the history of domestic service, even at its most mundane, suggests that it has always been a job like no other, involving unusual intimacies and frequently encouraging both employers and their charges to invest in a fantasy of friendship.

From medieval times, litigious servants have sought redress in the courts (legal records offer some of the earliest evidence of their lives). But historians have long found servants to be awkward customers. Their numbers alone make a history of service daunting (in 1900, there were still more people working in domestic service than in any other sector barring agriculture). Though they were legion, so much about servants was singular. They were legally seen as dependents but in principle were free to leave. Their hours of work, time off and wages were often unregulated and the perquisites, or 'perks' of the job, such as the quality of their board and lodging, varied enormously. Working in comparative comfort behind closed doors, deferring to employers and perhaps silently envious of them, the figure of the servant represents all that is the opposite of the articulate, organised or collectively-minded. Feminised, indoor and intimate, domestic service is usually excluded from more heroic accounts of the making of the English working classes.

Yet domestic service was not simply a throwback to a pre-industrial world. The ideal of service was the cornerstone of 19th-century life, informing the language and structure both of public institutions and family life. The Victorians elevated dependence into a moral and social good. The idea of serving others (perhaps in the new civil 'service' or as a 'servant' of a bank or indeed, in the 'services') was strengthened indoors by an evangelical Christianity. Domestic servants drew satisfaction and self-respect from their devotion to duty, though few were so inspired as Hannah Cullwick, Arthur Munby's maid and scullion in the 1860s. Up to her elbows in grease and muck, she welcomed the filthiest chores, as her diaries record, partly as a test of her humility and of her faith in a salvation achieved by hard work. But 'being drest rough & looking nobody', also gave her the freedom to 'go anywhere and not be wonder'd at'.

Service could mean betterment, though rarely did a servant rise far above her station (Cullwick eventually married her master but she obstinately resisted playing the lady). In Merlin Waterson's *The Servants' Hall* (1980), which describes 250 years of domestic history at Erddig, the Yorke family's modest country house on the Welsh marches, we learn that Harriet Rogers preferred to be a lady's maid and housekeeper than remain at home on an isolated farm. The Yorkes encouraged her reading and broadened her horizons but she remained single all her life and quietly put away her numerous Valentine cards. Servants made choices, though not in circumstances of their own choosing. If we fail to recognise this, they remain typecast as trouble makers or arch conservatives, as rogues or dupes or victims.

Servants haunt the 18th- and 19th-century domestic novel, conjuring up the fears and fantasies of their employers. As Daniel Defoe's diatribe of 1724, 'The Great Law of Subordination Consider'd', testified, the unruly servant was a sorcerer's apprentice who could send not just the kitchen but the whole social order spiralling into anarchy. In Jane Austen's *Mansfield Park* (1814), when Fanny Price returns home to Portsmouth from her posh relatives, her first sight is of Rebecca, 'a trollopy looking maid' who is 'never where she ought to be'. Rebecca's sluttish ways speak volumes about the moral impropriety of the family. Like Samuel Richardson's Pamela before her, Fanny is herself a servant morally worthy of a better station in life (Charlotte Brontë's Jane Eyre is one of her descendants). Her social climbing will reform but not threaten the upper classes. She looks forward to generations of middle-class mistresses whose superiority depends on keeping others firmly in their place.

It's almost impossible for us to see service except through an optic of class antagonism or exploitation. Yet the attachments between servants and their employers were often complex. No man, as they say, is a hero to his valet – certainly not Charles Darwin, whose butler, Joseph Parslow, douched and dried him everyday for four months, while Darwin tried hydropathy for his chronic diarrhoea and nausea. Parslow, who numbered among his many tasks donning leather gaiters to gather flower spikes from ditches or ferrying plant specimens back from Kew Gardens, often cradled Darwin like a baby in his arms. Thomas and Jane Carlyle got through servants at a rate of knots (one was dismissed by him as a 'mutinous Irish savage'). Prostrated by headache, Jane was often comforted by another maid-of-all-work, Helen Mitchell, who rubbed her cheek with her own and soothed her mistress with companionable tears.

Servants might be officially invisible but they were central as providers, especially when their employers were at their most needy. The English upper classes have frequently recalled cold childhoods warmed only by confederacies with the servants. Rudyard Kipling's first memories, in *Something of Myself*, were of his Portuguese ayah and the Hindu bearer, Meeta, who held his hand and eased his fear of the dark. 'Father and Mother' were associated with painful partings. Service, in other words, has always been an emotional as well as an economic territory. The valet, the housekeeper and the girl who emptied the chamberpots all knew this as they stepped over the threshold of someone else's house.

In most painting, as in literature, servants appear in supporting roles. But an exhibition at the National Portrait Gallery – 'Below Stairs: 400 Years of Servants' Portraits' – gives faces to some of those whom history has effaced. British art frequently followed the Italian convention in which a servant, a page or secretary, a horse or dog, might be included to enhance the stature of the principal subject. Literally so with Van Dyck's portrait of Queen Henrietta Maria painted in 1633; she was quite tiny but standing next to dwarf Jeffrey Hudson added several cubits to her height.

Servants were among the first commodities to be displayed, along with the fashionable silks and porcelain, in small-scale 'conversation pieces', family portraits from the 1720s. There are also plenty of walk-on parts for servants in genre paintings: pretty dairymaids in tidy farmyards, grooms exhibited with prize hounds in sporting scenes, ruddy-faced, fleshy cooks amid the slaughtered meat. Only rarely does a tremor of personality disturb these still lives.

'Below Stairs' concentrates on individual portraits of servants that have survived thanks to their employers' affection or caprice. The majority are 'loyalty' portraits, meant to be exemplary and instructive, testifying to the benevolence of the masters as much as to the virtues of their staff. Erddig's enlightened squires had individual, informal portraits painted of the whole household, from the lowly 'spider-brushers' to the cook, coachmen and gardeners, often with humorous scrolls attached detailing their lives and work. Loyalty portraits were popular too with the university colleges, museums, banks, clubs, hotels and other institutions. Paintings elevated trusty employees to the status of a symbol.

In their accompanying catalogue, curators Giles Waterfield and Anne French rightly warn that such portraits are anomalous. Only large establishments were likely to commission costly pictures and most British servants worked for the ever-expanding middle classes in far humbler situations. Rather than the butler or the housekeeper, the typical domestic in the 19th-century home or lodging-house was the 'maid-of-all-work' or 'slavey', like Dickens's 'Marchioness' in The Old Curiosity Shop, whose half-starved existence comically belies her inflated title. Usually a young girl, often straight from the workhouse, such general servants came cheap (until the 1940s the majority of Barnardo's girls went straight into other people's kitchens).

Life-size or full-length, looking you straight in the face, it's a shock to encounter sympathetic images of people so often caricatured, reduced to cartoon or grotesquerie. Artists aimed at more than mechanical likenesses, 'mere face-painting', as William Hogarth dubbed it. Bored with their patrons, painters were sidetracked by the servants whose faces were free of cosmetics and whose figures were less inert than those hampered by the trappings of wealth. George Stubbs's portrait of Freeman, the Earl of Clarendon's gamekeeper, for instance, shown moving in for the kill, is a force in his own right. Elderly servants, unlike their employers, didn't need to be flattered: the woodcarver with his spotted neckerchief, the weary housekeeper and the messenger at the Bank of England are given all their blemishes and wrinkles.

Loyalty portraits frequently commemorate long service and nothing is dearer to the conservative imagination than the image of the old retainer. Yet at the great houses, where the rewards for long service were most enticing, the speed at which servants could be hired and fired was often breathtaking. Even at Erddig there were clear limits to liberality. Elizabeth Ratcliffe, a lady's maid in the 1760s, was a talented artist who could put her hand to a mezzotint as easily as to her mending, but after one of her successes her mistress wrote to her son vetoing further exploits lest 'I shall have no service from her & make too fine a Lady of her, for so much say'd on that occasion that it rather puffs her up'. There are almost no portraits of ladies' maids in British art. Since the maid often dressed in the mistress's cast-offs, her Ladyship was afraid, perhaps, of being upstaged.

In reality, though, most servants have always been comers and goers, migrants arriving in the city and hoping to send money home, moving on to marriage or a better place. Ultimately, the servant portrait is poignant because it's a contradiction in terms. Its subjects, who often in life couldn't call their souls their own, are proudly dressed in a little brief authority. But even the most amiable portrait of the servant is always a portrait of the master.

In the 19th and 20th centuries, photography took over the loyalty convention, with group portraits of uniformed servants, often displaying their badge of office – a broom, a saucepan or a garden fork – formally posed outside the house. Such photographs remind us that live-in service does not belong to the distant past (I have one such memento of my grandmother in her days as a skivvy). Servants' testimonies, like those in the sound archives at Essex University, are often full of bitterness and shame. In her autobiography, *Below Stairs* (1968), Margaret Powell remembers how deeply humiliated she felt when her mistress told her to hand newspapers to her on a silver salver: 'Tears started to trickle down my cheeks; that someone could think you were so low that you couldn't even hand them anything out of your hands.'

Between the wars, as other employment became available, women, and particularly the young, voted with their feet. The decline of live-in service revealed just how hopelessly dependent many employers were. In the 1920s, for instance, Lytton Strachey's sisters, Pippa, Marjorie and Pernel (the former dedicated to women's suffrage, the latter principal of Newnham), had to ask

their younger relatives to turn on the oven on the servant's day off. Dependence was often a matter of pride rather than practical incompetence. Opening
the front door was especially unthinkable since servants were the gatekeepers
to the outside world. Well into old age, Siegfried Sassoon, in impoverished
isolation at Heytesbury House, kept up a façade of grandeur by asking visitors
to come by the servants' entrance.

Of course there were people who remained a lifetime in other people's
families, who were unstinting and generous and who believed what they were
doing was worthwhile. Julia and Leslie Stephen's cook, Sophie Farrell, who
was passed around Bloomsbury circles for many years, went on signing herself
'yours obediently' to 'Miss Ginia' (Virginia Woolf) all her life. Others were
snobs who missed their privileges and the kindness of their employers. Once
the old models of rank and deference collapsed, lives foundered; Frank Lovell,
for five years head footman at Erddig, made a new start as a chauffeur just
before he joined up in 1914 but the war years left him adrift. Disappointed and
unsettled, he drowned in 1934, leaving his wife and young son believing it to
be suicide. Servants often found it hard to adjust to a more democratic world.

But so did their employers. Although socialists and feminists might campaign for the poor, plenty assumed that housework was beneath them or that
others were more suited to it. Margaret Bondfield, minister of labour in 1931,
annoyed fellow Labour party members by refusing out-of-work Lancashire
mill girls unemployment benefit if they turned down domestic training. The
feminist Vera Brittain, whose unconventional household was shared with her
husband and Winifred Holtby, her friend, depended on the servants, Amy and
Charles Burnett, for years. It didn't prevent Brittain from bemoaning the lot
of 'the creative woman perpetually at the mercy of the 'Fifth Column' below
stairs'. Writers and artists wanted uninterrupted time and their servants duly
emancipated them. Grace Higgens, for instance, 'the Angel of Charleston',
made it possible for Vanessa Bell to be a painter, cooking and cleaning for her
for more than 40 years. 'Ludendorff Bell', as her son Quentin called her, kept
up the Victorian habit, nonetheless, of starting every day by giving her orders
to the cook, who stood waiting while her mistress sat at the breakfast table.
For all the photographs and portraits Bell made of Grace, they could never be
pictured side by side.

By the 1950s, few British women expected to 'go into' service but that
is hardly the end of the story. In the last decade or so the domestic-service
economy – an army of cleaners, child-minders, nannies and au pairs – has been
rapidly expanding (Allison Pearson's recent apologia for the career woman,
I Don't Know How She Does It, goes guiltily over the old ground of the mistress
victimised by a manipulative underling). In this country much of the cooking

and cleaning is done by low-paid casual workers, often migrants, in private houses as well as in hotels, offices and schools. Racial assumptions, as well as class feelings – as Barbara Ehrenreich and others have argued – are fostered by this division of labour.

All of us begin our lives helpless in the hands of others and will probably end so. How we tolerate our inevitable dependence, especially upon those who feed and clean and care for us, or take away our waste, is not a private or domestic question but one that goes to the heart of our unequal society. We rely constantly on others to do our dirty work and what used to be called 'the servant question' has not gone away. The figure of the servant takes us not only inside history but inside ourselves.

12

Experiments in Memoir-writing

1939:50 YEARS ON[*]

The war was still on when I was a child, though I never wore a gas-mask or heard a siren. In the 1960s we played 'Nazis and Jews' in the street, taking it in turns to be seven-year-old Gestapo, or to hide in door-ways, dodging passers-by. Always, the victims got away. We played 'French Resistance' in the municipal rec, made our own 'papers', cutting photos out of Freeman's catalogues and drawing detailed plans of escape to the churchyard. The 'Yankees' were our heroes, and I was in love with an eight-year-old pilot, who parachuted out of the trees to 'make contact' with me.

Had I seen war films by then, whose vocabulary seems so much the language of those fantasies? Kenneth More reaching for the sky, Virginia McKenna as Violet Szabo, *Albert RN*; or was it the landscape that formed the territory of recall? Bombsites were where we made our 'dens', weaving our way back from Picture Club across broken glass, balancing on blown-away ledges.

Relics were everyday. Grey army blankets on the beds, the sausage-shaped kitbag used for the laundry, Dad's khaki shorts. So many sentences started, 'during the war', 'just after the war', and 'before. . .' that war was always imminent. I didn't know when 'it' had 'broken out'; I knew for sure, it hadn't simply ended. In fact, like the Anderson shelter still there in 1966 at our grammar school, beached up like some white whale next to the empty building where we held our seances, memories are often out of bounds. Memory isn't a lane we wander down; it's a sea we swim in, and the backwash of the past leaves its own tidemark.

---

[*] '1939 50 Years On' first published in the *New Statesman*, 1 September 1989.

As the accounts of 1939 start to flood in, anniversaries can provoke a parody of remembrance. Public history and private memory are so frequently out of kilter that naming dates defeats their own object. Instead of conjuring up a past, anniversaries repel it, channelling the overflow of the years into this or that day.

The war we officially remembered was the Great War. Remembrance Day itself, Armistice, it was that war which had dates, places and soldiers in it, 'up to their necks in muck and bullets', not the second. A war of real names, Passchendaele, Somme, Bapaume, unpronounceable but sad-sounding, like the roll-call on local walls where you always looked for your own. I watched through my fingers (how old?) as a TV camera panned across documentary footage of the trenches, to crawl down a muddy tunnel and confront a skeleton in uniform hunched in a dugout. Later, all battlefields were to look like Flanders.

Soldiers didn't feature very much in my own family. Only sailors, who seemed somehow less bloody, and more smiling – Jack tars, matelots, marines – boys more obviously from back home, caps less sinister than helmets. Sailors weren't linked to torpedos – their element was the seaside, a stroll along that other kind of 'front.'

Even my father, who was in the army, had 'only' been a military policeman; his stories were all jokes about jeeps and melons; the Middle East meant photographs of his motorbike, and his Alsatian dog ('Aloof') – and teaching me to count up to ten in Arabic. It had no more to do with the fighting than the satin sheath with the mandarin collar an aunt brought back from Singapore, which I inherited for dressing up; and the life-sized Koala Bear in their front room whose leather paws were my idea of heaven.

Fragments from far-off, like holiday souvenirs and not the spoils of war. The real battles had gone on at home, though stories only got grimmer as I grew. My father, just a boy, firewatching, all his old haunts burning, impressing on me images of bodies he should not have seen; my mother, an abused evacuee, told it piecemeal over the years.

Mine was a whole generation of infant listeners who grew up steeped in the folklore of the Blitz: of Mrs B who rushed out during an air-raid, leaving her teeth in soak, got back to find the house flattened and her choppers, still there, grinning at her; of sudden changes of mind that meant survival – *Laurel and Hardy* at the Alhambra instead of the *Krazy Gang* at the Palace – 'all the two and sixpennies went up in smoke'; of Ida Turner or June Bailey dyeing her hair when the sirens went and ending up cerise pink, not auburn, for the duration. These were our epics, comically on the knife-edge of horror, not tales of martial prowess, told time and again to children who were never there.

If I had been a boy, it might have been different. I might have built model airplanes, known the names of generals and sought out bits of uniform to keep. I'd have learnt earlier the facts that I learnt later, envied exploits of the sort that *Victor* carried every week. And I'd have been a parachutist not an undercover agent, when we chose parts in the playground. Maybe. Even so, there are some things bigger than boyhood. Out along our common stretched a line of memorials – Balaclava, Inkermann, Ypres, Dunkirk – to me, they were so many indistinguishable crosses, anchors, bells tolling to the same war and the same men.

When we sang songs, I never knew which war was which because it didn't matter: 'Goodbye Dolly, I must leave you', as familiar as knowing that it was a long way, to Tipperary. The Siegfried line with its washing, as intimate and as remote as bluebirds over the Dover cliffs; Picardy and Piccadilly blurred into one. All merged into that melancholy strain of loss, at the end of the evening, when the grown-ups grew maudlin and weary: 'When this crazy war is over, oh, how happy we shall be.' Which war, and when? These were songs about parting and reunion, not about fighting. Like the requests for *Family Favourites* played loud every Sunday, Jean Metcalfe's soft tones calling Cologne and Hong Kong, so many talismans against separation, against being stranded in the land of 'BFPO'.

To me it was a continuum. Not the pre- and postwar which historians are so fond of but a long line of Saturday teas and Sunday best, stretching back as far as my grandmother. It was her life and not the nation's that bounded my sense of the past. Something essentially undisturbed which carried on working, just like the women. Like many families, it was the miraculous continuities, not the traumas of disruption which we hallowed. What was left of the past and went on, just the same, after the war, that made 'getting back to normal' more desirable, and more impossible, than change. What dates were these, and on which maps?

And I still don't know where my family's war took place. It certainly made too much present of a few years past, but we all knew the future would be just like looking back: we could all meet again, couldn't we, in some endless sing-song? My darling, just you wait and see.

IN PORTSMOUTH*

Fortitude Cottage in Old Portsmouth, so the publicity tells me, is named after HMS Fortitude, a 74-gun 'ship of the line' that was part of the fleet which took on the French in the Napoleonic Wars. A tall bow-fronted house, it's a bed and breakfast done out 'boutique-style', with white duvets, chocolate suede furnishings and modern ceramics. It was built on the site of a 16th-century cottage burned down in the Blitz and was recently renamed in keeping with the cobbled streets and battlements of the old garrison town. Across Portsmouth Harbour there's a glimpse of Nelson's flagship, the Victory, one of the tourist attractions in the 'historic dockyard'. Much more dramatic, as I sit at the breakfast table, is the Isle of Wight ferry, lumbering into view between the narrow streets like a great white whale.

I've booked in to avoid spending another night at my parents' sheltered housing. I can get to sleep in the guest-room only after the hard-of-hearing turn off their blaring TVs and only until dawn brings the more sprightly out for an early constitutional, clattering down in the lift and cheerfully banging the iron gates under the window. I also want to spend the morning at the local records office following up some family history. The host at Fortitude Cottage asks me how it feels to take a trip 'down Memory Lane'. I explain that my parents and brother still live here and I've been visiting the city all my life. 'Was Portsmouth a good place to grow up in?' one of the other guests asks, overhearing us. They are from East Anglia, anxious about recent flood warnings, and down in Portsmouth to buy a new yacht. As a Pompey girl, born and bred next to the football ground in Fratton, I naturally know nothing at all about sailing (though I know that 'F' stands for frigate and chanted 'Boney was a warrior, rah, rah, rah!' in the playground, assuming it referred to a skeleton). I nod smilingly at their Swallows and Amazons vision of me messing about in boats. When I was a child the seafront meant swimming and ice-cream cornets on the beach; crisps and lemonade at the pier; the funfair. I have faint memories of fishing boats hauled up slipways with their nets full (my friend Carole put me off by saying that mackerel ate sewage), but the pleasure craft whose masts now bristle and clink in the marinas around the harbour were unknown.

Portsmouth certainly meant the dockyard (not yet 'historic'), the city's main employer until the 1970s. My father's last job before retirement was as a fitter for Hampshire Engineering, a small maintenance firm contracted to the naval establishments, which tackled everything from fiddling with air-locks in

---

* 'In Portsmouth' first published in the *London Review of Books*, 7 February 2008.

radiators to climbing down inside huge industrial boilers and descaling them
with acid. A man of philosophic temperament, given to quoting from Voltaire,
who salts verses of poetry away in his wallet, my father is one of those millions
who left school at 13. His brief apprenticeship as a carpenter was cut short by
the outbreak of war. He tried his hand at most jobs in the building trade, and
at worst had to dig roads: 'a jack of all trades', he always says, 'master of none'.
Now 81, he has spent the last two years in and out of hospital with multiple
myeloma, a cancer which attacks both the blood and bones, It frequently
affects elderly men and is sometimes linked to the accumulation of 'toxic
insults' from working with pollutants or chemicals. Exposure to asbestos over
the years – roofing, ships' lagging, dust from dry walls – has also thickened the
lining around his lungs and may be partly responsible for his condition. Two
of his old workmates died of asbestosis.

Yesterday I went up to the blood clinic with him. He doesn't want a
chaperone but can get dizzy and forgetful. My mother has arthritis in her hips,
and is all but housebound, hobbling on two sticks. She can't manage his hospital visits any more, defeated by the long corridors. She waited eight weeks
to see the hip man, a pleasant, serious, overburdened consultant who told
her she might have to wait another four months for an operation. She comes
into the category of 'middle urgent'. Those who live alone or have other
additional illnesses are considered worse off. A private hip-replacement costs
about £12,000; they live on their state pensions and none of their children
can afford it. So my mother rations her painkillers as if they were luxuries
and trusts to the emergency buzzer in the flat which summons Careline, a
24-hour medical service. Most of the old ladies wear pendants with red alarms
like makeshift jewellery over their jumpers and blouses because 'you can't
rely on landing in the right spot'. According to new EU regulations, Janice,
the daytime warden, who keeps a weather eye on all the residents, is not
allowed to pick up anyone who has a fall. She can cover them with a blanket
but mustn't touch them – officially, that is. My mother thinks the new rules
are driven as much by fear of litigation as human rights. Her hairdresser,
Anne, is no longer supposed to help her elderly customers off with their coats
or position them under the dryer. She might accidentally break a brittle bone
and find herself being sued.

Portsmouth used to have three general hospitals: the Royal, near the dockyard, where I was once X-rayed for a rogue hairgrip; St Mary's, a short walk
from our house, where they poured sulphuric acid on my verruca till it went
black and dropped off; and Queen Alexandra at Cosham, a few miles outside
the city, and largely remote from our lives. The Royal closed in 1978 (a Sains-
bury's later appeared on the site) and St Mary's has been 'streamlined', so 'QA'

takes all-comers from the city and most of South-East Hampshire. It perches
on the slopes of Portsdown Hill, close to where in the 1860s Lord Palmerston
had yet more forts built against the French (known locally as 'Palmerston's
Follies'). My father makes the eight-mile round trip for blood tests and trans-
fusions, including a monthly intravenous dose of pamidronate, a drug that can
lessen bone pain. Mostly he avoids the aptly named 'patient transport', which
can take half a morning going round collecting a motley crew of invalids. Last
time the vehicle was a clapped-out boneshaker and he felt every bump and
jolt. Instead my parents blow their pension on an Aquacab, which glides up the
motorway in twenty minutes but costs £8 each way, and even more in rush
hour. Clinic hours have been cut just as patient numbers have increased, so it's
pot luck with appointment times.

Dad has learned to be flexible. For radiotherapy he must go to St Mary's,
though its machines frequently break down and his records sometimes get lost
in transit. The specialist for his skin cancer, though, is at the Haslar in Gosport, on the other side of Portsmouth Harbour. Once a naval hospital, Haslar
was built on a creek to prevent pressganged sailors from absconding when
their convalescence was over; it's best reached by ferry and then bus. Dad was
impressed by the naval surgeon who operated on the tumours around his groin
and by the well-swabbed wards, kept in shipshape order. Haslar has never had
a case of MRSA. Despite its proximity to the naval and military barracks, its
hydrotherapy pool for the wounded and disabled, only ten years old, and its
spotless reputation, the hospital – a grand stone edifice in the neoclassical style –
is scheduled to close. The building's period features and proximity to the sea-
shore make it a developer's dream. Staff and patients will eventually decamp to
Queen Alexandra, which is destined to become a supersized general hospital
of 1200 beds by 2010.

The haematology clinic at QA is a stuffy, makeshift space without enough
seats (chairs with armrests are at a premium). Tracey, the duty nurse who must
spend every day doing this, greets my father with a joke or two, and asks each
new arrival courteously; 'Would you mind if I weigh you?' He has lost weight
again. We sit drifting in the drowsy fog of hospital time, startled when Dad's
name comes up. The doctor consults the computer and recites figures – his
haemoglobin is up, the paraproteins are down – as mysterious to us as the
FTSE index, though we get the gist. The omens are good. He has to go on
taking the tablets. I write it all down for my mother, who has read up on the
disease and understands the pathology. She has long got over the shock of having to administer complex chemotherapy at home, including a long course of
thalidomide which left my father's feet numb. Their sideboard holds enough
poison for them to start their own branch of Exit.

The pharmacy is a strenuous walk. There's a sign announcing a long wait for prescriptions so we shuffle back to the lifts and down to the canteen for lunch in the bowels of the hospital. With the monstrous appetite brought on by steroids, Dad rapidly polishes off a pork chop, greens and mash, and then wanders over to the counter without his stick. If he keels over he could be bedridden for the rest of his life, but he returns safely with a dish of stewed apricots and custard, wondering why they don't keep the plates hot. He mentions, as he always does, with disbelief, that the nurses have to pay for their dinners and to park their cars. After a mug of hot chocolate, we go back to the pharmacy, where a senior chemist talks us carefully through the medicines, all with different regimes. Back home we hand over the booty and my parents count their blessings. 'He'd be dead without the drugs,' Mum says.

When my father was first diagnosed and looked unlikely to last six months, I started recording his memories. He came to Portsmouth from Birmingham in the 1930s as a child of five or six, not long after his mother died of TB. 'The old man', his father, had grown up in Pompey, left home to escape religion – my dad's grandfather was a strict Salvationist – and returned, swallowing his pride, to look for work. My father recounts again and again the memory of a 'moonlight flit', a scene familiar from many working-class autobiographies, the family secretly moving house in the middle of the night to avoid paying the rent, their few bits and pieces piled up in a wheelbarrow. Listening to his tales my mother butts in with jokes if he gets maudlin. She's a local girl and they met at a youth club in 1948 when she was 16. He was 22, barely out of demob and very wet behind the ears, despite having been a military policeman in Cairo, with a motorbike and a boxer-dog. Dad's first trip to hospital was the only time in nearly sixty years that my parents had slept apart. She can't sleep without the warmth he generates in bed.

I began my father's family tree for his 70th birthday, following a line of Henry Herbert Lights (masons and bricklayers to a man) back to Shrewton, a village in Wiltshire. Genealogy often gets short shrift from professional historians; it's seen as self-indulgent and myopic, obsessed with the idea of origins. But as the branches proliferate, individuals become families; families become neighbourhoods and groups; groups become classes. The records are impossible to fathom unless you come up for air and take in the horizon. What seems parochial is always connected to the national; the national to the global. On his mother's side, my father's family left farm-labouring in Herefordshire in the 1830s to work in the needle factories of the Midlands, in those outlying villages that fuelled Birmingham's industrial revolution. The Lights from Wiltshire migrated south to Portsea, the dockyard area of Portsmouth, which flourished during the wars against the French. Portsea's fortunes followed those of the navy. When William Cobbett surveyed 'that hellish assemblage' of Portsmouth, Gosport and Portsea on one of his rural rides a few years after the peace of 1815, house-lettings had already dropped to rock bottom and an 'absolute tumbling down' was taking place. By the 1850s it was an industrial slum.

In my morning's stint at the records office, I track my mother's forebears, Murphys and Millers. They also congregated in Portsea, eking out a living in its tight mesh of unpaved, filthy streets, courts, lanes and rows. I don't know how William Murphy, a shoemaker born in the 1820s, and his wife, Lydia, survived the cholera epidemic of 1849, but they turn up thereafter in different lodgings, mostly on Albion Street, notorious for its beer-shops and brothels (one of their seven children was Flora, my mother's grandmother, whom she never knew). Albion Street was wiped off the map, belatedly and pointlessly, in a purity drive in 1911. Even when I was a child, half a century later, train-loads of prostitutes would arrive from London whenever a fleet was in and set up shop in nearby Queen Street, still Portsea's main thoroughfare.

Family history can be deflating. I wonder whether to tell my mother that her 'Uncle' Tom Murphy (actually a great-uncle) was probably a fraud. She remembers visiting him as a schoolgirl. He lay in state upstairs, an aged invalid in his nightcap, smoking a clay pipe. The windowsills were decked with ships in bottles and he had 'sailed the China seas' in his youth. If so he must have been quick about it. The records give a different version of his twenties and thirties: paraffin merchant, shop-hand and then servant at an Italian coffee-house in the Strand. But maybe he managed a trip or two. In any case, tall stories, fabrications, become the myths families live by and carry emotional truths as historical as the census. People who never thought they had any history to speak of often talked themselves up.

On the way out of Portsmouth Museum, which houses the records, I take in the permanent exhibits, including the 'Living in Portsmouth' gallery, where the re-created 1930s kitchen looks uncannily like our own did in the 1950s. I note that HMS Fortitude ended up as a prison ship, joining all those other hulks where revolutionists, poachers, pilferers and cut-throats rotted or awaited transportation. And in a glass case a figure from my childhood greets me: the mechanical Laughing Sailor, a ventriloquist's dummy with staring eyes and a maniacal grin, who presided over the entrance to the amusement arcade at Clarence Pier. A penny in the slot sent him into hysterics. He too is out of commission.

At lunchtime I call in again at my parents' and find that they are trying out fish and chips from the new shop on the corner. I serve Dad and make myself a cheese sandwich while my mother, listing to port, fries an egg, not fancying the look of the batter. She finds the chips suspiciously 'bendy' and thinks they were cooked earlier and just warmed up. Most of their groceries are now ordered online or from the milkman, a shy, gangly bloke she has coaxed into conversation. ('What's your name?' she asked him finally. 'I can't go on calling you "Milkie".') He stows things away for her on the top shelf of the fridge, or on the kitchen surfaces, so she doesn't have to stoop for anything. I go out and do a bit of shopping for them, ignoring her warning against the prices at Waitrose ('About a pound of carrots, but get a paper bag if you can'), and then I change the sheets and pillowslips on the double bed, a job which usually takes them half an hour. Dad takes the washing round to their communal laundry, my mother following at a snail's pace in case he forgets to put the machine on or puts conditioner in the wrong compartment. On the train back to London, I feel relieved and imagine them taking their afternoon nap, sitting up straight in their armchairs. Later they will go back to collect their washing and I will be at Waterloo, and by then it will be dark.

A CHILD'S SENSE OF THE PAST*

When I recall how I first knew about the past, I hear a medley of grownup voices telling stories, weaving in and out, like the soundtrack to some lost film, until one or other suddenly breaks through the hubbub to regale the audience, and the cacophony subsides into a chorus of 'well, of all the . . .' or 'some people, I ask you!', or 'hang on a minute, and another thing. . .', on and on, each vying for their turn like soloists in an unending improvisation. (Another fainter noise is heard in the background: the clatter of trays and teaspoons, cups settling in their saucers.) Stories weren't so much told as staged. My mother, for instance, would spring out of her seat, adopt a comic walk, eyebrows raised, her hands slicing the air for punctuation, and others would follow suit, striking attitudes or aping accents, gesticulating for effect. Timing had to be nicely judged since the aim was to embroider a tale without making too much of a palaver. The point of a good story was in how you told it. But the past, when I first heard of it, had no dates. There was 'when you were just a toddler' or 'not even a twinkle in your father's eye' or 'when your Dad's Dad was alive'. Time was measured in people, by their length and breadth, as it were, like hands for a horse, a physical spanning in which the listener's size was also gauged. (Recently, asking my mother which year my father's father died, she thought and said – 'that was when you were still in your pram'.) Time flew backwards in generations, like a kite, leaving you a tiny figure, holding on, tethered.

The past was an enormous, seamless stretch without horizon, as daunting as Southsea Common on our Sunday promenade, all that grass, reaching from the main road across to the beach, much too far for a small child to manage. Portsmouth, the city where we lived was saturated with the past but the different stories about different times had been plunged into one big wash in my mind, swirling round indiscriminately. The sailor biting on his rum-soaked handkerchief as the surgeon hacked off his leg with a handsaw (as told on a trip to Nelson's 'Victory', moored in the local dockyard) was as recent, and as remote, to me as the bedbugs which my mother said she used to pick off her bedroom wall with a bar of soap or singe off with a candle when she was a kid. One of the terrifying 'dares' of a Saturday morning, when I was being minded by my brother and sister, was edging our way across the glass-strewn windowsills of a bombed-out house: there was an old Anderson air-raid shelter in our garden, yet my sense of that war was confused with the litany of names on the stone anchors and obelisks along the seafront: Trafalgar, Inkermann,

---

* 'A Child's Sense of the Past' first published in *New Formations*, 67, Summer 2009.

Passchendaele. My father's stories of close shaves during the Blitz – he and his mates safe in the front of the stalls at the Prince's while other boys had sneaked upstairs to the circle and been blown to smithereens – mingled with what he told me on family outings, bluebelling or 'wooding' on Portsdown Hill, high up overlooking the town. There were the forts out at sea shimmering in the distance and here was Fort Widley nearby on the Hill – all of them 'Palmerston's Follies' erected as a bulwark against a French invasion. I had no idea who – or when – Palmerston was.

Before I went to the grammar school I played in the street and made up my own stories for my gang of friends to enact, tales from the past which were added to our store of dressing-up clothes, as we cut off each other's heads or escaped from concentration camps. We raided the past like a props department to supply us with imaginary sets, borrowing from whatever we had seen at the Gaumont Picture Club – Kenneth Moore in *Reach for The Sky* or Virginia McKenna as Violette Szabo in *Carve Her Name with Pride* – furnished a few wartime scenarios, I remember – or from the BBC children's serials at Sunday teatime (*Kenilworth* and *The Three Musketeers* come to mind). When *Doctor Who* came on the television, I loved the idea of time-travelling, the Doctor collecting companions by chance from the centuries, the wild, kilted Jamie from the killing-fields of Culloden and Victoria, a prissy, crinolined Miss from her stuffy, upholstered home. This was the past of outings and trips, to be dropped in on, like a series of wishes granted by the genie; they were spots of time without causation or consequence. When I began to borrow books from the Carnegie Public Library I revelled in a more, not less porous present into which I could expand. My mother, who was the reader in the family at that time, never touched non-fiction and neither did I. *The Arabian Nights*, Grimm and Andersen, fairytales and the myths of ancient Greece and Rome took up where my weekly comics like *Playhour* or Children's Hour on TV, peopled by talking animals and toys, left off. Here was another shapechanging world in which a person became a star or a flower or at worst, a spider. I loved to be transported – 'up the wooden hill to the Land of Nod', I'd repeat, holding on to the banister, as I went upstairs to bed.

A child's world is perhaps always amorphous, searching for shapes to contain it, drifting between parallel universes, overlapping with, but not matching, where the adults live, full of multiple, shifting dimensions, more like a kaleidoscope of patterns than a stable view. This inner world is protean, can make infinite space of a nutshell; its walls are thin and airy; yet they can also stretch and insulate. This is the boundlessness of boredom, of fear, and of play; the place where the child is perhaps most itself and most inaccessible, and, where even at the bleakest of times, when all the colour is drained and the walls begin to buckle rather than bend, something which is isolated, is also preserved. If this world exists in time then it is the time of dream and nightmare; of fugue rather than narrative. The past may be part of its material, its repertoire, the stuff for a burgeoning ego, for the reverie and woolgathering which makes up the fabric of a self. Historical thinking, perhaps, involves separation, distinction and discrimination, a boundary, however temporary, between the self and others.

When I was small I liked to crawl behind the cupboard in my brother's bedroom. I discovered there a gas tap from the days when we lived upstairs in three rooms and this was our kitchen. I couldn't remember those times but that tap was evidence, cold and decisive, and I liked to stroke it. It was a part of history, an anchor, where personal experience, as relayed to me by the adults, remained vague and misty. Their past was not real to me, or rather it was as real as all the other make-believe in my life. I knew from an early age that my grandmother had been an orphan, dumped in the local institution with her baby brother, and shunted into domestic service at twelve. I don't think I was at all harrowed by the stories of getting up at five to skivvy, carrying cans of water, 'blacking the ranges'. I found it thrilling, as fabulous and glamorous as Cinderella covered in ash. Her stories added lustre to her because they gave her a past and she had lived to tell the tale. But it was many years before I could think of it as history. I only had her word for it, after all. To be history it had to become bigger – I would now say 'collective' – and be held at arm's length.

I absorbed the adults' stories, as perhaps all children do, like a sponge. What strikes me now is not that it was hard to know about the past as a child but how uncomfortably close, how awfully intimate it could be, rubbing shoulders with the present, fraying its fabric. No distance between then and now, only a hairline fracture. The past was just around the corner, leftover from yesterday like the spent fireworks we collected from the pavement and gutters the morning after Guy Fawkes's, a faint whiff of gunpowder still in the air. The past lurked and lingered in all sorts of things and could easily be surprised. It particularly favoured the dark and the dangerous – the dank corners in the Round Tower at Old Portsmouth, for instance, where you could imagine, my mother said, all the people who had been imprisoned there or the soldiers who had worn out the steps, trudging to and fro. I was troubled by ghosts (ghost stories ran in the family); ghosts were where the past leaked into the present like dye. I certainly learnt that the past was perilous, stalked by legendary illnesses – whooping cough, scarlet fever, rickets, polio – which had ravaged my relatives; people in the past, they said, had had to live in pigsties and they died like flies. Women were its walking-wounded; in fact their legs, clotted with veins, seemed especially to have borne the brunt of the long march into the present. I was a sickly child and I may have been especially alert to physical frailty but I think we were all brought up with a dizzying sense of mortality, of time rushing past, a whirling dervish, or a wind spinning you headlong from past to present to the graveyard. Among the lines of poetry my father was wont to recite were those relentless ones from Fitzgerald's translation of 'The Rubaiyat' of Omar Khayyam:

> The Moving Finger writes; and, having writ,
> Moves on: nor all thy Piety nor Wit
> Shall lure it back to cancel half a Line,
> Nor all thy Tears wash out a Word of it.

They surface in my memory tied to another of his favourite tags, more mirthful but more doom-laded, 'Eat, drink and be merry: for tomorrow we die'. If the present was a raft onto which we were crowded, the past was always blowing up a gale. It was important to wrap up warm.

Everything the grown-ups said about their own childhood and the past, the vehemence with which they animated it, made it seem stronger, smellier, dirtier, louder and brighter than the present. It was a lot for the children to take in. We fidgeted on laps or made the tea and passed round the biscuits. We weren't encouraged to be raconteurs. I think everyone craved the limelight yet at the same time dreaded showing off or making an exhibition of themselves. Naturally the adults took up the most room since they were making up for lost time. A great many of the stories that I heard as a child dealt in extremity of one sort of another – poverty, cruelty, suffering – but they were told for their entertainment value and shared theatre, always for a laugh. The hilarity made it safe, temporarily at least, to venture across a minefield of undetonated memories. On the other hand it was their being stories, the very making of a narrative which protected against any random flak. A story gave durability and duration to what had been broken or fleeting. Perhaps the main reason that I couldn't distinguish between my family's past and that of our city was because the grownups couldn't either: they didn't seem to have enough of a continuous past to separate from it. The past was inchoate, embryonic, pressing on the membrane of the present; stories helped bring it to birth.

This was why the sing-song became such an important ritual in our life as it did in so many other families; it gave us the continuity, or the illusion of it, which allowed us to see ourselves as a group with a past. When my mother's family got together and sang they overflowed with strong feeling, heady stuff, often nostalgic in the original sense of painfully longing for home and for the peace of a perfect union: 'A garden of Eden' we'd sing, 'just made for two, and nothing to spoil the view' ('*If you were the only girl in the world, and I was the only boy*'). But the songs also celebrated the unattached, spontaneous and casual – strolling, roaming, tramping, being of no fixed abode. Needs were declared minimal – 'All I want is a room somewhere, Far away from the cold night air' – and the best things in life were free. The sing-song was a make-shift, eclectic form – 'What shall we have now?', someone would ask, and bystanders in the pub would chip in with their own requests. It was robust, inventive, and compensatory, drawing at random on a repertoire of melodies and music-hall renditions, going back to my grandmother's childhood (the Boer War marching song, 'Goodbye Dolly, I must leave you') and forward to the Beatles ('Yesterday' was an inevitable favourite, relished for its melan-choly) or Rogers and Hammerstein. These weren't 'traditional'; in fact we borrowed shamelessly from the Irish or the Cockneys ('Maybe it's because I'm a Londoner' we'd sing gaily). I didn't learn any English folk songs until I was at school when Ewan MacColl and others introduced them on the radio. The singsong, in other words, was an invented tradition. My parents were fond of a drink (and had as rich a vocabulary for the shades and nuances of inebriation as the Inuit do for snow), but the singsong depended on a new, quite recent drinking culture, one in which men, women and children (if the landlord was lenient) all sat together on plush velvet seats in the 'lounge', quite unlike the spit and sawdust public bars in which my grandfathers had drowned their sor-rows, gone home with their fists flailing, or more often than not, had to be fetched before they drank the housekeeping money. The idea of meeting in the pub as a family to sing on a Saturday night was a domestication of the old order. Of course the singsong was a fabrication. That was its point. It wrought a harmonious present out of rows and rivalries and it mended a past full of rents and tears. (I was a keen performer but whenever I remember my solos, I see my sister's face, furious). Singsongs were also one of the few times when children were on equal terms with the adults and could join in without the usual put-downs that peppered grown-up conversation – 'what do you know about it?' or 'who asked for your opinion?'.

I think now that we were fashioning a shared past from something as yet only imminent in the history books, which hadn't yet turned into history (or 'history from below'): the lives of the vast majority of city dwellers, the great unwashed, the itinerants and unrecruitables, the 'unskilled', the people at the bottom of the heap whose tenancies were always precarious and whose footholds on the social ladder were slippery, like our own. Though I didn't know it then what I took to be a tradition of song was evidence of our lack of tradition, of our migrations and relocations and flittings, of people who had come from the villages to work in the city in the nineteenth century, found themselves beached up in the tenements and slums, and in my parents' own time, bombed out and re-housed. This may be one reason why family history as an amateur activity or hobby is now so popular: it constitutes a narrative; it offers an umbilical cord; it resettles. Genealogy used only to belong to the wealthy; only they owned a past and laid claim to a continuous history based on their claim to land and property. Tracking my own family and their many branches back into the late eighteenth century, as I now have, I find they were constantly on the move. If we became the 'lumpenproletariat' (from the German for 'ragged') then this class was made not born. This is the history that needs writing.

ON MOURNING*

It's four years since my husband, the historian and socialist Raphael Samuel, died of cancer at the age of 61. In the weeks after his death, I wrote about him every day. I filled a boxfile and an A3 ringbinder with anecdotes and observations, physical descriptions and characteristic phrases; I made notes on what he had told me of his childhood, on our marriage, on his work, on what we called his 'Communist unconscious'; I even listed his shirts. I couldn't stop writing; I was restless and, at times, euphoric. I accumulated thousands of words. I thought about writing an article. I knew how I wanted it to begin, with a quotation from one of Raphael's love letters, written when I was coming up to London to visit him, a fortnight after we'd met:

> Dear love,
> Further to my previous note, for God's sake, don't buy any vegetables. I have the two big aubergines we bought on Sunday, the fat cauliflower, the half pound of mushrooms, a giant beetroot, a bag of fresh herbs, two baby marrows, and sundry greens . . .

Raphael's succulent inventory was meant to woo me – I was a vegetarian at the time – but its seriousness was even more seductive, making me laugh out loud. After he died, I hankered after this sense of urgency more than anything. It was appetite in its purest form, and appetite was the only antidote to the deathly.

Writing was a way of staying close to Raphael; it was something we both did for a living and it shaped the rhythms of our domesticity. Scribbling random notes on the back of used paper (a habit of Raphael's), I was also impersonating him. Behaving like the lost person, employing their gestures, finding that you use, quite involuntarily, their turns of speech, is a common response to loss. It's a version of the searching which confirms the absence but also incorporates the presence of the dead, making tangible and visible again what perishes first of all – the body of the beloved. Raphael wasn't dead for me yet and writing kept him in suspended animation. In the months to come I understood better the myth of Mausoleus, whose widow eats his ashes. What easier way to take in a death and to digest its consequences (what therapists call 'internalising')? For me words were necessary to this incorporation; I was looking for ways to feed on my loss.

---

* First published in the *London Review of Books*, February 22 2001.

There was something manic in my writing: perhaps it was a last-ditch attempt at playing God, a compensation for the helplessness I'd felt watching Raphael die. I hadn't been able to stop that happening but now I felt that I, and I alone, had the key to his life. I was preparing the materials for a vast biography and at the same time imagined producing a succinct, authoritative piece which would allow me to have the last word. I see now that writing kept the grief at bay (though I collapsed periodically, leaning against the house walls for support or lying doubled up on the bathroom floor); that words were insulation and ballast, staving off the sense of weightlessness, the untethering which makes the bereaved kindred to the mad.

Raphael was diagnosed with cancer in the spring of 1995. I wrote a convoluted, poetic account of what it felt like to live with the illness (I called it 'The Fifth Season', since by the time I finished it we were into our second spring). It was never published and he never read it, but it was in part a response to Susan Sontag's attack on the idea of illness as a metaphor. Metaphors seemed to both of us then a possible defence, protective colouring – provided there were plenty of them, proliferating like vines. For instance, instead of the militarist notions of 'invasion' and 'bombardment' which Sontag had shown to be so insidious in medical thinking, we played with the idea of cancer as dissident or anarchist, a disease of the diaspora. Cancer was a precarious state, and metaphors offered a temporary hold, even a saving grace; the capacity to interpret and reinterpret was a knowing refusal of diagnosis as a death sentence; metaphor, a species of reprieve.

Formlessness, however, is a condition of mourning. I went to see a Howard Hodgkin exhibition at the Hayward Gallery shortly after Raphael died. I stood before an oil painting called *Lovers* in an ecstasy, dazed by the red and green swathes of bright, primal colour swooping like a rainbow and running right off the canvas, spilling over the black frame. A dialectical union of opposites, it figured that dissolution of boundaries, the falling in love which mourning restages. Like love, grief stops history in its tracks; it has duration without narrative. (For the lover time concertinas into unbearably fleeting moments: for the mourner each minute is monumental.)

Like other fledgling mourners I was not conscious of trying to 'master loss', as Freud puts it in *Beyond the Pleasure Principle*; all my efforts went into projection, into being with the deceased: wanting, in fact, to die. The sobbing, the dry heaving and violent racking of the body, the 'dissolving' into tears, all make the physical separation between the living and the dead seem less hard and fast. Those early months of mourning were, as we say, a blur. But mourning works against the will, by compulsive repetition. Eventually the repeated repetitions (all those anniversaries counted in days, then weeks, then months and years) force one to register that the absence feels different, if only by being, like the pain, more familiar. However stymied the mourner feels inside, however inert, outside changes remorselessly. So for example, the general election that May was a terrible wrench; an assault on my inwardness.

Of course I had to abandon the 'article' – editing, cutting or finishing anything about Raphael's life seemed psychologically impossible. As well as being grateful, I was shocked at how swiftly Raphael's closest male friends could write about him, how readily they occupied the public space. Perhaps mistakenly, I linked their capacity to find that authority with a different relation to grief, one in which anger was more allowable (and triumphal feelings, too). Getting something out of your system – and that includes writing about it – requires aggression; writing alienates. I found myself wondering whether, compared with their male peers, women have always written less about the death of people they loved.

Raphael wasn't 'famous' in the sense that film-stars are famous, but he was a public figure: a political activist who had been a member of the Marxist Historians Group and the old New Left; a teacher who had been at the same college, Ruskin, for thirty-odd years and had helped to shape the culture of adult education; a historian whose work had been part of a collective effort to change the practice of social history, and a writer and critic who had debated and engaged with these questions on radio and TV and in the press. Raphael's life was intensely peopled: he worked by constant consultation, and friendship – comradeship – was a principle of life for him.

He was 51 when I married him, twenty years older than me. He had had other love affairs and long companionships, had brought up children and made alternative households in the house in Spitalfields which he had first rented in 1962, and where I now live alone. He had not only kept in touch with ex-lovers but continued to work with them. That I would have to share the process of mourning and memorialisation was obvious from the beginning – about three hundred people came to the funeral at Highgate Cemetery, which sensibly was microphoned (this immediately made it a more public occasion, as did the presence of a press photographer, which I found unbearable). I received a mass of condolence letters, many from strangers who, like the hundreds at the memorial held the following April at the Conway Hall, talked affectionately and possessively about 'Raph'. None of this made me less territorial, even though I knew it was pointless to try to monopolise the dead. Rivalry among the grieving feels shameful and is usually hushed up in families. It may be more exposed in a public death where there are fewer shared rituals (especially on the secular Left). We had no politics of memorialisation; we had to make it up as we went along.

I remember some colleagues coming to the house from the University of East London to examine Raphael's books with a view to a donation. He had set up a centre for London history there in the last months of his life. I thrust photographs of him under their noses: here he is on holiday in his swimming trunks; basking in the sun; drinking Spanish brandy! I wanted to insist on 'the private man' I felt constantly in danger of losing as that other chimera, the public figure, loomed ever larger. But I knew the division was illusory, especially in Raphael's case. In the introduction to *Village Life and Labour* (1975), the first volume of the History Workshop Series of books, he wrote:

We need to know about the inner life of the household – the competition for authority and love, the allocation of domestic roles – if we are to give a convincing account of the way it is shaped by external forces . . . the same is true of moral discipline and social control: they are generated from within as well as imposed from without.

Interiors – the inner life of the home, but also of the self – are not outside history but places where history is made. This was literally brought home to me, as it usually is to the bereaved, when so many of my household habits no longer made any sense. It seemed as if the whole house had to be reincarnated, lived in differently, if I was not to feel redundant. By the first anniversary of Raphael's death all the work for his second volume of *Theatres of Memory* had been decanted into *Island Stories* and his study made into a sitting-room with a fitted carpet (the height of corruption). I had a party to mark the new room; no one found it heartless, I think.

Thom Gunn has a poem in *The Man with Night Sweats* in which he imagines the dead watching the living on TV, until, after a few episodes, they get bored and feel excluded and begin, at last, 'weaned from memory', to join the snowy battalions of the truly dead. After four years I can begin to let Raphael cross the Styx. He hasn't haunted me much, which is a shame. He has hardly appeared in my dreams after those frantic nightmares of the first year, fugues in which I sought and found him in madhouses and cancer wards, tormented, sick and abandoned. There have been one or two signs, however, from the underworld. Around the third anniversary I dreamt that Raphael was in the US (the place, given his residual anti-American feeling, that he was least likely to be). We talked on the telephone and it was good to hear from him (Raphael spent half his life on the phone, cradling the receiver lovingly under his chin). A connection had been made at least.

Then, in the run-up to the last anniversary, I had another dream which I take to be a psychic advance of sorts. Raphael was back. He had been away for some mysterious reason but now he had returned to Britain and I rushed round to where I knew I'd find him, slightly puzzled that he had not got in touch, but excited at the prospect of seeing him again. I dashed upstairs and knocked and there he was: wedged between teetering columns of books and almost invisible beneath a cliff of files (the setting suggested the North Gallery at the old British Library, where I used to unearth him at closing time). He was courteous and perfectly friendly but somewhat embarrassed. Clearly he was eager to get on with his work. I immediately woke up with a sad but satisfying sense that he had left me (how clever the unconscious is): he didn't need me anymore so it was fine for me to be living my own life. This time I didn't need the Atlantic to let me off the hook.

Proust says that grief decays more even than beauty, crumbles into dust, leaving fewer and fewer traces of itself. Certainly I can no longer taste the ashes in my mouth. But mourning – and Proust observed the anniversaries of his mother's death (even the monthly ones) devotedly – is the kind of remembering that leavens or deadens a life. In the first volume of *Theatres of Memory*, Raphael described memory as an activity, a dramatic process in which the relation to the past is constantly improvised, re-enacted and thereby made new. A theatre is the opposite of a mausoleum. As a historian Raphael had more past in his life than most. Not least, what weighed on me personally, the vast tranche of papers, the body of his work, which filled the entire house over five floors. Throughout my mourning I have wanted two opposite, impossible things: to hold on tightly and belligerently to absolutely everything; to be free of it all at one stroke. Coming across some tatty scripts with their edges scorched from being against a hot waterpipe, I longed for the whole lot to go up in smoke and our house, which was as Dickensian as Krook's, to combust spontaneously.

But the fear of being overwhelmed by the past is matched by the fear that there will be nothing left to show for a life; mourning lurches between the compulsion to remember and the desire – at times far more frightening – to forget utterly. More frightening because, perhaps, it heralds our own mortality, our disappearance eventually into history. In the last four years I've returned over and over to what one of my closest friends said when I lamented that I was 'just a chapter in Raphael's life'. Instead of reassuring me as I wanted, she said gently but boldly; 'Perhaps you don't like the idea of him becoming a chapter in yours.'

In a sense, all the writing that is produced in the wake of a death is hopeful – from the brief announcement in the paper to the fullest biography. Writing is a form of resurrectionism: a faith in the life to come. Perhaps inevitably the recent literature of mourning emphasises the survivor's story: it has been one of the central ways of plotting the 20th century. But what seems as compelling to me now is to find space in the writing of history or biography for those times when the story seizes up, when there is no progress, only stasis or repetition; the times out of time when we are helpless or sick, wounded or crazy. Poetry has always stolen a march on prose when it comes to picturing loss. I think of Tennyson's weaving together of sporadic moods, arrested moments and broken states in *In Memoriam*; how he winnowed down the years into those three Christmases which grant the reader the consolation of a narrative; how determined he was to ring out 'wild bells' at the New Year, over and over again, to celebrate and renounce the mourner's glimpse of eternity.

PART III

WRITING LIVES

13

A Woolf in Dog's Clothing: *Flush**

'There is nothing like a dog story for bringing out people's characters . . .'
Virginia Woolf, 'Gypsy, the Mongrel'[1]'

THE ANIMAL WITHIN

Anyone who cares to go dog-spotting in Virginia Woolf's diaries and letters
will swiftly realize that the most constant presences in her life were canine.
Woolf grew up with dogs (her father, Leslie Stephen, had been 'unthinkable',
according to his biographer, without a dog)[2] and her early journals bristle with
accounts of being 'out with Gurth', 'that extraordinarily ubiquitous dog',[3]
in the new department stores in Oxford Street, at concert halls and libraries.
Dog-walking, like cycling (which Woolf's sister Vanessa took to early on),
was a modern emancipation: with a canine chaperon, the relatively advanced
Edwardian young woman could haunt the streets in safety. Rambling across
London squares, or, later in her married life, on the Downs in Sussex, Woolf
always had a dog in tow. One of them, a red cocker spaniel called Pinker,
or Pinka in deference to her sex, a gift in 1926 from Vita Sackville-West in
the heyday of their friendship, became the model for Flush (her photograph
graces the first edition as a frontispiece). Yet Virginia Woolf in her middle years
was not, according to her nephew, 'a dog-lover': she kept her distance from
that relationship as from so much else she had inherited from the nineteenth
century, tempering her accounts of canine existence with a characteristic mix
of sympathy and raillery (Pinka's fleas, her fatness and − alas! her smell are all

* First published as the introduction to the Penguin Classics edition of Virginia Woolf's
Flush, 2000.

chronicled).[4] One of the impulses behind *Flush* is to mock, however kindly, the intense attachment which Elizabeth Barrett formed for her spaniel, a doting affection which kept them both in thrall.

One of *Flush's* forerunners can be found early on in Virginia Stephen's writerly apprenticeship, in an obituary of 'Shag', the Stephen family dog.[5] Shag was 'the last of the family to live in the old house' in South Kensington from where, after the recent death of her father, Virginia and her siblings had boldly moved to Bloomsbury. It begins on a breezy note by disparaging the 'impertinence' and 'foolhardiness' of pet-keeping. But 'On a Faithful Friend' (as its sentimental title suggests) is soaked in Victorian pathos. The story of the stone-deaf, half-blind terrier returning from an enforced retirement (he had been ousted by a younger dog) and going home to die, was meant to 'glad-den the heart' of Sophie Farrell, the family cook, who had accompanied them across London and who had never taken to Gurth, the newcomer.[6] Wherever they feature in Woolf's writings, dogs evoke the vulnerabilities, as well as the comforts, of dependency. Sophie Farrell and Shag were to be refigured, much more guiltily, over thirty years later, as 'Crosby and Rover' in *The Years*: this time both old retainers are put out to grass (and in Rover's case put out of his misery) by the younger generation making modern lives.[7] In writing the biog-raphy of Flush, Virginia Woolf was in some ways going back over old ground, back into the nineteenth-century home, into older forms of family life and feeling. *Flush*, however, was to be 'an escapade', a fantasy of leaving the past behind without pining, of being footloose and fancy-free.

When Pinka died in 1935, Woolf wrote that 'a dog somehow represents – no I cant think of the word – the private side of life – the play side'.[8] Animals took her, as so many of us, back to the nursery; their real or imaginary presence in her life fuelled her earliest creative exploration of the world. Her child-hood had been crowded with all kinds of creatures (the family pets included a squirrel, a marmoset and a mouse called Jacobi). One of her earliest memories, before she could read, was of her father drawing animals for his children – 'as fast as we could demand them' – or twisting paper beneath a pair of scissors, 'and out would drop an elephant, a stag or a monkey'.[9] Her mother, Julia Stephen, wrote and read them her own animal stories (where pigs, bears, mon-keys, always return gratefully home like wayward children).[10] Woolf relished exotic as well as domestic species (at one of her frequent visits to London Zoo, she particularly enjoyed a 'very wombatty wombat').[11] All her life she used the animal nicknames, or 'pet names' which her family had invented for each other in childhood as a form of relationship to herself and others, a teas-ing vocabulary of endearment and silliness: she was 'Goat', 'Sparroy', 'Ape', depending upon whom she was addressing (she often signed herself as a dog);

new friends were instantly attributed animal personae or characteristics: Ethel Smythe, the last of Woolf's intense female friendships, was 'an uncastrated wild cat'.[12] Playing at being an animal made it possible in a late Victorian household to solicit 'a petting', for a respectable English young lady to ask for physical affection and reassurance – 'so, kiss your dog on its tender snout and think him me', she wrote to one close friend;[13] it was one way that longings, otherwise taboo, could be spoken. The Woolfs (or 'Woolves' as they were sometimes called) used this child's play as a code for the amorous pleasures and velleities of married life: 'Love from every animal', Virginia typically closed a letter to her husband, 'Come along marmots and do your jublimmails'.[14] Dog correspondence with Vita made up a large part of the erotic fantasy-life between them. Woolf's 'internal zoo'[15] comprised a whole menagerie of creatures allowing the expression of her private experiences and feelings, whilst keeping them partly concealed.

But there was a dark side to animality. If it was an acceptable way of overcoming a reticence about the body and its needs, it also unleashed a fund of metaphors and imagery for what was dangerous or disturbing in human behaviour, for unmanageable feelings of rage or terror; it was a habitual and traditional language of insult, hatred and hostility. The animal as predatory or wild – the bestial – was for Woolf, as for others, frequently a metaphor for sexual aggression and for human acts of force; it could signal, by association, the fears roused by other denigrated or demonized groups, as well as be the means by which they are dehumanized. These surface in Woolf's first novel, *The Voyage Out*, when her heroine, after being passionately kissed for the first time, dreams that she is trapped in a dank, oozing tunnel

> alone with a little deformed man who squatted on the floor gibbering, with long nails. His face was pitted like the face of an animal.[16]

In the 1930s Woolf reworked the language of animality to find ways of writing privately about what she felt to be her most painful and shameful experiences, especially those of a sexual nature: she looked back on her home as a 'cage' where she was 'a nervous, gibbering, little monkey'.[17] 'Brutishness', both personal and political, is one of the major preoccupations of her last novel, *Between the Acts*, written during the Second World War.

Flush, as Woolf was to write over and again, was meant 'only for a joke',[18] but like all jokes, it makes light of material which otherwise, and elsewhere, had powerful resonances. *Flush* was published in 1933. It followed in the wake of *The Waves* and was gradually pushed to one side by Woolf's drafting of 'The Pargiters', an experimental 'essay-novel' which was to take much tormented rewriting before it evolved into her novel, *The Years*, and her overtly feminist essay, *Three Guineas*.[19] *Flush*, though it played the part of light relief from these serious works, has much in common with them, not least in exploring the place of physical experience in the making of a life or personality, a question which *The Waves*, a kind of group biography, had broached. Woolf-hoped 'The Pargiters' would deal, amongst other things, with 'the sexual life of women'.[20] It took its cue from a speech she gave early in 1931 (the year she began *Flush*) where she acknowledged that writing about 'womens bodies for instance – their passions'[21] was the sticking-point of her imagination: 'telling the truth about my own experiences as a body', she wrote frankly in a later version, was the greatest 'obstacle' in her way as a woman writer.[22] Trying on a dog's body for size allowed Virginia Woolf to inhabit a different physical existence (what could be more down to earth than a life lived on the paws or through the orifices?) whilst simultaneously covering her tracks. But venturing beyond the confines of respectability, even in the guise of a nineteenth-century pet spaniel, meant encountering what was threatening as well as liberating about the animal within: Flush, in other words, is a Woolf in dog's clothing and thereby hangs the tale.

A DOG'S LIFE

Pity the poor animal who is born to be a writer's pet! For if ever a creature's independent existence is likely to be undermined, who is more at risk than the dog or cat cooped up with an author? And perhaps no animal lived more of a dog's life in this respect than the Victorian cocker spaniel Flush. A gift in 1841 from the writer Mary Russell Mitford (who had already translated her own dogs into verse) to Elizabeth Barrett, a poet obliged through illness to conduct more of her life in writing than in person, Flush was bandied back and forth in their letters as a token of their friendship; then, since his mistress promptly fell in love with another writer, Robert Browning, and conducted much of her clandestine courtship by post, his fate as a literary device was sealed; he featured in their correspondence as symbol and simile for all the shades of romance, the pretext for decorous flirtation, or the occasion for a lovers' tiff.[23] Attachment to Flush was, for both poets, a measure of devotion: 'yours as your hand is, – or as your Flush, rather', wrote Robert Browning: '*I* am *your* Flush, and *he* is mine', declared Elizabeth Barrett in the heat of the moment, when her spaniel had been snatched by thieves, and the love-affair was reaching its own crisis.[24]

Although Elizabeth Barrett could not anticipate that, nearly a century later, Flush's biography would be composed for him, she was quite untroubled by the idea of putting words in his mouth.[25] She saw a telling expression in his silent looks, a pleading significance in the twists of his tail; every twitch and every scratch, every snuffle or sniff, spoke volumes in 'Flush-language' (and filled pages in her copious epistles). At times he was barely a dog at all, he was her 'loving friend', 'the first person', she wrote, 'who wakes me'; he could recognize (according to his mistress) the letters 'A' and 'B', could count to three (he might eventually, she hoped, manage dominoes); and since letters and numbers were within his reach, why not writing too? Miss Barrett's most extravagant fancy was to elevate him into an author: out and about in London he had 'the air of one taking notes' and she was 'by no means sure that Flush wont bring out as good a two volumes of "Travels" some day – of notes and documents – as anybody from the new world'.[26]

Yet far from being merely an imposition on a much put-upon animal, this ventriloquy was part and parcel of Elizabeth Barrett Browning's benevolent and liberal philosophy. Her 'philo-dogism', as she called it,[27] shared in that radical shift of attitude towards animals, which, in the nineteenth century, brought so many cats and dogs in from the cold. Flush's mistress might object to 'the mar-tyrdom' of 'a sporting valuable spaniel' in 'the London streets prison',[28] but her very protests acknowledged that a dog bred initially for its worth was now seen as sentient and suffering. As they lived inside private apartments and familial rooms, nineteenth-century pets took up residence more and more inside the minds and imaginations of their owners; and as they shared the private lives of humans, they were credited with private lives of their own.[29] Since Miss Barrett could identify with Flush, she made no bones about speaking for him. And anyone wishing to understand what it felt like to be Elizabeth Barrett in London in the 1840s, might begin with what she says, not about herself, but about her spaniel.

So when Virginia Woolf sat in her garden at Monk's House in Sussex in the summer of 1931, perusing again the famous love-letters between Elizabeth Barrett and Robert Browning, and laughing out loud at the picture of Flush, she was apparently picking up where Flush's mistress had left off.[30] It was Eliza-beth Barrett who first identified Flush's position with her own. He was the diminutive companion and ministering angel – 'dear faithful loyal Flushie' – who had foregone the pleasures of 'the sunny moor' to share her darkened life in the back bedroom in Wimpole Street; she sent their likenesses to her friend, Richard Horne, commenting humorously on the resemblance of Flush's silken ears to her own ringlets; her letters delight in the similarities between them.[31] Flush, she told Miss Mitford, was horribly 'spoilt'.[32] Fed on paprika chicken, cream, and ginger cake (Elizabeth's leftovers which she gave him the taste for), he was childish in his sulks and scenes. But who was the pampered, useless dependent, 'chained' to the sofa in Wimpole Street, if not Elizabeth Barrett herself? Feminist reviewers of *Flush* immediately saw that, with the hindsight of the 1930s, Woolf had reversed the perspectives: Flush's story was in part a 'psychological biography' of his mistress,[33] his 'imprisonment', as Rebecca West put it, a 'symbolic representation' of Elizabeth Barrett's own.[34]

Woolf's relation with her Victorian predecessor was double edged. She had already written a brief account of the poet's life shortly before she began *Flush*, in her critical assessment of Barrett Browning's novel-poem, 'Aurora Leigh' (itself an epic tale of a woman writer's emancipation), which seeks to reclaim the poem from obscurity.[35] Though she admired Barrett Browning's 'lively and secular and satirical' mind (all modern, indeed Woolfian, virtues, we might note) and her 'shrewd and caustic humour', the Victorian 'poetess' had long exemplified for Woolf the cost as well as the achievement of nineteenth-century womanliness.[36] Woolf's own escape, as she saw it, from the stifling demands of the late Victorian family together with her modernist aesthetic of impersonality, made her ambivalent towards what she deemed a too personal and loosely expressive, feminized art, the product of an intense, secluded life.[37] Elizabeth Barrett Browning's 'ardour and abundance' were a sign of weakness as well as strength: 'Mrs Browning', she wrote tartly, 'could no more conceal herself than she could control herself.'

In 'Aurora Leigh' Woolf mentions Elizabeth Barrett's love for Flush as evidence of her overwrought, hot-house life: his loss affected her, Woolf suggested, 'as the loss of a child might have affected another woman'. *Flush* gives us both the story of that mutual attachment and a more modern tale of successful separation, a weaning from anxious emotionalism, and a gaining of a new expansiveness (which is nicely caught in Vanessa Bell's contrasting drawings of the claustrophobic Wimpole Street and the light, bare Casa Guidi in Florence). In Italy Miss Barrett becomes Mrs Browning, properly absorbed in her husband and baby rather than her dog; she is emancipated enough, at the end of the story, to return to Wimpole Street and visit it unscathed (it is only, she feels, that the house wants cleaning). Flush, meanwhile, has had the run of Florence and learns to stand on his own four feet; facing death, he is his own master, choosing to make his way home. *Flush* is Woolf's fantasy of making peace with the past; the little dog embodies a freer relationship to emotional and physical ties.[38]

Flush is one of Woolf's many forays into what her contemporaries called 'Victorianism', which they felt as a psychological as well as a material encumbrance The Wimpole Street back bedroom, shrouded by blinds and cluttered with busts and bric-à-brac, where young Flush finds himself buried, is an image of the overheated and crowded private life of the Victorians, 'tangled and matted with emotion' – as Woolf wrote of her own childhood home.[39] Writing from Flush's point of view guaranteed Woolf an amused distance from Barrett Browning and from the reverence that had long been afforded her femininity, her courtship, marriage and motherhood.[40] More than one reviewer felt that Barrett Browning was thereby diminished (Robert Browning, with his dandified lemon-coloured gloves, is also somewhat reduced): readers of this biography will learn little about her and still less of her poetry; the former appears to Flush as vague 'enthusiasm', whilst the latter is as baffling as her penchant for 'table-rapping' – the nearest we come to understanding Barrett Browning's spiritual beliefs.[41] Woolf wrote of Mrs Browning in 'Aurora Leigh' that nowadays 'nobody troubles to put her in her place'. *Flush*, in its waggish way, does that.

In coming to terms with the Victorians, *Flush* was very much of its time. Writing about the Brownings reached a new peak between the wars – between 1928 and 1931 alone, eight new biographical volumes were published,[42] and an edition of Barrett Browning's letters to her sister Henrietta, which Woolf drew upon for *Flush*. But its immediate prompt may have been Rudolph Besier's play, *The Barretts of Wimpole Street*, whose version of the story was on everyone's lips in the autumn of 1930.[43] Besier had added a Freudian twist to the romance, turning Edward Moulton Barrett, Elizabeth's father, into a sinister, repressed villain, and hinting at an incestuous impulse behind his veto on her marriage.[44] Not surprisingly, Barrett's descendants were appalled and wrote to the press to protest;[45] the play was slightly 'toned down' before it came to London, though it retained one scene which has Mr Barrett dandling his niece on his knee and kissing her 'roughly' on the lips. British theatre audiences, however, took this kind of sex-talk in their stride (particularly since a tyrant patriarch made the romance, which Besier treated as sacrosanct, even more exciting).[46] Woolf, in fact, wanted stronger meat; she saw the play and thought it 'rather feeble', though 'the astonishing story' was not, she added, an exaggeration.[47] More importantly, perhaps, Besier had put Flush fully in the limelight as the only witness to the courtship and as Elizabeth's vulnerable surrogate: the part was faultlessly performed by a canine actress, though of the wrong sex and hue, a 'Miss Tuppeny [sic] of Ware'.[48]

The Barretts of Wimpole Street also kindled discussion in the press about the ethics of biography. Mention was often made of Woolf's close friend and rival, Lytton Strachey, whose *Eminent Victorians* (1918) and bestselling *Queen Victoria* (1921) had set the tone after the war for an ironizing reassessment of nineteenth-century values.[49] Irreverent and entertaining, rather than sanctifying or didactic, Strachey's biographies aimed at lightening the load – moral and literary – of weighty Victorian lives.[50] He favoured economy in life-writing,

the suggestive detail selected from an already written life rather than the amass-
ing of new evidence. For Strachey the subjective nature of interpreting historical fact made biography an art, one which, under the influence of psychology,
was now free to conjure his subjects' thoughts, memories and feelings – 'the
subtle, secret lines of their inner nature'.[51] One of the impulses behind *Flush*
was to cock a snook at Strachey: 'I meant it for a joke with Lytton', she wrote
to her friend, John Lehmann, 'and a skit on him'.[52] Like all parodies, though,
Flush was liable to bite the hand which fed it.

For Woolf had her doubts about 'the new biography' as she called it.
Although she relished its 'lack of pose, humbug, solemnity', she was sceptical
about how far biography could go in trespassing on the techniques of fiction
in order to marry 'the granite like solidity' of historical truth with the 'rainbow like quality of personality': biography was ultimately driven by different imperatives. And whilst she approved the fact that the biographer was no
longer hero-worshipping or writing hagiographically, as many Victorians had
done, she observed that the new approaches threw as much light on the biographer as on his subject: biography had become unacknowledged autobiography, a form of self-portraiture (this might be, she commented provocatively,
its most appealing aspect). She feared, nevertheless, that the ironic approach
to the past, 'though it has its tenderness' risked elevating the biographer at his
subject's expense.[53]

In May 1931 Woolf read Strachey's latest collection of biographical essays,
Portraits in Miniature, deciding that 'the compressed yet glowing account' suited
his methods better than 'the larger scale'.[54] Writing the life of a dumb animal allowed her to cut down to size the biographer's all-but god-like claims
to omniscience, a self-conscious analogy with the way pet-owners ventrilo-
quized. *Flush* suggests a more modest biographical relationship: our view is
always limited as well as framed by our own perspective; and though Flush
may be party to secrets, he cannot repeat them – the lives of others, like the
past itself, are simply not open to our eavesdropping.[55] In *Orlando* (1928), her
other spoof-biography, Woolf had already played self-consciously with the
limits of life-writing: her protagonist swashbuckles through four centuries and
changes sex en route. Woolf suggested that since the lives of those usually
omitted from the historical record – like the lives of women – do not neatly fit
the conventional plots and categories of biography, they call in question how
history itself is understood. *Flush* was to queer the pitch differently.

Woolf intended *Flush* to be a 'lark', 'something to boil my pot', a pamphlet
dashed off for fun in a few weeks.[56] It was written, like *Orlando*, after the efforts
of *To the Lighthouse*, to 'ease the brain' (in the summer of 1931 she had just finished proofing *The Waves*).[57] In fact it proved laborious. Woolf abandoned the

draft after a few weeks and it hung fire for a year. Flush's life, unlike Orlando's, could not give her the pleasure of pure fabrication; her methods came much closer to the writing of a full-scale biography (*Flush* is, in some ways, a trial-run for *Roger Fry*). It meant keeping careful reading notes, turning to canine 'authorities' (not all of which were finally listed) – a history of British dogs, the rules for the Kennel Club – to promote a history from below.[58] The first draft was unwieldy, packed with quotations from Barrett Browning's letters, which would have to be winnowed. She had also begun writing 'A Tap on the Door' (an early title for *Three Guineas*), was 'bathing' herself in the Elizabethans for the second series of *The Common Reader*, and making up her 'Letter to a Young Poet'. Then Lytton Strachey died early in 1932 and much of the point of the book evaporated.

When she resumed *Flush* in July 1932, the idea still made her laugh uproariously, and she enjoyed some of 'the freak' of the writing,[59] but it was now 'cuckooed out' by 'The Pargiters' written at a great rate from October.[60] In late December Woolf took up *Flush* again to 'cool' herself from the heat of this other project, and was dejected to find that it wouldn't do: 'Oh what a waste – what a bore!' she declared, it was at once 'too slight and too serious' and she felt 'landed' with it.[61] More setting of teeth, rewriting and polishing, in order to get back to 'The Pargiters' (which now represented freedom for her imagination), and 'that abominable dog!', as he was sadly dubbed, was finally 'despatched' at the end of January 1933. 'Nobody can say I dont take trouble with my little stories,' she wrote rather ruefully in her diary.[62]

Woolf's drafts suggest how much biography's tendency towards ventriloquy, made more obvious when one tried to write 'the lives of the dumb', gave her pause for thought.[63] *Flush* was bound to be caught between two stools: it was meant to expose Strachey's limits, but could only do so by following his methods, taking the leap from the written record into re-interpretation and into the use of fictional techniques (like internal monologue). Woolf rapidly dropped her initial attempt at inferring Flush's life from his owners' (with its series of cumbersome repetitions of 'he must have felt' or 'he must have thought'), and reshaped the narrative around shocks and raptures which were purely his. Flush's life now had separate highs and lows: jealousy and fury made Robert Browning, not Mr Barrett, the villain of the piece, so several pages on 'bloodsucking' fathers were cut;[64] smell took precedence over sight (the Wimpole Street scenes give us 'a terrific whiff of the past'),[65] and Flush's difference from his mistress was emphasized as much as his sympathy with her: 'She spoke; he was dumb. She was woman; he was dog. Thus closely united, thus immensely divided, they gazed at each other.' 'The Life, Times and Opinions of Flush the Spaniel', a working-title whose mock-heroic tone distanced her subject, became '*Flush*', a dramatic unity in which the life-course and the growth of a sensibility were one.[66] And as Woolf invented Flush's imaginative universe more entirely, so, in the manner of 'the new biography', she revealed more of her own.

A DOG'S BODY

Flush's early life could take its place as a case-history alongside any of Freud's. Leaving Miss Mitford's and the freedom of the fields, he relinquishes his polymorphously perverse puppydom and learns to enter human culture by repressing his instincts, 'the alternate rages of lust and greed' which Wimpole Street and 'the lessons of the bedroom school' teach him is the sign of civilized behaviour. He becomes a thoroughly bourgeois pet. But where Mrs Browning romantically afforded Flush a selfhood, Woolf's Flush is post-Romantic, and prone to twentieth-century angst. He finds selfhood itself a bone of contention:

> Was not the little brown dog opposite himself? But what is 'oneself'? Is it the thing people see? Or is it the thing one is? So Flush pondered that question too . . .

Flush may be 'the first animal to be an Eminent Victorian',[67] but he is also clearly a species of Canine Modernist.

Flush's dumbness speaks to Woolf's sense that what matters most in a life may not be able to be put into words; may be momentary, unconscious, inchoate: 'Can words say anything?' she has Miss Barrett wonder, 'Do not words destroy the symbols that lie beyond the reach of words?' Flush's existential crisis comes when he is snatched by dog-thieves and taken to Whitechapel, where he languishes miserably, half-starved and parched, believing himself abandoned, for several days. Mewed up in his own incommunicable world, his canine collapse is a version of that solipsism which Woolf dreaded, of being immured in one's own subjective viewpoint, dissociated from the body, in an interminable, formless present ('a lunatic dislocation', as one reviewer of *Flush* called the episode).[68] Like Rhoda in *The Waves*, Flush loses the boundaries of his newly-won ego and learns how precarious his identity is. Whitechapel is a bourgeois nightmare – the return of the repressed – where Flush encounters humans who are more animal than himself and Woolf plays safe with her own fears of the animal within.

'Whitechapel' is Woolf's own confection. The Whitechapel scenes gave Woolf the most trouble to write;[69] she had entirely to invent Flush's terrors (he left no record of them), and as part of her attempt to write more 'lowlife scenes', they are self-consciously literary and melodramatic.[70] Elizabeth Barrett was vague about her visit to the dog-stealers in 'Manning Street, or Shoreditch, or wherever it was'.[71] Like most mid-Victorians (including Thomas Beames, whose contemporary account of the slums or 'rookeries' of London, Woolf turned to), Barrett did not discriminate between conditions here and in other more central parts of London.[72] She never wrote directly about Whitechapel: what Woolf calls 'the most vivid passages' in *Aurora Leigh* which may have been inspired by fetching Flush home, are a description of the poor of 'St Margaret's Court' in St Giles, a different area in the vicinity of Oxford Street, and of the rural poor who loot and set fire to the house of her hero, Romney Leigh. In an ironic note Woolf mocks the 'distortion' inevitable given Barrett Browning's narrowly sequestered view.[73] But whilst she avoids the vicious mid-Victorian language of infection and contamination for the poor (Mrs Browning compared the inhabitants of St Giles to ooze, slime, pus, vermin and plague), she picks up on the animalizing vocabulary of the 'pack' and of the racially indeterminate 'mob'.[74]

By the time Virginia Woolf's mother was slum-visiting in the 1890s, the East End had come to epitomize working-class poverty in London, and was established in the hearts and minds of the respectable as 'Outcast London', 'the dark continent', 'the Netherworld'. Woolf's Whitechapel owes as much to the language of degeneracy as it developed in the late nineteenth century, to social investigators such as Charles Booth (a friend and relation of her mother's), and to the fiction of Gissing and Wells, as it does to the imaginative universe of Barrett Browning, Dickens or Mayhew.[75] The denizens of Whitechapel, in Flush's fevered vision, are strange throwbacks, 'demons' who 'pawed and clawed', 'horrible monsters', 'whether beast or human'. It is the 'hairy ruffians sprawled on the floor', regressive types both physically and psychologically, who are the real brutes. Woolf borrowed Thomas Beames's emphasis upon the slums as 'only a stone's throw' from Wimpole Street, 'cheek by jowl'; but the sense that 'mixed up with that respectablity was this squalor', is made more intimate and conflictual. The tripartite structure of *Flush* sets 'Whitechapel' firmly against 'Wimpole Street', as its antithesis, offering readers a psychological as well as a geographical map. Arguably, Woolf self-consciously suggests a topography of repression – of the limits, inside as well as out, on which respectability depends. But it also suggests the terror which the loss of such boundaries might bring; all Flush can do is flee.

In fact Flush would hardly have found Whitechapel 'reeking smells' offensive (dogs, as the Bible tells us, return happily to their own vomit); his fastidiousness is a measure of where our allegiances should lie. For though Woolf is able in *Flush* to explore the unpolite sense of smell, it is smell as sensibility which reigns supreme. In Italy Flush becomes the ideal aesthete, savouring the stones of Florence without any of his experiences suffering 'the deformity of words'. He takes his pleasures but is neither aggressive nor mindless (as he would be in Wimpole Street or Whitechapel). Flush never fights with other dogs but he doesn't run with the pack either; he remains a loner. The only canine call of nature he responds to is the 'the hunting horn of Venus', but nothing could be further from 'mating':

> Now Flush knew what men can never know – love pure, love simple, love entire; love that brings no train of care in its wake; that has no shame; no remorse; that is here, that is gone, as the bee on the flower is here and is gone.

Flush 'embraces' his spotted spaniel, lying 'tranced' side by side in an egalitarian but unlikely position. In *Flush* Woolf wants to liberate the experience of the senses from the trappings, as it seems, of the body.

What a long way Woolf's Flush comes from Mrs Browning's 'hairy Faunus', her erotic image of those animal spirits which were restored to her in marriage and maternity![76] For if Flush eschews the phallic position, he cannot be the object of affection either; he's never stroked or fondled or made a fuss of; and he doesn't go in for grooming. Flush is a spaniel who doesn't lick himself, let alone others (he's pretty much a drool-free dog), and who has passed through the oral and the anal stage of development without ever looking back. He reacts violently to the 'repulsive presence' of the 'helpless, weak, puling, muling lump' of the Browning baby: not only jealous or angry, he feels, inexplicably, a deep disgust at the 'live animal'. In old age, Flush loses the last vestiges of doghood along with his hair[77] (a necessity brought about by the scourge of Italian fleas), the 'coat', which like a coat of arms is the insignia of his pedigree. He is 'emasculated' and thereby freed: ' "You are nothing" ', the mirror tells him, 'To be nothing – is that not, after all, the most satisfactory state in the whole world?' The final triumph for Flush is to become a 'nobody'. As an image of physical emancipation, being no body, a non-entity, might appear a mixed blessing. But the metamorphosis into a spaniel can be seen as a way of imagining a different physicality beyond human sexuality and its relentless opposition of masculine and feminine.[78]

Flush may also be a retort to Lytton Strachey's sexualizing of biography. Woolf had particularly disliked *Elizabeth and Essex* (published a month after her own Elizabethan fantasia, *Orlando*, in 1928), where Strachey took a Freudian view of the English queen's love-affair, elaborating the scanty historical evidence in order to attribute unconscious sexual motivation to behaviour

and character.[79] Strachey saw Elizabeth's capacity to survive as due to her
'femininity': 'Only a woman could have abandoned with such unscrupulous
completeness, the last shreds not only of consistency, but of dignity, honour,
and common decency'.[80] Subtitled *A Tragic History*, Strachey's account had its
protagonists helplessly driven by their sexual desires and their bodily histories.
Woolf disapproved of Strachey's 'suppression of irony' without which there
was little room for manoeuvre.[81] In *Orlando* she had played fast and loose with
the question of sexual difference; as a spaniel perhaps she sought another way
of escaping the biological determinism which dogs Strachey's view of men
and women.[82]

Flush pillories the obsession of the English with pedigree and breeding, and
their assumption of superiority, especially abroad, of being 'top dogs'.[83] Woolf
makes fun of some of the ways in which 'dog-fanciers' in the nineteenth century elaborated their own discriminatory systems of canine rank, mirroring
their social and racial prejudices about 'the lower orders'.[84] But in Italy the
rules of the Kennel Club can be mocked precisely because the discontents of
English civilization are kept safely at bay (in Florence the peasants are decorative and charming; they aren't churlish or smelly like the 'great unwashed' at
home). In Italy Flush can be a democrat without actually losing caste; he may
end his life mingling with 'the many-coloured mongrels' in the Florentine
market-place but he does not become one of them. Though he no longer
looks like a spaniel, he never forgets where he came from. Flush sees out his
days rehearsing his memories to younger dogs. In this, as in so much else, he is
a scion of the 1930s, a modern who shores up his parlous sense of himself by
the remembrance of things past.

There is another dogsbody in the story whose life came much closer to
home. Woolf's absurdly long note on 'the extremely obscure' life of Lily Wilson, Elizabeth Barrett Browning's maid, draws attention to the way in which
the servant is usually pushed to the margins of history or biography. Archly
insisting that Lily's life-story cannot be told, Woolf begins to do just that.
Woolf knew that the maidservants of history had even less than a dog's chance
of their biographies being written. In *A Room of One's Own* she had urged
that 'a supplement' be added to history, 'so that women might figure there';
she described 'the pressure of dumbness, the accumulation of unrecorded life'
which 'all these infinitely obscure lives' generated.[85] Woolf had used the phrase
'the lives of the obscure' before, chronicling her own kind, the daughters of
educated men, but here she includes 'the women at the street corners with
their arms akimbo . . . the violet-sellers and match-sellers and old crones sta-
tioned under doorways'.[86] All need recording. 'It is much to be regretted',
she wrote, in *Three Guineas*, 'that no lives of maids, from which a more fully

documented account could be constructed, are to be found in the *Dictionary of National Biography*'[87] – suggesting another supplement, this time to her own father's *magnum opus*. And 'Wilson' is noted here again.

And yet Woolf's irony is always slippery. Her note on Lily Wilson takes away with one hand what it gives with the other. Lily, like Sophie Farrell,[88] is in part a nostalgic figure for Woolf – 'the glory of the British basement' – and her note half-celebrates those lost class-relations which, in fantasy at least, seem to her so settled (Woolf's 'violet-sellers' and 'match-sellers' would be equally as much at home in the 1850s as in the 1930s). Woolf's suggestion that Lily Wilson 'spoke almost as seldom as Flush' and that her appearance is far less familiar than his, is deliberately tongue-in-cheek, but, by association, 'Wilson' is somewhat diminished. Though Woolf acknowledges 'the extreme precariousness of a servant's life', her harmonious picture of the maid 'exalted' to the rank of the family does nothing to disturb the reader's comfort. Finally Woolf leaves her in the rosy glow of her sunset years, partially obscured by a cloud of contented reminiscences. Lily Wilson is consigned to silence, however knowingly, by Woolf: the last words go to her mistress whose conventional epitaph 'may serve'.

We do not need to know more about Lily Wilson to read between these lines.[89] The stress which Woolf placed on the 'inscrutability' of servants – 'the all-but-silent, the all-but-invisible' – the idea that their lives could not be made sense of, was one way of side-stepping the potential conflict, the anger and resentment, which seeing their point of view and hearing their stories necessarily revealed.[90] When she was writing *Flush*, Woolf was in the midst of furious, agonizing scenes with her only servant, her cook Nelly Boxall, who had been with her since 1916, and whom she tried many times to dismiss. She saw relations with servants as part of the 'rubbish heap' left by the older generation which needed to be swept away.[91] Both Woolf and Nelly Boxall were casualties of the past, no longer able, or willing, to act out the old roles of the Victorian household. Far from being silent, Nelly Boxall had plenty to say for herself (Woolf hated the sound of her servants' voices; they talked too much rather than too little). Woolf's diaries suggest how much guilt, rage and spitefulness was fomented by what Woolf deemed Nelly Boxall's 'dependence and defencelessness'.[92] Yet without Nelly there would be no writing, and Woolf's vitriolic outbursts are equally full of self-loathing. Who, *Flush* bids us ask, was the more dependent of the two?[93]

In the late 1920s and early '30s, Woolf was increasingly alert to the dangers of trying to speak for working women. Introducing a book of testaments from members of the Cooperative Women's Guild,[94] she was honest but intransigent about the limits of her identification with their concerns, arguing that any sympathy she might feel was 'fictitious' since she could not share their experience of poverty and want. Her view that 'the imagination is largely the child of the flesh'[95] shaded, however, into a sense that the physicality of these lives might be the problem, that these women might have no interior life to speak of. Woolf admired the 'extraordinary vitality' of working women. Yet she tended to identify their lives with their writing, and see both as a kind of raw material, too fragmentary or shapeless, too unselfconscious to be included in 'literature' (such is the status of her charwoman, the gormlessly named 'Mrs Gape', in her *Letter to a Toung Poet* written at this time).

Like dogs throughout the ages, Flush, then, is not only a stand-in for his mistress, but for the human servant whose loyalty and whose liberation were far less easily incorporated into the historical record. When communication broke down between them, Woolf degenerated into calling Nelly 'an untrained animal':

> How can an uneducated woman let herself in, alone, into our lives? – what happens is that she becomes a mongrel; & has no roots any where. (13 April 1929)

Servants were neither one thing nor the other, go-betweens, and, as a term for 'mixed breeding' and unknown origins, 'mongrel' could easily turn into an insult. One of Woolf's last stories, written in 1939, does make the mongrel the heroine, 'Gipsy', 'a dog of the people'. But Gipsy's owners also acquire Hector, a dim-witted, aristocratic hound, who is eventually, from preference, given away: 'imagine you have two maids; you can't keep them both . . .', says the owner. Gipsy pines for her patrician companion and this time the shaggy dog story ends, or rather doesn't – unlike the old story of Shag – not with death or reconciliation, but with 'a sense of vast empty space', Gipsy's unexplained disappearance. The story doesn't work and it wasn't published. Perhaps, unlike *Flush*, it wasn't escapist enough.[96] Rather than imagine the life of the mongrel, setting off on its own path, without mistress or master, Woolf chose to leave the future blank.

TAILPIECE: A MONGREL IN THE MARKET-PLACE

The jury is still out on *Flush*. Readers will decide for themselves whether they belong to the ranks who find it 'agonizingly short' or who agree that an essay 'surely would have done justice to this subject'.[97] A mixed press is inevitable, given that *Flush* is a literary cross-breed, a hybrid like all biographies ('eared in one way and tailed in another', as Woolf wrote of her hero's less salubrious companions), but even more *sui generis*: a dog story for grown-ups, it also straddles what Philip Larkin called those 'uneasy marches between *humorous* and *children's*'[98] where no British writer can tread with impunity. For all its brevity, *Flush*, like *Orlando*, is a protracted joke and its facetiousness can be wearing. Though few will go as far as the sniffy reaction of one literary editor who declared it the 'most tiresome book Mrs Woolf has yet written',[99] it seems perfectly reasonable to find *Flush* irritating and amusing by turns, given that Woolf was trying to have it both ways.

Woolf was certainly in two minds about the spaniel: 'that foolish witless joke', she told Vita. Going over the proofs of the manuscript, she thought it a 'silly book', calling it 'a waste of time'.[100] As publication approached, her mood was querulous. She dreaded the plaudits *Flush* would receive as much as the brickbats, assuming – rightly as it turned out – that the combination of dogs, humour and a woman writer would invite cultural condescension:

> I shall be very much depressed, I think, by the kind of praise. They'll say its 'charming' delicate, ladylike. And it will be popular . . . I must not let myself believe that I'm simply a ladylike prattler; for one thing its not true. But they'll all say so. And I shall very much dislike the popular success of Flush. (2 October 1933)

Flush was indeed showered with feminine compliments – 'delicious', 'delightful' and, most often, 'exquisite' (one fulsome reviewer compared it to a sampler neatly stitched); and the same terms were used to damn it with faint praise ('almost too like' the brilliant conversation of 'some charming hostess').[101] The lightness of *Flush* meant Woolf could now be taken less seriously: it marked 'the passing of a potentially great writer', and in a *Scrutiny* article on Strachey, whose pernicious influence on Woolf's recent work was detected, it was taken to represent, along with *Orlando* and the second series of *The Common Reader*, her 'deterioration and collapse'.[102] *Flush* fed the animus amongst a younger generation, especially the more left wing, which was to contribute to the picture of her as an effete stylist, isolated from contemporary reality, and to the decline of her reputation in Britain over the next thirty years.

Flush was indeed enormously popular. It was reviewed across the board in the British Isles, from the expected periodicals and literary columns to the local and evening press, popular weeklies, monthlies, and family or women's magazines; even the church digests were fans of *Flush*: *The Catholic Herald* and *The Quaker* carried reviews; the *Methodist Recorder* thought it lovely; *The Christian Science Monitor* quoted it at length. It appeared in lofty company with other biographies and memoirs (in the publisher W. H. Smith's *Trade Circular* it sat next to Winston Churchill's *Marlborough*);[103] or downmarket with other animal books and stories (*The Animal Register* evoked 'the shot-silk poetic texture of *The Waves*', whilst the *London Mercury* grouped it with *Horsemanship As It Is Today* and *The Compleat Jockey*). It went into a cheap edition in time for Christmas and was chosen by the Book Society for its October list and in America by the Book-of-the-Month Club; requests for photos came in; there was even talk of a motion-picture.[104] Reviews from the cuttings-agencies poured in from across the globe to Monk's House in Sussex: from the *Auckland Weekly News* to the *Natal Mercury*, the *Jamaica Times* to the *Winnipeg Free Press*. *Flush* became her bestselling book to date: *Orlando* had sold over 8,000 copies in the first six months; *Flush* sold nearly 19,000.[105]

Flush made Virginia Woolf all but a household name, a commercially successful writer as opposed to a purely acquired taste. 'Readers who dread Mrs Woolf's "difficulties" need not alarm themselves,' wrote the *Daily Mail*; 'the first of her books that is likely to appeal to a public at all general', the *Irish Independent* agreed.[106] All this made the author queasy. She remained defensive, even dismissive, of *Flush*, feeling the need to justify it to her friends as a joke, one that had grown too long, something of which she was 'rather ashamed'.[107] Mixing her markets stirred her anxieties about becoming other people's property. Woolf always sneered most at the 'middlebrow', and yet here was the *Huddersfield Weekly Examiner*, amongst many other local papers, praising *Flush's* 'singular charm' and 'marvellous insight', and reviewing it alongside Galsworthy.[108] One of the final ironies about *Flush* is that what began life as a coterie publication, a private joke, became her most accessible work, perhaps the only one to reach the common reader.

If Woolf feared a kind of literary miscegenation and a loss of control, she also chafed at those discriminations which she was unable to relinquish, and went on pressing painfully at the limits of her imaginative sympathies even as she came up hard against them. Woolf jibbed against the unwanted publicity which followed *Flush's* success (she wrote to *The New Statesman* proposing the foundation of a Society for the Protection of the Author), but it was fame as a kind of fetter against which she was also reacting. In her diary she followed in Flush's footsteps, advocating a 'philosophy of anonymity' in order to go on experimenting:

> I will not be 'famous' 'great'. I will go on adventuring, changing, opening my mind & my eyes, refusing to be stamped & stereotyped. The thing is to free ones self; to let it find its dimensions, not be impeded. (29 October 1933)

In the work of the 1930s Woolf returned to this idea of anonymity, wondering whether it was possible to remain 'immune', detached from aggression and slavishness, in what were much more threatening circumstances. *Flush* embodies the small hope, which was to take shape even in the most fragmented moments of Woolf's writing, that the structures of a society, its hierarchies and divisions, like those within a person, could be transformed without erupting into anger or violence.

Over the years *Flush* has remained largely beneath the notice of the critics: 'the kind of novel that Noel Coward would, and did, admire' is one ambivalent assessment.[109] But *Flush* deserves its place, however lowly, in that more generous understanding of Woolf as a writer which recent Woolf scholarship and biography has enabled, that sense of her as someone for whom, as E. M. Forster remarked, 'literature was her merry-go-round as well as her study'.[110] *Flush* belongs firmly in the 1930s, the decade which saw Woolf trying to combine the critical and the creative – 'the facts as well as the vision'.[111] 'Oh Lord,' she wrote, apropos of *Flush*, 'how does anyone pretend to be a biographer?'[112] a question which was increasingly to preoccupy her in the years to come.

Woolf's freedom, as she was the first to admit, was tied to 'a short length of capital',[113] and writing was a means of straining at that leash. *Flush* is both the simplest and the most artful of Virginia Woolf's books, revelling in the fantasy of writing as a purely escapist activity. In a more generous literary culture which can, unlike Woolf's own, celebrate the vagrant and enjoy the mixed, there does not have to be an underdog amongst her works. Every dog, as the old adage goes, has his day.

BIBLIOGRAPHY

The following is a list of short titles used:

Diary	*The Diary of Virginia Woolf*, ed. Anne Olivier Bell, 5 vols. (Hogarth Press: London, 1977; Penguin Books: Harmondsworth, 1979)
Essays	*The Essays of Virginia Woolf*, ed. Andrew McNeillie, 4 vols. (Hogarth Press: London, 1986–94)
Letters	*The Letters of Virginia Woolf*, ed. Nigel Nicolson, 6 vols. (Hogarth Press: London, 1993–4)
Moments of Being	Virginia Woolf, *Moments of Being*, ed. Jeanne Schulkind (Hogarth Press: London, 1985)
Passionate Apprentice	Virginia Woolf, *A Passionate Apprentice; The Early Journals 1897–1909*, ed. Mitchell A. Leaska (Hogarth Press: London, 1990)

Virginia Woolf	Hermione Lee, *Virginia Woolf* (Chatto & Windus: London, 1996)
Crowded Dance	*The Crowded Dance of Modern Life*, ed. Rachel Bowlby (Penguin Books: Harmondsworth, 1993)
MHP	The Monk's House Papers at Sussex University Library

NOTES

1. *The Complete Shorter Fiction of Virginia Woolf*, ed. Susan Dick (Hogarth Press: London, 1985), pp. 267–74.
2. F. W. Maitland, *The Life and Letters of Leslie Stephen* (Duckworth: London, 1906), p. 364.
3. Leaska, *Passionate Apprentice*, p. 243.
4. Quentin Bell, *Virginia Woolf* (Triad: London, 1976), Vol. II, p. 175. He found her feeling for animals 'odd and remote', although it seems simply to have been not proprietorial.
5. 'On a Faithful Friend' first appeared in the *Guardian* (18 January 1905); reprinted in *Essays* I, pp. 112–15.
6. Letter to Violet Dickinson, 8 December 1904: *Letters* I, no. 200.
7. Shag had perhaps already been resurrected in Chapter 4 of Woolf's first novel, *The Voyage Out*, where the Dalloways, great dog lovers, tell the story of a Skye terrier who had been run over (as Shag had been). Their sentimentalism is of a piece with their love of England and Empire, and Woolf is marking her distance from it all.
8. Letter to Ethel Smythe, 2 June 1935: *Letters* V, no. 3025.
9. 'Impressions of Sir Leslie Stephen', *Essays* I, pp. 127–30; and 'Leslie Stephen, the Philosopher at Home: A Daughter's Memories', *The Times* (28 November 1932). Leslie Stephen was also wont to cover his books as he was reading with deft pencil sketches of animals; his copy of Robert Browning's *Ferishtah's Fancies* (1884), for example, sports a dog on the front endpaper and a kangaroo at the back, whilst Ruskin's *Fors Clavigera* (1871–8) carries bears, a tortoise and a fox: *Catalogue of Books from the Library of Leonard and Virginia Woolf*, ed. G. A. Holleyman (Holleyman and Treacher: Brighton, 1975).
10. The unpublished stories are collected in Julia Duckworth Stephen, *Stories for Children, Essays for Adults*, ed. Diane F. Gillespie and Elizabeth Steele (Syracuse University Press: 1987). Amongst Woolf's earliest efforts at fiction are a number of fragmentary animal stories: see, for example, 'Manchester Zoo' and 'The Monkeys', in *MHP*, nos. A24a and A23j; two other unpublished tales involving animals, written for children in the 1920s, 'Nurse

Lugton's Curtain' and 'The Widow and the Parrot' (the widow's dog is yet another Shag *redivivus*), can be found in Dick, *Shorter Fiction*.

11. 29 January 1905: Leaska, *Passionate Apprentice*, p. 229.

12. Letter to Ethel Smythe, 14 August 1932: *Letters* V, no. 2620; Hermione Lee gives a brief but highly illuminating discussion of the intimate place of animals in Woolf's life: *Virginia Woolf*, pp. 111–12, 332–3.

13. Letter to Violet Dickinson, I September 1907: *Letters* I, no. 381.

14. Letter to Leonard Woolf, 4 October 1929: *Letters* IV, no. 2076.

15. Lee, *Virginia Woolf*, p. 529.

16. *The Voyage Out* (first published 1915; Penguin Books: Harmondsworth, 1992), p. 68.

17. 'A Sketch of the Past', in *Moments of Being*, pp. 116; 69. This unfinished 'autoanalysis' was begun in the spring of 1939; it goes back over some of the material in her earlier (also unpublished) memories of childhood, 'Reminiscences' (1905), and in '22 Hyde Park Gate' and 'Old Bloomsbury', written to be read to a close circle of friends in 1920. These can also be found in *Moments of Being*.

18. See, for example, her letters to Lady Ottoline Morrell, 23 February 1933, to Hugh Walpole, 15 April 1933, and to Vita Sackville-West, 30 September 1933: *Letters* V, nos. 2707, 2726 and 2799.

19. For the evolution of these texts, see *The Pargiters: The Novel-Essay Portion of* The Years, ed. Mitchell A. Leaska (Hogarth Press: London, 1978).

20. Woolf noted in her diary on 20 January 1931 that she had 'conceived an entire new book': *Diary* IV.

21. Speech before the London National Society for Women's Service on 21 January 1931: Leaska, *The Pargiters*, p. xxxix.

22. 'Professions for Women', published posthumously in *The Death of the Moth* (1942), and reprinted in Bowlby, *Crowded Dance*, p. 105.

23. Alethea Hayter explores this theme briefly in *Mrs Browning: A Poet's Work and its Setting* (Faber: London, 1962), p. 67.

24. 15 January 1846 (Vol. I, p. 402), 5 September 1846 (Vol. II, p. 522): *The Letters of Robert Browning and Elizabeth Barrett Barrett 1845–1846* (Smith, Elder: London, 1899).

25. A few years before Flush's birth she had urged Miss Mitford, who had been sending canine 'memorabilia' in her letters, 'You certainly should write Dash's memoirs!': 29 September 1837, *Elizabeth Barrett to Miss Mitford*, ed. Betty Miller (John Murray: London, 1954).

26. ? May 1841, 21 September 1841: ibid.

27. 2 May 1837: ibid.

28. 28 December 1840: ibid.

29. For a discussion of these new sensibilities and a rich and suggestive account of the history of human relations with domestic animals, see Keith Thomas, *Man and the Natural World: Changing Attitudes in England 1500–1800* (Penguin Books: Harmondsworth, 1983); on nineteenth-century animals in particular, see Harriet Ritvo, *The Animal Estate: The English and Other Creatures in the Victorian Age* (Harvard University Press: Cambridge, Mass., 1987); and see also the discussions on pet-keeping in A. Manning and J. Serpell, eds., *Animals and Human Society: Changing Perspectives* (Routledge: London, 1994).

30. Letter to Lady Ottoline Morrell: *Letters* V, no. 2707.

31. See Barrett Browning's poem, 'To Flush, My Dog', one of Woolf's 'authorities', which first appeared in the *Athenaeum* (22 July 1843); the picture was sent in a letter of 5 October 1843, suggesting it be given a place on the frontispiece of Horne's collection of essays, *A New Spirit of the Age*, to which Elizabeth Barrett had contributed, as an excellent substitute for herself: *The Letters of Elizabeth Barrett Browning to Richard Hengist Horne*, ed. S. R. Townshend Mayer (Bentley: London, 1877), 2 vols.

32. ? May 1841; 18 August 1842; 7 January 1843; 23 June 1843: Miller, *Elizabeth Barrett to Miss Mitford*.

33. Rose Macaulay, 'The Spaniel of Wimpole Street', *Spectator* (6 October 1933).

34. Rebecca West, 'Two Poets Through the Eyes of a Spaniel', *Daily Telegraph* (6 October 1933). West also detected spaniel-like qualities in Barrett Browning's 'lolloping' poetry.

35. Woolf's 'Aurora Leigh' was first published in *Yale Review* (June 1931) and the *Times Literary Supplement* (2 July 1931); an essay based on those articles appeared in *The Common Reader*, second series (Hogarth Press: London, 1932). Robert Browning was well known to Leslie Stephen; Woolf's copy of Barrett Browning's autobiographical epic was given as a Christmas present to her half-sister, Laura Stephen, by Robert Browning himself in 1873: Holleyman, *Catalogue*, section 1, p. 1. There are no other poetical works by Barrett Browning in the list.

36. As a young woman in 1906, Woolf had written of Elizabeth Barrett in more violent terms, seeing her as leading a 'victims's life', 'forced to acquiesce in her position as a life-long prisoner . . . guarded by a mad gaoler in the person of her father': 'Poets' Letters', *Essays* I, p. 102; Woolf used similar language for the demands made by her father in her own childhood home after the death of her mother: 'Reminiscences', in *Moments of Being*.

37. Lola L. Szladits has suggested how much Woolf's description of Elizabeth Barrett's early life has parallels with her own: 'The Life, Character and Opinons of Flush the Spaniel', *Bulletin of the New York Public Library* (April 1970).

38. *Flush* is, amongst other things, a rewriting of the more conservative form of Victorian animal story which acts out an emotional drama of loss and deprivation through the traumas of the helpless animal, whose sufferings are like those of the orphaned child – Anna Sewell's *Black Beauty* comes obviously to mind. Such waifs and strays were usually restored to the domestic bosom. So powerful was the appeal of this kind of story that the popular magazine *Everybody's Weekly* (6 January 1934) misread Flush's liberation as a callous form of abandonment: 'World's Most Devoted Lover Was A Dog – And his mistress forgot all about him'.

39. 'Old Bloomsbury', *Moments of Being*, p. 183.

40. It is hard to overestimate that reverence. The Browning romance and marriage was turned into legend via letters and gossip almost as soon as it was made known to friends and acquaintances in the 1840s (in their courtship the couple themselves had played with mythologizing their roles in what Elizabeth Barrett called 'my own especial faery tale'). Later memoirs (which began with Miss Mitford's chapter on 'Married Poets' in her *Recollections of a Literary Life* in 1852), and especially those of meeting Mrs Browning in Italy, stressed her angelic womanliness (made more ethereal by her illness); Sophia Hawthorne (the American novelist's wife), for example, typically remembered 'her fairy fingers' and her 'spiritual radiance': *Notes in England and Italy* (London, 1869), pp. 392ff.; Mrs Sutherland Orr, in the first *Life and Letters of Robert Browning* (Smith, Elder: London, 1891) joined in the throng of voices who confirmed that 'her moral nature was as exquisite as her mind was exceptional' (p. 141), whilst Mrs Richmond Ritchie (Anne Thackeray, Woolf's 'Aunt Anny') struck a typically idealizing note in her entry on Mrs Browning for Leslie Stephen's *Dictionary of National Biography* (Vol. VII) in 1886, praising her 'sweetness of temper and purity of spirit'. The publication in 1899 of the courtship letters, with the revelation of Mr Barrett's prohibition on marriage, had the effect of obscuring the poetry even further by dwelling on the life and person; thus – 'a poet in every fibre of her, but adorably feminine' was the judgement of the *Edinburgh Review* 189 (1899), pp. 420–39. Woolf's father reviewed the courtship correspondence when it was first published, and, while he condemned Elizabeth's father as a 'preposterous despot', he too eulogized the poets as 'an ideal pair of lovers', emphasizing that Browning was 'a man of undisputed pre-eminence in his art' and Elizabeth Barrett 'a woman worthy of him': Leslie Stephen, 'The Browning Letters', *The National Review* XXXIII (1899), pp. 401–15. The thrill of the story seems to have reached utterly rhapsodic proportions in the Edwardian years: see, for example, Lilian Whiting's ecstatic account in *The Brownings: Their Life*

and Art (Hodder & Stoughton: London, 1911). For more on the mythologizing, see the epilogue, 'A Century of Criticism', in Gardner B. Taplin, *The Life of Elizabeth Barrett Browning* (John Murray: London, 1957);
Hayter, *Mrs Browning*; Daniel Karlin, *The Courtship of Robert Browning and
Elizabeth Barrett* (Clarendon: Oxford, 1985).

41. *Punch* (12 October 1933), for example, took the view that 'admirers of
the poetess will not like this clever book', whilst *Country Life* (14 October
1933) called *Flush* 'a subtly disparaging picture of 'Ba' and Robert'.

42. They were mostly romantic or novelized biographies which saw the lives as a
period piece, caught in the aspic of the letters, and said little about the poetry:
see, for example, Dormer Creston, *Andromeda in Wimpole Street* (1929); Car-
ola Lenanton, *Miss Barrett's Elopement* (1929); David G. Loth, *The Brownings: A Victorian Idyll* (1929); Harriet Gaylord, *Pompilia and Her Poet* (1931).
An exception is the work of American writer Louise Schutz Boas, whose
Elizabeth Barrett Browning (1930) also reclaims *Aurora Leigh* as a feminist poem
(noting how it borrowed from *Jane Eyre*), and (unlike Woolf) makes the connection between Mr Barrett's mentality and his growing up in Jamaica as the
child of a slave-owner. See also Taplin, *Elizabeth Barrett Browning*.

43. Besier's play had first been aired at the Malvern Festival on 20 August
1930, under the direction of Mr Barry Jackson, opening in London on 23
September at the Queen's Theatre. It was made into a Hollywood film in
1934 with Norma Shearer as Elizabeth (there was a less successful British
remake in 1956).

44. In fact Mr Barrett was against any of his children marrying. Her father,
Elizabeth Barrett wrote to Robert Browning, 'never *does* tolerate in his
family (sons or daughters) the development of one class of feelings' (16
September 1845: *Letters of Robert Browning and Elizabeth Barrett Barrett*, Vol.
I, p. 203), and six months later she blamed this on 'the miserable conception of the limits and character of parental rights . . . after using one's children as one's chattels for a time, the children drop lower and lower toward
the level of the chattels' (4 March 1846: ibid., Vol. I, p. 534). For differing
discussions of Mr Barrett and of Elizabeth's devotion to him, see Karlin,
The Courtship, and Cora Kaplan, 'Wicked Fathers', in *Sea Changes: Culture
and Feminism* (Verso: London, 1986).

45. In a letter to *The Times* (29 August 1930), three of Elizabeth Barrett
Browning's nephews attacked the play for its 'disgusting charge' against
Edward Moulton Barrett, their grandfather, and its 'gross violation of the
canons of literary decency'.

46. Contemporary reviews suggest how knowingly the period was now looking back on the Victorians and restaging the past. *The Play Pictorial* (no. 345,

no date) praised *The Barretts of Wimpole Street* for appealing to the 'mental independence' of 1930 (it was billed as a comedy), and for attacking that 'most Victorian of prisons', the family, whilst *The Times* (21 August 1930) was relatively untroubled by Besier's use of 'imaginative licence', commenting only that the portrayal of Elizabeth's father was almost laughable thanks to 'twentieth-century fancies about "Victorianism" '.

47. The exact date of Woolf's theatre visit is unclear; she tried to get tickets shortly after the opening in October: *Letters* IV, nos. 2245, 2393 and 2399.

48. *The Play Pictorial* (no. 345) carried a large black and white photo of the dog. Woolf later wrote to an American fan of *Flush* that the 'dog who acted his part here was black – but there can be no doubt that Flush was red': *Letters* V, no. 2715.

49. 'Dishonour Thy Father!' (*Observer*, 7 December 1930), arguing in favour of biographical freedom, refers to the 'new school of biographers, who claim, with little warrant, to have been inspired by Mr Lytton Strachey'. See also, for discussion of Besier, 'The Ethics of Biographical Drama', *Daily Telegraph* (2 October 1930).

50. Strachey, like Woolf, often conjured the past in terms of its fabrics and furniture, memorably describing Queen Victoria as 'a part of the establishment – an essential part as it seemed – a fixture – a magnificent, immovable sideboard in the huge saloon of state'. *Queen Victoria* was dedicated to Woolf, and there are many similarities between her evocation of the Victorian period in *Orlando* and Strachey's.

51. Lytton Strachey, *Elizabeth and Essex* (Chatto & Windus: London, 1928), p. 10.

52. Letter to John Lehmann, 31 July 1932: *Letters* V, no. 2615. Woolf later wrote to Ottoline Morrell after she had finished *Flush*: 'I was so tired after the Waves, that I lay in the garden and read the Browning love letters, and the figure of their dog made me laugh so I couldn't resist making him a Life. I wanted to play a joke on Lytton – it was to parody him': *Letters* V, no. 2707. Woolf's first draft originally had Flush dying in one long voluptuous swoon of reminiscence, in the manner of Strachey's Queen Victoria – a *tour de force* already much imitated – but Woolf decided to 'cut it out, when he was not there to see the joke': letter to David Garnett, 8 October 1933, *Letters* V, no. 2801.

53. 'The New Biography', Woolf's review of Harold Nicolson's biographical cameos *Some People*, appeared in the *New York Herald Tribune* on 30 October 1927; reprinted in *Essays* IV, pp. 473–80. The Hogarth Press had published Nicolson's *The Development of English Biography* in 1927, with its attack on the 'Victorianism' which had descended on life-writing (p. 113).

See also Woolf's assessment in a later essay, 'The Art of Biography' (1939), reprinted in Bowlby, *Crowded Dance*, pp. 144–51. For a nuanced account of Victorian biography and of the modern challenge to it from Strachey and Woolf, see Laura Marcus, *Auto/Biographical Discourses: Theory, Criticism, Practice* (Manchester University Press: 1994). But she ignores *Flush*.

54. 19 May 1931: *Diary* IV.

55. Leslie Stephen felt 'unpleasantly like an unjustifiable eavesdropper' while reading the courtship correspondence: 'The Browning Letters', p. 13.

56. According to John Lehmann, 'it was intended as a booklet for Christmas': *Virginia Woolf* (Thames & Hudson: London, 1975), p. 94.

57. Woolf's first holograph draft is dated 21 July 1931; her second, 26 July–8 October 1932. The first reference to *Flush* is in Woolf's diary entry for 7 August 1931 (*Diary* IV); and in the letter of 16 September 1931 when she wrote to Vita Sackville-West requesting a photograph of her dog, Henry (yet another cocker spaniel), because of 'a little escapade by means of wh. I hope to stem the ruin we shall suffer from the failure of The Waves': *Letters* V, no. 2436; and see also no. 2726. Woolf used many similar terms to describe the writing of *Flush* as she did of *Orlando*, at least to begin with.

58. See *Virginia Woolf's Reading Notebooks*, ed. Brenda R. Silver (Princeton University Press: 1983). The reading notes for *Flush* are undated.

59. Telling the story to John Lehmann, she laughed so much that she became 'red in the face and tears were streaming down her cheeks, before she retired incapable of going on': cited by Hermione Lee, where she discusses Woolf's capacity for 'laughing herself silly' (her wild displays of choking and hooting laughter troubled many of her friends), as containing 'a dangerous, reckless, perhaps also a sexual element': *Virginia Woolf*, p. 110.

60. Leaska, *The Pargiters*, and see entries for 15 and 19 January 1933: *Diary* IV.

61. 19 and 23 December 1932: *Diary* IV.

62. 3, 21 and 26 January 1933: *Diary* IV.

63. Woolf's holograph manuscript for 26 July 1932, when she resumed *Flush* after a year's gap, begins with a mock-serious musing on the difficulties of writing the 'lives of the dumb': 'How are we to interpret', it asks, 'the inmost lives of those who cannot write, who have left no love letters or documents of any sort behind them?' Woolf's answer is that modern biographers must interpret body language.

64. Mr Barrett reappears in *Three Guineas* as a textbook example of 'infantile fixation' (a Freudianism which Woolf uses loosely). And Crosby and Rover (the maid and dog who feature in *The Years*) crop up again,

Woolf suggests, as the kind of harmless topic which women may 'drag' in to lower the temperature of a heated discussion with men about the differences between the sexes: *A Room of One's Own* with *Three Guineas*, ed. Michele Barrett (Penguin Books: Harmondsworth, 1993), pp. 257–65.

65. 'Old Bloomsbury', *Moments of Being*, p. 182.

66. Woolf's working title was reminiscent, perhaps, of Laurence Sterne's novel of the 1760s, *The Life & Opinions of Tristram Shandy*, which she delighted in. There was much of the eighteenth century in her first draft: Flush's theft was called a 'rape', and, in the minifying manner of Pope's mock-epic, his low angle was offered far more as a corrective to human folly. One of his literary forebears can surely be found in Francis Coventry's *The History of Pompey the Little or The Life and Adventures of a Lap-Dog* (1751), though Flush is a middle-class animal and not the toy of aristocrats.

67. The phrase belongs to David Garnett who recognized *Flush* immediately as a 'teasing tribute to Lytton Strachey': *New Statesman and Nation* (6 October 1933).

68. E. J. Scovell, review for the *Literary Supplement* to the feminist periodical *Time and Tide* (14 October 1933).

69. Woolf records that she was writing a third version on 5 January 1933: *Diary* IV.

70. Hermione Lee makes this point: Ethel Smythe had criticized *The Waves* for not being 'Dickensian enough': *Virginia Woolf*, p. 620.

71. 7 September 1846: *Letters of Robert Browning and Elizabeth Barrett Barrett*, Vol. II, p. 527.

72. Henry Mayhew, for example, in his *London Labour and the London Poor*, 4 vols. (1861), tended only to single out eastern districts when there was a special trade or activity to be surveyed, such as the clothing industry or conditions in the docks. Charles Kingsley, whose novel *Alton Locke* (1850) was one of the influences upon Barrett Browning's *Aurora Leigh*, chose the East End for his grim description of a 'sweater's den' for the same reason. Dickens, of course, rarely wrote about the East End. See P. J. Keating, 'Fact and Fiction in the East End', in *The Victorian City: Images and Realities*, eds., H. J. Dyos and Michael Wolff (Routledge & Kegan Paul: London, 1973), Vol. II, pp. 585–602; and Robert Mighall, *A Geography of Victorian Gothic Fiction* (Oxford University Press: 1999).

73. Woolf's own view was hardly much wider. Although her walks took her through the City of London and she knew some of the poorer districts in the centre of town, the East End – Whitechapel, Shoreditch, Bethnal

Green – would have been out of bounds. In March 1931 Woolf visited the docks of London with Vita Sackville-West, Harold Nicolson and the Persian Ambassador; in an essay for a series on 'The London Scene', she noted what she called 'the sinister dwarf city of workmen's houses': 'The Docks of London', first published in *Good Housekeeping* (December 1931); reprinted in Bowlby, *Crowded Dance*, pp. 107–12.

74. The 'interfusion' of St Giles and St James in Elizabeth Barrett Browning's poem is a kind of miscegenation across the classes in which the racial and animal or 'savage' blur; Aurora Leigh sees amongst the poor 'such strangled fronts [foreheads], such obdurate jaws' as 'twit you with your race': *Aurora Leigh*, IV. 590–91.

75. The publication of Charles Booth's *East London* (1889), the first volume of his *Life and Labour of the People in London* (17 vols., 1891–1903), 'marks a culminating point in the discovery of the East End': Keating, 'Fact and Fiction', p. 595; see also Gareth Stedman Jones, *Outcast London: A Study in the Relationship between Classes in Victorian Society* (Oxford University Press: 1971). In a review of Gissing's fiction, Woolf commented, 'What a strange place it is – this Nether World! [the title of Gissing's novel of 1889] There are women as brutal as savages, men who are half animals . . .': 'The Novels of George Gissing', *Essays* I, p. 357. Woolf's first draft of *Flush* drew more obviously on Darwinist language: she referred to the poor as 'apes and chimpanzees', and to the way St Giles reached out 'a claw' or 'the black paw of Shoreditch might stretch and pounce'. Early in 1932 Woolf was reading *The Science of Life* by H. G. and G. P. Wells, and J. Huxley (Cassell: London, 1931), which gives, amongst other things, a theory of the evolution of the species and of the individual: 2 February 1932, *Diary* IV.

76. 'Flush, or Faunus', Mrs Browning's sonnet to her spaniel, published in *Poems* (Moxon: London, 1850 edition).

77. Being shorn was of course one of the new freedoms for women in this period. Woolf had her hair bobbed and 'shingled' in 1927, 'the most important event in my life since marriage – so Clive [Bell] called it': *Diary* III, p. 127.

78. Readers who find Flush too ladylike might like to think of alternatives – the brawling canine virility of Jack London's *The Call of the Wild* (1903), for example, or Kipling's *Thy Servant a Dog* (1930), whose fawning 'Love of Master' and self-punishing sense of discipline are hard to read without cringing. Perhaps the best one could hope for from Woolf's male contemporaries would be the phallic tenderness of a *Lady Chatterley's Dog*. (The relation to cats, especially amongst modernist males – Lytton Strachey, T. S. Eliot, for instance – would be another tale.)

79. Strachey had read Freud and dedicated *Elizabeth and Essex* to his brother and sister-in-law who were Freud's English translators. The original plan for his book was an analysis of love-affairs, including the Browning romance: Michael Holroyd, *Lytton Strachey: A Critical Biography* (Heinemann: London, 1968), Vol. II, pp. 523, 585.

80. Strachey, *Elizabeth and Essex*, p. 13. He also suggested that Elizabeth had suffered an early sexual trauma and that her lifelong virginity was therefore of an 'hysterical origin'. It is hard not to read this as a veiled reference to Virginia's virginity which, from the early days of their friendship, was as much a topic between them as Strachey's *amours*. Strachey had protested at 'the lack of copulation' in *To the Lighthouse*, and in turn disliked *Orlando*: Holroyd, *Strachey*, Vol. II, p. 531.

81. 15 June 1929: *Diary* IV.

82. After publication Freud wrote to congratulate Strachey on being 'steeped in the spirit of psychoanalysis', and suggesting it was 'very possible that you have succeeded in making a correct reconstruction of what actually occurred': Holroyd, *Strachey*, Vol. II, p. 616.

83. If *Orlando* is Woolf's love-letter to Vita Sackville-West, then *Flush* is its antithetical postscript, marking, one hopes, more of a distance from her fascination with the English upper classes and their 'breeding' – both their animals' and their own. Leonard Woolf, like Vita, bred from cockers: see 30 June 1935, *Diary* IV. MHP hold a file of certificates for his prize-winning dogs and cats.

84. Thus, typically, a sportsman on safari described his animals as 'dogs of high and low degree, from the purebred English greyhound to the Kaffir cur': Ritvo, *Animal Estate*, p. 90. Ritvo also discusses 'the institutionalization of the Dog Fancy' in the creation of the Kennel Club.

85. Woolf, *A Room of One's Own*, pp. 41, 81.

86. Ibid., p. 81. 'The lives of the obscure' is Woolf's title for one group of biographical essays in *The Common Reader*, first series (Hogarth Press: London, 1925; reprinted 1984), where she sees an obscurity 'which is not empty but thick with the star dust of innumerable lives', p. 109. The essay on 'Taylors and Edgeworths' also mentions the way in which men blithely speak for their wives (tyrant fathers feature here too). Hermione Lee discusses Woolf's passion for 'the lives of the obscure', commenting that 'For Virginia Woolf, a revolution in biography is also a sexual revolution': *Virginia Woolf*, p. 13ff.

87. Woolf, *Three Guineas*, p. 297.

88. Woolf wrote a sketch of the Stephen family cook around the time of *Flush*: see 'The Cook', 14 October 1931, *MHP*.

89. Those who wish to learn more might turn to Margaret Forster's biography, *Elizabeth Barrett Browning* (Chatto & Windus: London, 1988), and to her novel, *Lady's Maid* (Chatto & Windus: London, 1990), which is based on what she had learnt of Elizabeth ('Lily') Wilson's life.

90. A similar sleight of hand takes place in Woolf's essay, 'Great Men's Houses', written around this time, where Woolf suggests we find out much about the history of the fraught marriage between Thomas and Jane Welsh Carlyle by attending to their lack of domestic facilities: the house was 'a battlefield – the scene of labour, effort and perpetual struggle'; she then implies that in the fight against dirt, mistress and maid were simply united as companions in arms: Bowlby, *Crowded Dance*, p. 118.

91. 13 April 1929: *Diary* III.

92. 11 March 1930: *Diary* III.

93. I explore the dimensions of this relationship more fully in a forthcoming book, *The Question of Nelly* (Viking: London).

94. The Cooperative Women's Guild was founded in 1883 to campaign for reforms and improvements in the lives of working women.

95. Introductory letter to *Life As We Have Known It*, by Cooperative Working Women, ed., Margaret Llewelyn Davies (Hogarth Press: London, 1931), pp. xxviii–xxx.

96. 'Gipsy, the Mongrel', written late in 1939 and sent to her agent in January 1940, was one of two 'dead pigeons' Woolf was glad to 'throw off' (the other was the essay, 'Gas at Abbotsford'): Dick, *Complete Shorter Fiction*, p. 304.

97. *Books of the Month* (October 1933); *The Yorkshire Post* (5 October 1933). There is a fat file of cuttings and reviews, pointing to the enormous popularity of *Flush*, in *MHP*.

98. Philip Larkin was reviewing the work of another woman writer, the poet Stevie Smith: see 'Frivolous and Vulnerable', in *Required Writing: Miscellaneous Pieces 1955–1982* (Faber: London, 1983), p. 153.

99. Geoffrey Grigson, *Morning Post* (6 October 1933).

100. *Letters* V, no. 2717; 29 April 1933, *Diary* IV. Woolf took some pleasure, however, in thinking that the six months' 'dogged and dreary grind' of *Flush* had made some home-improvements possible at Monk's House (a new garden pond, for instance): 2 September 1933, *Diary* IV.

101. Osbert Burdett, 'A Storyteller's Holiday', *The Listener* (11 October 1933); Scovell, *Time and Tide*.

102. 'F.C.', *The Granta* (25 October 1933); T. R. Barnes, review of the posthumously published *Characters and Commentaries* by Lytton Strachey, in *Scrutiny* Vol. II, no. 3 (December 1933).

103. The Hogarth Press publicity for their new books placed *Flush* alongside Freud's *New Introductory Lectures to Psychology* and *The Political and Social Doctrine of Fascism* by Benito Mussolini: *Publishers' Circular* (11 November 1933).

104. 20 October 1933: *Diary* IV.

105. Leonard Woolf, *Downhill All the Way* (the fourth volume of his autobiography, first published in 1967; Oxford University Press: 1980), p. 293; in America the Harcourt Brace edition sold 14,081 copies in the first six months.

106. *Daily Mail* (19 October 1933); *Irish Independent* (21 October 1933).

107. Letter to Vita Sackville-West: *Letters* V, no. 2799; letter to Lady Cecil: ibid., no. 2852.

108. 'If any human being, man, woman, dog, cat, or half-crushed worm dares call me "middlebrow" I will take my pen and stab him, dead': 'Middlebrow', *Collected Essays* (Hogarth Press: London, 1966), p. 203. Woolf had written this polemical essay in October 1932 to contribute to a debate in the *New Statesman and Nation*, but Leonard Woolf advised her not to send it: *Huddersfield Weekly Examiner* (21 October 1933).

109. R. Majumdar and A. McLaurin, *Virginia Woolf: The Critical Heritage* (Routledge & Kegan Paul: London, 1975), p. 25. Coward wrote to Woolf on 17 November 1933 to say how much he 'loved' *Flush*: 'it is quite exquisite and the most marvellous picture of an age', *MHP*. He had also been a great fan of *Orlando*.

110. E. M. Forster, *Virginia Woolf*, The Rede Lecture 1941 (Cambridge University Press: 1942), p. 10.

111. 25 April 1933: *Diary* IV.

112. Letter to David Garnett, 8 October 1933: *Letters* V, no. 2801.

113. Cooperative Working Women, *Life As We Have Known It*, p. xxvii.

14

Fascism, Fear and Feminism:
Virginia Woolf's *Three Guineas**

In the 1960s we used to sing a music-hall song in the pub whose rousing refrain began, 'Two lovely black eyes – Oh, what a surprise!' and went on: 'Only for tellin' a man he was wrong – two lovely black eyes!' It took me a while to realise that the singer was a woman who'd been beaten up by her bloke because the song made me laugh so much, especially when we all whooped in chorus on the 'Oh', raising our eyebrows melodramatically. Stories of men given to hitting their women weren't unheard of in my family, but I associated them with my grandparents' generation, like chenille tablecloths or mangles or the music hall itself. 'In the old days' there were men who liked their drink a bit too much and 'took it out' on the wife. Wife-beating, in theory at least, belonged to the dark ages. Hitting children, however, was commonplace; a mother slapping a toddler round the legs was a familiar sight in public, though hitting one across the face wasn't. Corporal punishment at school was routine (in Penhale Road Infants' we were rapped across the knuckles with a ruler) and in the course of his growing up my brother got thrashed with a belt, caned and slippered. There were limits, even so. When a sports-master at the grammar hit him so hard with a hockey stick that his back broke out in raw, crescentshaped welts, my mother went in a fury to the headmaster. She got an apology but the teacher kept his job.

I grew up with a colourful language of aggression, much of it centuries old, like the threats of a 'whopping' or a 'walloping', a 'good hiding' or a 'tanning' (or, less frequently, 'a leathering', which also harked back to the treatment of animal skins). Mostly it suspended violence over our heads like the sword of Damocles. Everybody menaced children all the time: parents, neighbours,

---

* First published in the *London Review of Books*, 21 March 2002.

shopkeepers, bus-conductors, you name it. 'I'll wring your neck!', 'I'll knock you to kingdom come!' (or, one of my favourite variations, 'into next week!') and 'I'll murder you!' were heard so frequently as to suggest a society of psychopaths. Taken more seriously were the quieter forms of intimidation, as when your mother asked, 'would you like to see the back of my hand?' or offered to 'give you something to cry about' (or, more ominously, 'something to remember'). 'Wait till your father gets home' was the ultimate deterrent. An afternoon spent in anticipation could feel like a lifetime.

I was rarely smacked and, of course, I knew the difference between a threat and a blow. A smack, when it came, was meant to relieve tension and to draw a line. But anger does not always go through all its stages like a kettle coming slowly to the boil. In my childhood a foul temper was treated with respect, as if it were a force of nature, like a hurricane or volcano, and more fool you if you put yourself in its path ('you know what his temper's like'). Adults were always seeing red or blowing their tops; they lashed out or got 'carried away'. Men who were 'too fond of their hands' – this was usually meant as an apology after the fact – 'didn't know their own strength'. It hurt to be smacked (and it was never, not once, fair), but I dreaded people getting angry: the shouting, the red faces, the raised fists, the fact that anything might happen in the heat of the moment. In the bullying culture typical of many English childhoods, you are meant to stand up for yourself and to fight back. Being punished and being 'brave' also entitles you to a certain amount of esteem. Being afraid, on the other hand, has nothing going for it.

I begin in this way because Virginia Woolf calls *Three Guineas*, her anti-war book, an 'enquiry into the nature of fear'. *Three Guineas* finds a kinship among fear's victims, a move which many readers thought wrong-headed or downright foolish when the book was published in 1938, and which is still hard to take. Woolf argues that until recently women of her class – 'the daughters of educated men' – had been utterly dependent: they had no claim to nationality, no right of citizenship; they could not own property; they were not able to travel or mix without a chaperone; they were excluded from education and they could not earn their own living; nor could they divorce their husband or limit the number of children they had. Theirs may have been a gilded cage, but they were nevertheless imprisoned and silenced by fear – 'the fear that forbids freedom in the private house'. They were afraid of the male aggression that surfaced in the angry opposition with which the majority of men met every stage of the struggle for equality. Woolf suggests that this fear, though it might seem 'small and insignificant', is connected to the fear at large in Hitler and Mussolini's Europe. She identifies the experience of those being persecuted under Fascism with that of her mother's generation; 'You are feeling in your own persons what your mothers felt when they were shut out, when they were shut up, because they were women. Now you are being shut out, you are being shut up, because you are Jews, because you are democrats, because of race, because of religion.' For Woolf fear is the controlling force, and is as destructive and as violating, to those who live in its grip, as physical aggression.

Three Guineas is Woolf's angriest book and her most overtly pacifist; its prompt and provocation was the question around which it revolves: what could women like herself do to help prevent war? Pacifists and warriors have long been locked in each other's arms: the study of anger has been the pacifist's task. *Three Guineas* belongs to that flood of pacifist writing in the 1930s which concerned itself with 'war psychology' and found the roots of warmongering in education (this was Bertrand Russell's position in his 1936 pamphlet, *Which Way to Peace?*) or in the greed and competition integral to capitalism (*The Roots of War*, published by the Hogarth Press in the same year, took this line). As Hermione Lee pointed out in her biography of Woolf, *Three Guineas* reiterates much of the debate over peace and war which split the Left in the mid-1930s, but whose complexity, it might be added, has disappeared beneath the weight of that derogatory term, 'appeasement'. Nor was Woolf's combination of feminist arguments and a pacifist stance new. Feminists during and after the First World War (many of them in Woolf's circle) had played a central role nationally and internationally in the establishment of pacifist organisations, arguing against the seductive emotional rhetoric of patriotism, and claiming that women had different insights and experience which made them especially effective in 'peace-diplomacy'. *Three Guineas* made a disturbing leap into the dark, however. As well as being Woolf's denunciation of Fascism it attempts to bring Fascism's emotional and psychic violence home to the British. The Fascist is one of us – a view which was for many readers simply too much.

Three Guineas looks to the psychological, to what goes on inside – 'in your own persons' – for an understanding of the way inner economies, disciplines and controls might generate as well as reinforce the economic and political structures without. It was Woolf's response to the worsening situation in Europe, her search for meaning beyond the horror and misery she felt at the 'idiotic, meaningless, brutal, bloody, pandemonium' of Hitler's rise to power and the increasing likelihood of another war. Woolf's republic of fear, where being dictated to feels the same whether it is by the state, by institutions or by individuals, is a boundless space, but it is also a deeply familiar one. Like Wilhelm Reich in *The Mass Psychology of Fascism*, written in the early 1930s, Woolf turns to the emotional and psychic structures of the patriarchal household and its sexual relations, maintaining that 'the public and private worlds are inseparably connected; that the tyrannies and servilities of the one are the tyrannies and servilities of the other.' The Victorian family, devoted to the father-figure, demanding the subordination of women and based on the jealous possessiveness of capitalism, shored up the pugnacity, greed and hypocrisy of public life. Both private and public life fostered the slavish worship of hierarchy and social status. Without the proprietorial mentality of the 19th-century paterfamilias, that confidence in 'the traditions of mastery' at home, the British Empire abroad would have been unimaginable, and the debacle of 1914 equally so. But for Woolf, not only is militarism only a stone's throw away from civilian masculinity, but all forms of masculine authority shade into authoritarianism. The political dictator differs only in degree from the suburban tyrant treating his home as his castle or ruling his family with a rod of iron. The university lecturer imposing himself on docile minds and the civil servant lording it in the corridors of power are both little Hitlers, swept together in Woolf's rhetoric: 'The whole iniquity of dictatorship,' she writes, 'whether in Oxford or Cambridge, in Whitehall or Downing Street, against Jews or against women, in England or in Germany, in Italy or in Spain is now apparent.' In *Three Guineas* the 1850s slide imperceptibly into the 1930s. Woolf's phrase for the ladies of the mid-19th century, 'the daughters of educated men', serves equally to describe those born twenty-five, even fifty years later.

Woolf offers a chapter in the psychosexual history of the English middle classes. *Three Guineas* wants to understand the warmonger but it is not a discussion of aggression (or of 'aggressivity') or of war in general; it wants to see the 'male habit' of fighting as a matter of 'law and practice' but it has nothing to say about female aggression. It maintains that only dictators make fighting the essence of virility (and concomitantly deem passivity cowardly and womanish), yet the history of feeling, which Woolf evokes, constantly sexualises aggression as a masculine trait ('your anger, our fear', as *Three Guineas* puts it). Naomi Black, the book's most recent editor, observes that 'violence against women goes virtually unmentioned' in Woolf's account. But behind the fear that men's upbringing might breed violence lies a deeper fear, approached tentatively but knowingly in the text through the use of ellipsis: the fear that male aggression always has an erotic component, that fathering might be founded on conquest, that the laying down of the law is always violent and is always what makes a man. In Woolf's account of heterosexuality, desire appears both masculine and predatory: it is 'dominance craving for submission', a mere will to power (this is the nightmare which haunts her last work, *Between the Acts*). In asking what women might do to help prevent war, *Three Guineas* wonders 'what possible satisfaction can dominance give to the dominator?' But it cannot tolerate identification with the aggressor for long.

Faced with the prospect of war, passivity is for Woolf the less tainted position. How might it be redeemed from the history of victimhood? *Three Guineas* follows much pacifist writing in proposing an esteem based on a different kind of inner discipline, a confrontation of the conflicting desires in the self, and a willing dispossession which comes close to Gandhi's ideas of passive or non-violent resistance. Those who have been the objects of exclusion and derision are already freer, Woolf suggests, from the 'unreal loyalties' that prompt belligerence: 'nationality, religious pride, college pride, school pride, family pride, sex pride'. Given the moral bankruptcy of capitalism and its 'adulterated culture' in which everything is mixed with the 'money motive', it is preferable to live modestly. To compete is to imitate: women should cultivate an attitude of 'indifference', ideally refusing to display any tokens of prestige or rank, flinging back any offer of public honours (Woolf turned down an invitation to give the Clark Lectures at Cambridge in 1932, refused the Companion of Honour in 1935 and honorary degrees from Manchester and Liverpool); they should abstain from any rituals which promote the 'desire to impose "our" civilisation or "our" dominion upon other people'. 'To be passive is to be active; those also serve who remain outside.' The most exhilarating impulses in *Three Guineas* incite an imaginary violence – 'Set fire to the old hypocrisies' – such as the demand for 'Rags, Petrol, Matches' to burn down any woman's college if its values are no better than men's. ('Let it blaze! Let it blaze! For we have done with this education!') Woolf knows that women must 'face realities' – take jobs, pass exams, earn salaries – but she is far more excited by renunciation and by the struggles of Florence Nightingale or Sophia Jex-Blake than by the achievements of her own generation. With its fear that 'the victims of the patriarchal system' might become the new 'champions of the capitalist system', *Three Guineas* tries to envisage a psychic and emotional space in which those who have been infantilised, those who see themselves as weak and helpless, might move beyond a sense of inferiority without assuming mastery in return (*Three Guineas* deserves a place alongside Frantz Fanon's analysis of the dependency culture of the colonised).

Three Guineas is Woolf's most utopian book; it is also her grimmest, most anti-social. Despite its brief millenarian glimpses of future peace, her pacifism refuses any faith in the brotherhood of man (it differs markedly here from Forster's What I Believe', published in the same year), since personal relations offer no sanctuary from power. Group gatherings or associations threaten to submerge individuals, she argues. They encourage 'the herd mentality', as 1930s psychology dubbed it, and that transcendentalism with which Fascism was mystifying 'the masses'. As the life around her becomes more intensely politicised, Woolf dreams of a Society of Outsiders, working without 'leagues or conferences or campaigns', without procedures, and above all, without leaders. Her Society of Outsiders is to remain disembodied. There are to be no meetings to further co-operative projects, nothing mutual except at arm's length. Only a few lonely individuals will manage this psychic economy, holding onto just enough to keep them going. Behind *Three Guineas* lies the terror of the concentration camp and the penal colony; Woolf's political heroine is Antigone, whose civil disobedience led to her immolation, walled up in her tomb. For the less brave there may only be room to retreat: to live, if necessary, without hope; to work, if need be, without love.

Three Guineas was fuelled by rage. It began life in 1931 as a sequel to *A Room of One's Own*. Woolf started to collect material to illustrate her views on women's exclusion from the professions and on patriarchal bullying, pasting clippings into scrapbooks and transcribing passages from her reading (this edition offers a full account of Woolf's research, much of which went into more than a hundred endnotes to the final text). By 1932 she'd already got 'enough powder to blow up St Paul's' but went on stoking the fires, adding to her 'cauldron' of ideas, as she worked on other projects. It drew heat from her 'essay-novel', 'The Pargiters', borrowing from its polemical 'interchapters' (Woolf eventually dropped them and the fictional remainder finally became *The Years*). Just thinking about the work filled her with a terrifying excitement – 'like being harnessed to a shark'. Everything was grist to her mill: the petitions for her signature she received daily in the post, political conferences, articles in the press, pamphlets and manifestos, exchanges and arguments with friends and family (especially with Julian Bell, her nephew, who was determined to join the Republicans in Spain; his death there in 1937 made the book seem more necessary). The drafting, when it began in 1936, raced and galloped violently. It was an explosive experience: 'It has pressed & spurted out of me,' she wrote, 'like a physical volcano.'

Naomi Black calls the gestation of *Three Guineas* a 'period of postponement' but the years of allowing her 'sizzling' brain to cool, as Woolf put it, enabled the transmutation of anger into what she wanted for the book: 'beautiful clear reasonable ironical prose'. *Three Guineas* is deliberately diffuse and yet elaborately structured, It is framed by a series of undated, unlocated first-person replies from an anonymous, rather arch lady to those asking for funds and support, Like a Chinese box, each letter contains within itself versions of other letters the writer has received and drafts of the replies which she may send. 'The fiction of the letters', in Naomi Black's phrase, acts as camouflage. Woolf's indictments, her ventilation of the airless world of masculine self-importance, her pillorying of the smug cliquishness of interwar Britain, and her history of professional misogyny, are handled lightly and satirically;

the endnotes frequently borrow novelistic techniques and, as Keynes rightly complained, 'made a mockery of our history': Woolf ridicules the wearing of 'pieces of metal, or ribbon, coloured hoods or gowns' to express 'worth of any kind'. *Three Guineas* includes photographs of a general, a herald, a university procession, a judge and an archbishop looking suitably absurd in full fig (they were mysteriously cut in the 1968 and 1977 reprints of the Uniform Edition). But every incendiary impulse, however much relished, ultimately hangs fire. Woolf worried while writing that she was being too conciliatory: 'I so slaver & silver my tongue that its sharpness takes some time to be felt.' Leisureliness and flippancy were antidotes to the 'braying' loudspeaker tone, which she so disliked, its association with the ego-politics of Fascism, and her fear that all political argument was likely to harden into orthodoxy and the taking of sides. *Three Guineas* refuses to dictate. Its irony protects the reader from the violence of its polemic.

Black's introduction makes plentiful use of quotations from Woolf's diaries but consistently omits or truncates those comments which suggest her ambivalence about the work or about politics in general (she is troubled, for example, by 'the vulgarity of the notes', by 'a certain insistence'). Black cites the diary entry dealing with Woolf's attendance at the crucial Labour Party Conference of 1935 where George Lansbury resigned as leader after a dramatic attack on his pacifism by Ernest Bevin – this was a turning point in the evolution of *Three Guineas*, the moment when the connection between feminism and Anti-Fascism seemed to fall into place. She passes over Woolf's shrugging dismissal of the political situation as a whole, written as if her exclusion from politics in the past left her utterly blameless in the present: 'Happily, uneducated & voteless, I am not responsible for the state of society.' Woolf's desire to be 'immune', and her belief that her art depended on an energy which came from being detached and uncommitted, often looks like a refusal of those ideals of agency on which so much feminism has prided itself. Black reassures her reader that Woolf was not as 'frivolous' about feminism in person as her writing sometimes is: *Three Guineas* is 'explicitly feminist', she insists, 'in spite of some coy denials', thus glossing that inconvenient passage which hankers to consign the word 'feminist' to the flames – 'an old word, a vicious and corrupt word that has done much harm in its day and is now obsolete'.

This edition, however, gives us an American Woolf, long known to be a different species from the native variety. Despite the English canonical ring of Blackwell and its imprint 'The Shakespeare Head Press', this series of Woolf texts relies on a team of Canadian and American scholars (with the exception of Andrew McNeillie), is aimed mostly at American students (Black annotates 'coalscuttles', 'margarine' and 'ironmongers', for example), and sometimes takes the marked-up American proofs as copy-texts, thereby publishing editions which Woolf's British public never read. North American critics did much in the 1970s and 1980s to combat the view of Woolf as an effete stylist, the Invalid Lady of Bloomsbury, and their painstaking textual scholarship frequently went hand in hand with a recovery of her feminism. Black thinks it 'odd' that the British, including the editors of the Penguin and Oxford World's Classics editions of *Three Guineas*, take issue with Woolf and highlight her ambivalences. But it's equally odd that a scholarly teaching edition should see its role as celebratory, preaching only to the converted.

It is astonishing that Woolf continued to stake so much on feeling disenfranchised – how much it still rankled, that old grievance of being 'uneducated'. So much, it seems, that she saw no incongruity in telling the men and women of the Brighton Workers' Educational Association whom she lectured in January 1940 that she was one of them: she didn't look at things, she said, from 'the leaning tower', those heights from which public school and university men surveyed the world. Not everybody believed her. Her claim that the 'daughters of educated men' were 'the weakest class' (since they could not even withdraw their labour) could seem deluded or at least myopic. Queenie Leavis's infuriated review for *Scrutiny*, 'Caterpillars of the Commonwealth, Unite!', was particularly scathing, not least about Woolf's inability to register any university other than Oxford or Cambridge, as though the London colleges and the redbrick universities, which had long awarded degrees to women, did not exist. For Woolf, 'the daughters of educated men' were not bourgeois because they lacked capital and owned little. *Three Guineas* does not recognise how much women of her sort had themselves generated and sustained the emotional and psychological territory of class, its cultural capital, investing in ideas of respectability and sensibility, and in their sense of being different from, and superior to, working women. Woolf did not include the power wielded by mistresses over servants in the tyrannies and servilities of the private sphere: tinpot dictators could only be male.

Naomi Black wants to believe that *Three Guineas* 'consoled' Woolf as war approached, even though Woolf was sometimes dubious, writing to one fan: 'Whether it made any impression I don't know, I doubt if ideas ever do,' (Black calls her 'disingenuous' when she writes that 'the book is a mere outline.') Woolf's diary suggests she was indeed pleased to have had her say but partly because she now felt entitled to return to 'the real world', the world of fiction which, like Sleeping Beauty, had been 'barred with brambles'. Woolf's isolation as war approached, the product partly of circumstance, partly of choice, may well have been freeing, but it may also have been a mistake. Who knows? Perhaps it was both. All we can say is that her refusal to repudiate passivity in her own creative life seems to become more self-conscious in the late 1930s. After thirty odd years as a writer, the desire to 'own no authority', as she put it, that negative capability which for her, as for other Modernists, came so close to the depressive position, felt like a precondition for her writing. Why accentuate the positive? Perhaps it's easier to legitimise an aggressive reaction to fear than the feelings of helplessness and self-hatred Woolf so often endured. But without accepting their paralysing force, it's hard to appreciate the scale of what she achieved. And hard also to understand why she was a writer, that most passive of activities. In April 1939 Woolf began drafting her memoirs and recalled how the long indistinguishable 'cottonwool' days of childhood would unexpectedly be broken into when 'something happened so violently that I have remembered it all my life.' She gave an instance of one such 'sudden violent shock'.

> I was fighting with Thoby on the lawn. We were pommelling each other with our fists. Just as I raised my fist to hit him, I felt: why hurt another person? I dropped my hand instantly, and stood there, and let him beat me, I remember the feeling. It was a feeling of hopeless sadness. It was as if I became aware of something terrible; and of my own powerlessness. I slunk off alone, feeling horribly depressed.

Against this memory of despair, Woolf immediately set another exceptional moment, a memory of satisfaction:

> I was looking at the flowerbed by the front door; 'That is the whole,' I said. I was looking at a plant with a spread of leaves; and it seemed suddenly plain that the flower itself was a part of the earth; that a ring enclosed what was the flower; and that was the real flower; part earth; part flower. It was a thought I put away as being likely to be very useful to me later.

Woolf hazarded that in her case the 'peculiar horror' of passively registering those blows was always followed by the desire to explain, the delight in consciousness and reason, in putting 'the severed parts together' and putting the shock into words. This 'wholeness' removed the blow's power to hurt: 'I go on to suppose that the shock-receiving capacity is what makes me a writer.' It's as if by the time she reached her late fifties she came to believe that not defending herself had allowed her to become an artist.

For all its fighting talk, *Three Guineas* is not a manifesto. It pulls its punches. It does not simply unleash Virginia Woolf's fury at the blows which the daughters of educated men felt they had suffered; such an expenditure of emotion (like the three guineas finally donated to help prevent war) would not, in the end, go very far. But neither does it censor. In a series of feints and passes, Woolf's writing resists and deflects the aggressive reaction, defuses the volatile emotion, making something else of it. For Woolf, as for Freud, sublimation, not retaliation, is the art of civilisation. Writing, in other words, is at best a way of becoming more mindful of one's anger.

15

Addicted to Diaries: The Romantic Journals of Jean Lucey Pratt*

The early entries in Jean Lucey Pratt's journals brought to mind Cecily's diary in *The Importance of Being Earnest*, where Wilde sends up, among other things, the predictable script of boy meets girl. Long before she knows Algernon, Cecily has charted the progress of their romance in her diary, but when they meet, and Algernon falls instantly in love as planned, Cecily won't let him read it: 'Oh no, You see, it is simply a very young girl's record of her own thoughts and impressions, and consequently meant for publication. When it appears in volume form I hope you will order a copy.' Cecily's diary is a ruse just like her modesty. It's a cover for her unladylike ambitions – to be an author and to be in charge of her life. Romance offers girls the opportunity to gain the upper hand, but a diary, to adapt a Wildean aphorism, gives a more lasting pleasure, the chance for a lifelong romance with oneself.

Pratt began a journal in 1925 and carried on writing until her death in 1986. She imagines her public from the start. 'Reader please be kind to me!' she writes winningly: 'I am only 16 at present, and just realising life and beginning to think for myself. It's all very thrilling in its strange newness.' Jean wants to be a romantic heroine rather than a bespectacled schoolgirl, and diary-writing gives her the leading role. Bored and restless, with only her widowed father for company, she is a fan of Rudolph Valentino and melodramatic tales of unrequited love or forbidden marriage. She longs to be an actress and 'live in a real world of Romance' (i.e. cinema): 'I should love to feel that I sway men's hearts to a danger mark, and women's too for that matter.' In search of her 'Ideal He' – 'someone slightly overpowering who dances divinely' – she wishes she were 'light and amusing and attractive' (she is podgy, shy and often

---

* First published in the *London Review of Books*, 17 March 2016.

tongue-tied). Pratt writes her journal in the holidays from boarding school, 'that strangely bittersweet prison'. She begins by breathlessly totting up her past 'beaux', who include a waiter in Worthing ('he used to gaze at me so sentimentally'), a nameless choirboy at the local church 'with rather deceitful blue eyes' ('he makes eyes at Barbara Tox and Gwen Smith now'), and 'Ronald', 'quite a common sort of youth, but rather good-looking', and 'another romance where I never said a word'. Next she lists her 'cracks', or crushes, at school, no longer conjuring the world of the silent screen but of Angela Brazil whose stories fed the appetites of those emotionally starved young ladies new to private education. Jean sighs after 'J.R.' (Jean Rotherham) – 'there is no sweeter sight on earth' – despite her inamorata being incommunicado for six weeks in the 'sicker' (sickbay). Her current 'wayward passion', she confesses, is for 'A.W.', Miss Wilmott – 'everyone knows I am gone on her.' Naturally this too is a hopeless love: 'she lives in a world of games and speed and swift thought . . . and straight, slim, eager girls.'

Jean is no dupe. She knows how mass-market romance is pedalled and how easily the heartstrings can be plucked. On holiday with her father, she watches 'filmacting' from a 'topping' perch in Mullion Cove, nothing sardonically that the actress's hair is 'suspiciously fair' and that the shooting of a love scene supplies 'some sob stuff gratis'. She becomes adept at writing sob stuff herself, imagining, for instance, how nobly she will behave when her father announces his intentions to remarry, ' "Why Jean, aren't you pleased?" Perhaps then I'd say, bravely gulping down the tears and smiling: "Oh yes, Daddy, I'm very pleased, but Daddy, have you forgotten mother so soon?" ' Her anguish is no less desperate for being heightened or sentimentalised. In her stuffy home, crying in public is seen as vulgar; affection is rarely expressed. Jean is both pampered and neglected. She dotes on her older brother – 'Pooh' – who works abroad but comes home a stranger. 'I anticipated too much,' she writes as the train takes him 'heartlessly' away again. 'The anticipation was far sweeter than the realisation,' a leitmotif that recurs in Pratt's diaries, and one of the prompts for writing them.

Her family are an echelon or two below what George Orwell, an old Etonian, called in *The Road to Wigan Pier* the 'lower-upper-middle-class', his family's shabby-genteel world peopled by clerics, servicemen and Anglo-Indian officials who were reduced to living on 'virtually working-class incomes'. Pratt's antecedents are in trade and business and she grows up in a semi-rural Wembley. Her father is an architect and a freemason; her brother an engineer with Pacific and Cable (the Pratts are possibly *middle*-middle-middle class or perhaps lower-middle-middle but not lower or middle *lower*-middle class). Jean's home life between the wars initially seems to belong to someone in a

Betjeman poem. She prays that God will help get her elected to the 'upper sects' of the tennis club committee; she accompanies her father to the Anglican church where he is a warden, to Conservative Club dinners in 'pale blue georgette' or to the Ladies' Night at the local council, where she swoons over Harold Dagley who wears 'such wonderfully creased flannels' (alas! he is fatally 'weak-chinned'). Becoming Jean means learning a finely tuned language of discrimination. What matters are the differences between the middle classes. The lower orders ('the plodding workers'), like the upper classes, are a race apart. Throughout the decades Pratt nervously patrols her class boundaries; she is easily embarrassed, frequently judgmental and perennially insecure. (Will bobbing her hair make her look 'cheap'?)

Her outlook begins to change when she attends classes in architecture at Ealing Institute and then at University College London, paid for by her father. Fitzrovia, where she rents a flat, takes a dim view of Wembley and its 'flaccidness': 'I am still stamped with the stamp of suburbia . . . this is sick-making.' Intense political conversation with male students take her further from home: 'Roy', who is 'delicate' but 'intensely selfish and lazy', expounds proto-fascist views of British superiority and male supremacy, while artists, actors and other acquaintances are 'socialistic'. 'Why shouldn't India be allowed to rule herself?' she wonders, and aged 22, undertakes a student tour of Soviet Russia on her own. Her daydreams, however, are all of rising above her station, imagining a soignée life as a dress designer perhaps, 'superbly accoutred in black velvet moving suavely up and down softly carpeted luxuriously lit rooms'. If only she had 'pots' of money, 'enough anyway to provide me with an adequate number of servants, trained people who will look to the care of my wardrobe and meals and all these petty irksome little details that take up so much of one's time'. At college she cultivates an image of herself as worldly and cynical. Sex, she announces airily, 'is only of relatively minor importance', too often 'sentimentally confused with love'. But while she talks the talk, her behaviour is less advanced. Feeling sexy makes her feel a 'bad woman' or – in the new jargon – 'oversexed' and she won't go further with any of her 'lovers' than 'a petting party'.

Pratt sets out to be entertaining. She keeps up a sprightly, unforced conversation with herself and nearly every entry reads as if it is hot off the press; sometimes lyrical, often droll. She becomes adept at deflating her more elevated sentiments, juxtaposing them with domestic mishaps and often banal titbits of everyday life. Her editor thinks she picked up lessons in parody from *The Diary of a Nobody* and that her comic timing owes something to the music hall. Debunking the Victorian or fuddy-duddy in a flip tone, however, is more Coward or Waugh than Pooter. (In later years she would look back and 'wriggle' at her facetiousness.) She is not always high-spirited. Her diary is also a commonplace book where she transcribes passages from authors whose wisdom inspires her – the popular left-wing novelist Ethel Mannin, for instance, who tells her that love is 'the greatest human happiness' or Walt Whitman, who advises that life is best seen as 'a series of episodes'. Her youth – she was born in 1909 – is overshadowed by the memory of the First World War and its heroicised losses. But is life, she asks herself, really a matter of giving things up for a higher ideal or is it made up of 'little things – washing up, typewriters and shoulder straps'? As a modern young woman with a modicum of education and a decent allowance, self-fulfilment, not self-sacrifice, becomes her mantra.

'Pretty mediocre' at architecture, Pratt transfers to a course in journalism, vowing to become a writer. She joins the Tomorrow Club, precursor of International Pen, but finds its literary milieu 'alarmingly refined' (Stephen Spender lectures on Poetic Drama, 'loathing the suburbs'). She gives up the *Daily Mail* and starts reading the *New Statesman*. In 1936 her father dies unexpectedly. At 26 Jean has £300 a year, rent from the family home, and a portfolio of stocks and shares, almost the amount of unearned income – £500 – that Virginia Woolf thought a woman needed to write and have a room of her own. Pratt takes the top floor of a house in Hampstead, buys a car and a fur coat ('a good dyed squirrel') and starts a novel. She encounters Hampstead communists and works briefly for the Popular Front ('What will the Conservative relatives say?') but finds the comrades sour, 'midgets with a grievance'. She keeps on falling in love but her romances come to nothing; her novel is rejected, as are her short stories and other novels that follow. Afraid that she is 'an engaging rabbit who will not leave its burrow', she turns to psychotherapy, embarking on two sessions a week for a month with Graham Howe in Harley Street. Howe proposed a course of enlightenment called 'The Open Way', integrating psychoanalysis with Eastern philosophy (he was to influence R.D. Laing). 'Learn to make the best of what you have,' he advises. 'If you can't have that, you have this. Learn to love this.' With war looming, and friends panicking, Jean decides London is bad for her and for her writing. In 1939 she moves to an isolated cottage surrounded by acres of woodland deep in Buckinghamshire.

Simon Garfield first came across Pratt as one of the anonymous volunteers who kept a diary for Mass Observation, the organisation set up in 1937 which sought to capture the mood and mores of the British public; he included her in three earlier anthologies of contributors (*Our Hidden Lives, We Are at War and Private Battles*, where Pratt appears as 'Maggie Joy Blunt'.) But Jean, he subsequently discovered, also kept what she called a 'real diary'. *A Notable Woman* includes material from both though the differences between them are hard to judge: neither here, nor in the anthologies, are the extracts from

Mass Observation complete; they occasionally overlap but the MO diary has been heavily truncated. Pratt was certainly 'addicted' to her diaries (her word) during the war, sometimes writing twice a day at some length. Self-pity or spleen, her shame at being lonely or periodically 'manless', the savage moods that come with PMT were kept for her private diary, but that too is dodgy evidence: 'Blue Moods' journal, she dubbed it at one point. Anything to do with sex was also not for official eyes. While her MO diary comments on the Blitz and Churchill's broadcasts, Pratt's other journal obsesses about 'F.', and whether to go to bed with him. As a German invasion threatens, she determines, aged 31, not to join the 'DUVs (Dried Up Virgins)'. 'Ought I,' she asks herself, 'to lose my chastity by this particularly unspectacular and neurotic little man with whom I am not in love (nor is he with me)?'

Taking a job in the publicity department of High Duty Alloys, an aluminium works making aircraft parts, she embarks on a series of 'amorous adventures', foggy though she is about biology – can she get pregnant without intercourse? And oh those Lotharios! 'F.' with his dirty nails and 'hideous' cap: 'I never felt less romantic about anyone in my life'; dapper men with toothbrush moustaches like 'H.L.', a journalist and soldier, who has a Greek wife but misses Jean 'damnably'; the 'feckless' Tommy Hughes – Irish, of course – a doctor and a communist; and 'Mac', the office philanderer, who has five girlfriends (three in Sheffield), a liaison that goes on for years. The 'sex war' is in full spate and Jean unbuttons: 'I could have knifed him!', she writes, when 'Mac' has the office junior in his sights. Women in respectable tweeds and twinsets are 'bitches', 'bits', 'blouses', 'husband-chasers'; men are 'mother-swathed' egotists or – if they are any good in bed – deemed 'Latin' lovers. Sex may be enjoyable but it 'oh, it MUST mean something!' Promiscuity is morally dangerous; being left 'on the shelf' even worse. Marriage is still the ultimate goal: 'I'd tackle it as a full-time job demanding all my intelligence and wit and charm. I'd have to submit myself to rigorous discipline, house-keeping, catering, cooking, grooming, clothes, health all kept at 100 per cent efficiency – but without any jarring or nagging!' Faced with this dauntingly tall order, she concludes: 'I'd better get on with my life as it is.'

With her Mass Observation entries kept to a minimum, Pratt's official despatches are more like bulletins in this volume. They cover more familiar ground. Yet it was a novelty for her, as for the majority of the population, to feel entitled to enter history and speak for the nation. Wartime gives her the licence to think about what history is and how it ought to be written: 'We shall discover in time that history is made by people. It is not a series of reigns, battles and party politics.' 'Feel like Pepys,' she writes, as she notes her diet. War intensifies her feeling of transience so she makes lists of commodities that 'are now part of the fabric of the nation', including Kruschen health salts, Pepsodent toothpaste, Senior's fish and meat paste. The sense of the past, however, is evoked as much by what she sees as unremarkable, like her anxiety that cakes in wartime will definitely have less sugar or her constant mincing of food for her cats' dinners. She dreads having to volunteer for anything, which is endearing. War planes are often overhead but she doesn't have to experience an air-raid to dread death by bombing: her imagination is on full alert. Typically, she mocks her own Sarah Bernhardt tendencies when she keeps herself awake half the night after writing a last letter disposing of her worldly goods, so moved and fascinated is she by inventing the scenes that might take place in her home after her death.

Pratt's small cottage on the edge of Burnham Beeches was hardly remote from civilisation but conditions were basic. Fending for herself – lighting fires, cooking, doing chores – was unusual for a woman of her class and generation. True, she has her 'Mrs Mopp' to do 'the rough', whom she treats with the requisite condescension, and tradesmen to help out (in Home Counties parlance they are always diminutive, as in 'a little plumber came today'); neighbours within reach, occasional visitors and lovers, but most of her time is spent learning to enjoy her own company. She is, she realises, 'one of 3 million surplus women in Great Britain' and increasingly an oddball. Gradually she breaks with some of the shibboleths of her tribe, reckoning that inherited income makes one 'fat, flabby, feeble' and that she likes other people far more than she does her relatives. The casual racism of her sister-in law writing from Trinidad saddens her and she fears her niece despises her 'for not being a Tory'. She even sells her fur coat.

Pratt's experiment in living alone becomes a lifetime. Yet she rarely sees this as an achievement. Drawing on her sessions with Graham Howe, she believes herself a casualty, 'crippled psychologically – just as much as a child's leg may be crushed and made useless by a careful car driver'. Her mother's death, her respectable upbringing – who knows what the 'accident' was? The feeling of 'being left by the roadside' persists, but her journal may offer 'a warning and an example'. Looking for models, she is particularly impressed by the 'fine scientific clarity' of W.N.P. Barbellion's *Journal of a Disappointed Man*, 'a nude study', as he put it, of his sufferings, including an account of multiple sclerosis. At the very least, she concludes, she might in time be considered as some sort of 'specimen'.

At the end Pratt's journals filled 45 exercise books. Thirty-four were written before 1952. Thereafter, a single volume is enough for two or three years; some years are missing altogether. She begins to fall out of love with 'prancing before mirrors in one's mind'. Far from being therapeutic, the journals are 'aspirins', stopping her from feeling; reading old journals is suffocating; old patterns repeat and there is no progress. Instead she looks for affirmation and approval in half-serious visits to palmists and clairvoyants, graphologists, and has her 'auragraph' taken at the Marylebone Spiritualist Association. She goes to Quaker meetings, studies Buddhism and Theosophy – 'I am a little put off Theosophy by Theosophists' – and reads Jung. For months on end her journal becomes an anti-diary, with lengthy quotations and meditations drawn from Krishnamurti or Marcus Aurelius, aimed at renouncing the ego. When she finally publishes a book (under a pseudonym), a biography of David Garrick's mistress, the actress Peg Woffington, she worries that success may change her. But 'nothing shattering has happened. What I expected I do not know. Did I think I would wake up famous?'

As her capital dwindles, she is preoccupied with money-making schemes. She contemplates running a cattery but takes in paying guests instead, a 1950s version of Airbnb, feeding them on 'cream cheese and grated sprout' sandwiches. Finally, she plunges into village life and sets up a bookshop, despite its being partly 'menial work': 'Sluggard, slut, craven and snob in me all shriek: "Oh you can't! You couldn't!"' 'Bringing culture' to 'those rich, starchy, atrophying Farnham Common women' is hard work; one borrower flings Sylvia Townsend Warner's stories back at her, crying 'filth!' and saying: 'I hope the author is not a friend of yours?' Jean runs the shop for 25 years, often at a loss, but without lowering herself to 'sidelines' of tobacco, sweets and stationery: 'oh God, I will not descend to that level!' In her sixties she is treated with Trimipramine for a lengthy depression – 'Why have we lived? Have we lived?' – though she self-medicates by getting 'tight' on Dubonnet. As parish clerk, props manager for the local am dram, and bookseller, she keeps busy, spasmodically chronicling change in the village and at home: the National Health Service ('really not as bad as has been made out'); a boiler for baths, though its behaviour is 'surly'; years spent fighting the M40; the blessings of formica and 'knotty pine'; the shock of a new hairdressing 'salon': 'Scores of little teenage girl assistants in pastel overalls attending two male operators. It was like a launderette . . . We are all being moulded to one pattern, made to look as the hairstylist and fashion designer dictates. We haven't a chance to be individual.'

In old age there are lapses into reaction, Wembley no longer has any 'good people' like her parents, but she writes with grace and humour about her frailties, game to try a long distance 'psychic operation' on her cataracts and gin and tonic as a cure for cancer. In her last years her journal is a rare indulgence rather than a necessity: the romance with her 'self' has all but evaporated.

A Notable Woman is a much reduced version of Pratt's journals, one million words winnowed down to a fifth of that. Garfield's edit has no doubt excised much chaff but four volumes of an equivalent length is a lot to lose. Despite a few deft summaries of ellipses, it is impossible to know what and where he has cut. He has also tidied up Pratt's garbled grammar, added punctuation, and tempered her use of exclamation marks. Frustratingly, there is no index. An editor, he rightly notes, cannot predict what will interest future readers. There was too much on cats, he says. There is plenty left. Jean got her first kitten (Cheeta) after her father's death, kept eight cats at one point, well aware of the spinsterly cliché and that at least one friend found they 'gave her the pip'. Cats were her longest lasting relationships and by her own account, her greatest loves. She reported on the fate of animals in wartime and was a regular at cat shows (including the annual meeting of the Red, Cream, Tortie, Blue-Cream and Brown Tabby society). In her bookshop cat books were her most successful line and after retirement she went on with a mail-order service. She was touched that the *Cats and Catdom Annual* of 1980 called her 'the Fairy Godmother of the Cat Fancy'.

Listening to Jean's voice across six decades creates a powerful intimacy and even, strangely, a feeling of responsibility, as if one were helplessly watching another human being drifting alone on a raft. The effect, perhaps, of a single volume spanning an entire life. Her longings to be elsewhere or to be someone else are utterly recognisable; her frustrations and disappointments poignant, and her dying with so much undone inevitable. It is also a tribute to her writing that she appears so vulnerable. Foolish, even self-deluded as she is at times, she seems brave in just keeping going. Ultimately nothing tells her who she is. Money, men, work, writing, cats, family, including a lengthy spell as a 'guardian aunt' – are only sufficient for the day thereof. Yet she cannot throw away her journals. The desire to be read and understood outlasts all else. For most of her life she wanted two things, 'a wedding ring and a publisher' but perhaps she was a better diarist for getting neither. These journals are a priceless find. I hope Cats Protection, the agency where they are now lodged, takes good care of them.

16

Writing the Lives of 'Common People': Reflections on the Idea of Obscurity*

'Everyday' lives; 'lives of the obscure'; the lives of 'common people', all these phrases are tricky and make me slightly uneasy, because they always conjure up the opposite categories, which come with the buzz of value added: extraordinary lives, celebrity lives, the lives of exceptional people. Take the unhappy distinction between obituaries in the British liberal newspaper, *The Guardian*: some lives take up a page or half a page, and others are given very short columns – those they call 'other people'. The ordinary tend always to be *other* people. Not you and me. But 'obscurity', we know, is a relative term. The servant was not obscure to her sister. It also hides assumptions about who matters and what matters, and how some lives count or do not count. This conference is, of course, a rebuttal to this.[1]

I'd like to begin with a biographical sketch which is in part a homage to Virginia Woolf since 'lives of the obscure' is her phrase, and her passion for life-writing in all its forms, has inspired many of us who work in literary or cultural studies and in the women's movement (which does not mean we are not aware of the sticking points of her imagination). Let me remind you of Woolf's biographical invention in *A Room of one's Own*. A 'what if' story: what if Shakespeare had been born a woman in Elizabethan England, agog to see the world and with 'the heart of a poet'? Shakespeare's sister 'Judith' isn't sent to school; is kept at home to work and is beaten if she picks up a book; is betrothed against her will and shamed into marriage. She manages to run away but can't find work in the theatre, is seduced and ends up killing herself, dying in obscurity, her gifts wasted.

---

* First published in the *Kenyon Review* online, Sept/Oct 2019.

In 1928, when she was talking to female students at Cambridge, Woolf's story of Shakespeare's sister pointed up the limits of women's lives, how power relations are built into everyday life and that nothing is 'outside history': the family and the household; the social conventions against the work; the strictures about marriage and lack of choice over unwanted pregnancies; and so on. This is where many of us start, using the idea of the everyday as a wedge for prising open the grand narratives of the past but also recognising that it is in our personal and social lives that we reproduce, say, the habits of command, or the divisions of labour; in our bringing up of children that we pass on our fears about others who are different; and so on. The everyday is not outside history but is its texture, its warp and weft. It is the fabric of the present from which the past is made.

Woolf, though, wanted Judith to be a writer of genius like Shakespeare. Her interest in this invention was not in the everyday life except as a form of confinement. Elsewhere in her work her lives of the obscure – the 'Mrs Browns' on trains, clergymen's widows, faded genteel spinsters, forgotten lady novelists and devoted daughters, are a kind of reclamation. She notes household habits and past-times; pets and tea ceremonies, and conjures a life from a variety of sources, not only the written or printed – diaries, letters, memoirs, household accounts – but objects: a bonnet, a shoe, a ballad or 'Miss Ormerod's' insect collection. But she also fictionalises, inventing dialogue, for example, imagining thoughts and longings. Woolf is often caught, I think, in a dilemma, which is a tension, between the historical or documentary and the literary impulse and, if you like, between researchers and readers: is the life *always* interesting or is it the way it is written that makes it interesting? I want to press on this a little harder.

My biographical sketch starts in the Jewish East End, in a family of three daughters living off Brick Lane in Spitalfields. Their parents, Jakov and Feigel Nirenstein, like thousands of others escaping the pogroms in Russia, arrive from Odessa in the 1900s. They are not among the poorest of the poor; Jakov manages a Hebrew bookshop which also sells religious goods, such as prayer shawls. The oldest girl, Minnie, has a musical talent like her uncle Laibel, a self-taught violinist who takes her to concerts. She is lucky. At her school in Clapton, East London, her gift is encouraged by her Fabian Headmistress, Dr Mary O'Brien who insists on the girls learning German after the war and gives promising pupils what she calls 'Shaw teas' – after the playwright – carrots and salad, promoting vegetarianism and free thought.

The family can't afford to send Minnie to university so Dr O'Brien puts her in for a place at the Royal Academy of Music, to study piano and composition. She is successful but at nineteen she is also terrified, afflicted by shyness.

For two years she stays solitary and friendless, too scared to eat in the canteen with the other students; a timid, ugly duckling of a Jewish girl. Nevertheless she does extremely well, learning composition under a well-known musician, William Aylwin; she wins a competition and her student pieces, including a 'Ballade' in the manner of late Debussey, are performed in South Kensington, and also at the Whitechapel Art Gallery in the East End, near her home. But the money runs out. After her father's death, her mother and sisters struggle to keep the business going. How could Minnie, without money or support, and with the pressure of family loyalty so strong, have put her music first?

Her story is less dramatic than Judith Shakespeare's. Minnie leaves college and goes back to help in the shop. Two years later, in 1931, a suitable match is made for her with a good Jewish boy, Berrill or Barney Samuel, a solici-tor and a graduate of Cardiff University. Theirs is a traditional Jewish wed-ding in Shoreditch, he, short and tubby and somewhat over-mastered by his top hat and she looking gawky in white lace. They are showered with pres-ents, including a modern hand-painted dinner service in blue and orange and brown, a set of fish forks and knives, and much of the paraphernalia needed to set them up for bourgeois life. Like others from the East End, they move to a sparkling new home close to Golders Green and Finchley, on the fringes of Hampstead Garden Suburb. Soon enough, her husband is dandling their baby boy in the sunny garden outside by the rockery.

★

Let's stop the clock. Is this an ordinary or an extraordinary life? What shape shall we give it? As historians we can make much of it, surely; as feminists; as those alert to different cultures. There are so many sources now to find and draw on that could put flesh on these bones. We can know for instance that the Jewish East End was alive with a culture that fostered many artists, musi-cians, and writers – Isaac Rosenberg, David Bomberg spring to mind; there are websites like that designed by Nadia Valman at Queen Mary College, London to take us on a tour. A historical imagination might equally be excited by life in Hampstead Garden Suburb with its experiments in housing and new forms of social life; its rejection of Victorian aesthetics with its modern interiors, pale painted walls, Ercol wooden chairs and fitted kitchen units. The sociologists among us might want to chart the contrast of different worlds and social classes *among* the Jewish migrants from Shoreditch and Whitechapel as they found themselves in north London. What are now very pricey suburbs – Parliament Hill, Kentish Town and even Hampstead – were far less salubrious between the wars, full of multi-occupied houses, cheaply rented, with two or three

generations crammed; the roads studded with Polish cafes and Russian baker-
ies and corner shops selling everything from hat pins to candles to rat poison.

Pause here to ask: what are we writing the life for? If it is to reveal exclu-
sions, occlusions – as I certainly wanted to when I researched the servants who
worked for Virginia Woolf, and who were never more than their first names
in most accounts of 'Bloomsbury', we have the advantage of what has been
called 'the archival turn': so many institutions now, like the Royal Academy
of Music, have their own records and we have access to decades of scholarly research, including women's history. There are secondary texts, such as
Sophie Fuller's *Guide to Women Composers*, which tell me Minnie was not the
only woman student of composition between the wars. Hers was a remarkable generation of women. Among her close contemporaries were Elisabeth
Lutyens (born 1906), Grace Williams (1906); Elizabeth Maconchy (1907),
Imogen Holst (1907), the daughter of the composer. If chance had sent her to
the Royal College of Music and not the Royal Academy, Minnie might have
found a milieu. Except that these other women were able to support themselves or had family connections in the musical world – Lutyens, for instance,
married Edward Clark, who was secretary to Schoenberg and was responsible
for bringing his music to the BBC.

All this is biographical 'background' can be brought to bear on the individual life – its frustrations and possibilities in the interwar years. But there are
other questions. What we might call 'History with a capital H', wars, political
regimes, laws, economic changes and so on, impact differently on different
lives at different times. If I return to Minnie's life in the late 1930s, I find both
she and her husband are members of the Labour Party and also running an
agency to get Jewish children out of Nazi Germany. Then Minnie's closest
family – her sisters and their husbands – join the British Communist Party.
Their evenings are spent at branch meetings and discussions; their weekends
on the street canvassing, protesting, leafletting; informing others about the
fight against fascism. More of the family join and their social circle becomes
entirely that of Party members; their dentist and their grocer even. Politics
avalanched into Minnie life: it took up all her hours. Eventually it broke up
her marriage and led to divorce, a scandal in those days, and to Barnett's family
cutting off from her.

Another pause for thought. To be a Communist was a complete social
identity. Family life and political life were one, and in theory, at least, under
Communism there was to be no private life: the self was to be subordinated
to the struggle. Writing that life, writing any life, is about how the self is conjured, or narrated; a history of ideas about selfhood is implicit or explicit in
what we write which may be inappropriate or culturally out of kilter. How to

do justice to Minnie's life at this time? And how also to avoid the enshrinement of childhood as *the* origin of the self, that view which tells us that the child must be father to the man or mother to the woman – a view that determines, indeed over-determines – much biographical writing. Childhood becomes the key that unlocks the inner sanctuary of the person.

Yet this period of Minnie's life was a radical break. It liberated her from domesticity; it emancipated her from religion – she was 'against God', she told her son. And joining the Communist Party was, for her, as for many women from very different worlds, an education, a place where she could argue and be taken seriously as a rational human being. For Minnie, self-fulfillment was not the aim – not 'individuality', that prize so often awarded by biography or seen as feminism's goal. Being part of the group, acting together was what mattered; putting one's 'self' and its needs *second* for the public good. She was freed, to put it differently, from the burden of personal ambition.

Equally too, a sense of collective memory or of belonging to a generation may be as relevant or even more important to a life than individual experience. Writing about his growing up in France, the philosopher Michel Foucault, born in 1926 insists that 'nearly all the great emotional memories' of his childhood were 'related to the political situation'. [2] Recently, Luisa Passerini in her *Autobiography of a Generation*, has tried to find a way to capture group experience and her own relation to it, including her years in psychoanalysis, by weaving her own story and reflections into a web of documents and interviews with students, women, and workers involved in the Italian struggles around 1968. Her book is broken into different parts; different voices, using memory to call official accounts of the period into question but also – since she is an oral historian – assessing those memories critically, looking for their tropes, their repetitions and contradictions. Memory can also be deluded.

The relation, in other words, between the singular and the representative, is a tension which takes different forms and emphases in life-writing, whether the case study, the extended biography or the memoir. And 'once a life has been turned into stories', 'it becomes those stories', cautions Jeremy Gavron in his account of his mother, Hannah Gavron, a young feminist sociologist who killed herself in 1965 when he was four. In *A Woman on the Edge of Time*, Gavron wants to make his mother representative of her times, without her being merely a reflection of history, crushed, if you like, by context or background, or fashioned into an example of a readymade interpretation or theory. It means that he too eschews the extended narrative and writes a fragmentary text.

And then – another pause – the so-called 'non-eventful'. After the war, now in her forties, Minnie married Bill Keal, a sheet-metal worker from working-class Liverpool, the love of her life. She was calling herself Minna by then, more romantic, less Cockney than Minnie. Should we end it here? She left the Party, as so many did, in 1956 after the invasion of Hungary by Soviet troops and the revelations about Stalin's purges, though she stayed a left-winger. They moved to a 1930s semi-detached house, not unlike her first home with Barnett, outside a small town in Buckinghamshire and she worked in an office. Sometimes she gave piano lessons to local children. Minna retired when she was 60 and entered what she felt was the autumn of her life. An ordinary life after all?

★

Of course I have created the sense of ending by narrating Minna's life in this way. Writing a life is always a question of how we represent time – from the life to the day and its passing – but also the different paces or velocities of time. When I wrote *Common People*, I was struck, for instance, with how different a child's experience of time is, especially when well-meaning Victorian social investigators were puzzled that slum children seemed happy playing their games in filthy streets or diving for pennies from wharves. But the children did not know themselves to be poor. It was not their 'background' but their foreground. They had not yet made a narrative of themselves in those socially-divisive ways.

The arbitrary shape of a life given by clock time or chronology; the kinds of time we inhabit; how we don't live our lives progressively, though much may be spent in anticipation, and the alchemy of memory which itself changes over time, all need consideration. Old age, say, a great deal of which may lived in memory, is a good example of what doesn't count in a conventional biography. It is usually the winding down; twenty years maybe get twenty pages because 'nothing happens'. Then there are the breaks in a life which are as formative as any progress, those times out of time: falling in love, childbirth, mourning, breakdown itself, when time enters another dimension, elongating or shrinking like a Surrealist clock.

In *Common People* I wrote too about the ways in which time in families is generational, repetitive, cyclical; how events in women's lives differ to those of men. I used my own family history and ended up following many different branches of my forbears going backwards across the centuries, a hectic process, which also speeded up historical time and undid periodization. Whirling across the centuries, backwards, places become a kind of 'flow', not static as they are on maps; communities come and go; cities turn back into fields. I found I needed a mentally split screen to see generations emerging and to track the multiple narratives, full of uneven, un-matching developments. So many of those handy divisions and short-hands historians rely upon, like 'the country and the city' or 'pre-industrial and industrial', became unsettled. Kinship creates a different geography. I found, for example, when I discovered my grandmother, Evelyn Light, whom I never knew, aged ten in the census of 1900, that she had cousins and siblings working as labourers on the farm; others travelling the country as railwaymen; still others working in local factories: one grandmother ran her own pub; another worked as a housekeeper to a baronet in London. She was living on the outskirts of Birmingham – was it a rural or an urban life?

I also included memoir in *Common People*, as a jumping off point, memories of my grandparents and their stories. This was in part an antidote to working in cyberspace – with its instant access to information and instant intimacy: the pace of the inner life, of reflection and memory can be an opposite, resistant current. Memory was a slowcoach and it also allowed me the breathing space of an image. Plus memories, like dreams, are an emotional inheritance which shape us as much as land or property – the tall stories others tell, and those with which we grow up, are a legacy, part of who we are.

My family history became a group biography of sorts about the migrant English and the Irish poor. They were mostly agricultural workers, sailors and servants or itinerants – or forced labourers, like those transported to Van Diemen's Land. I had very few objects, photographs, gravestones, let alone dwellings; some lived in the forest, for example; many in slums that are now demolished. But I had an astonishing amount of information about their lives; their work; their neighbours; their travels; their illnesses, loves and religious beliefs. Innumerable records can be accessed – many online – including over forty years of a British census and parish registers, state records, local government materials, to state only the most obvious, which give us endless insights even if they must so often be read against the grain (I spent some thrilling hours looking at the sanitation committee minutes for the burgeoning naval town of Portsmouth which taught me why some areas became slums. Only the 'best' streets and avenues were cleaned by private contractors in the days before it was a council or corporation responsibility. An argument, if ever there was one for publically-owned services).

I had no diaries and few letters, no 'ego-documents', as historians sometimes call them. But being a literary critic I am particularly sceptical about all written sources, particularly about the ways they constitute an idea of the self and a sensibility. Our letters are often a kind of theatre or a duet, narrating and dramatizing, say, a love affair or a dull day. Diaries are a different kind of performance; we tell ourselves what we already know; they are at once too much and too little. They are great deceivers, as Leonard Woolf argues in his selection of Woolf's diaries which give a picture of her, he maintains, as a person far gloomier than she was in day to day life. My own diaries, written at tedious length over the decades, are pretty airless; History with a capital 'H' doesn't feature much but they certainly show an enormous investment in the idea of a self – did that change over time?

I return to my question. Whether it is the life of the person or of the group, we still ask what are we writing the life for? And for whom? And where? Writing and recording lives is always in a context and that shapes what we can do and what we can't say. It is not a one-way traffic but may have huge effects, on knowledge but also on the wider world, of which that knowledge is always part. Family history, the apparently bland and much scorned, poor relation of the historical profession, is a good case in point. In Turkey recently the population registers went public and the system crashed as people rushed to find out about their ancestors and where they had come from.[3] This mattered to them personally but it rapidly also created deep unease. It revealed that scores of Turks had Syriac, Greek, Jewish and Armenian forbears who converted to Islam, and thereby gave the lie to the idea of a pure Turkishness which the current government is promulgating. In a climate of political repression and persecution, this was a very risky thing to learn. Family history is always part of the national story, or part of its unravelling.

★

Finally, let me return to Minna in her sixties giving occasional piano lessons to local school children. Social and economic forces set limits to our lives but there is always contingency, times when chance, the wild card, intervenes. One of her pupil's examiners for piano was a young composer, Justin Connolly. Idle chat led to him politely asking to see Minna's student work. He was so taken with it that thanks to a gift from Minna's son (for she was an old age pensioner by now), he gave her lessons, and then arranged for her to continue with another composer, Oliver Knussen.

Minna now opened her ears to modern music, to Bartok and Stravinsky; she embraced the 'new' – new to her – musical language of Schoenberg and Webern and she began writing music again. A string quartet at seventy; a wind quintet, then a symphony, nearly half an hour of music, which took her five years – and she felt rejuvenated. Her symphony was premiered by the BBC at the Proms in the Royal Albert Hall in her eightieth year. As Minna Keal, composer, she became exceptional. She graciously accepted a Royal Academy Fellowship from Diana, Princess of Wales, loathing monarchy, but delighted with the honour from other musicians and her old college. She was taken up by the media because of her unusual career and sometimes treated as a 'Geriatric Phenomenon', featuring in books on how to live your old age, invited onto radio and tv. In 1992 BBC 2 devoted a television documentary to her (entitled 'A Life in Reverse'). It showed her buying a ticket to London at her local station, and beaming when the conductor told her he had seen her on the chat show hosted by Terry Wogan. 'I'm almost famous', she replied, with a laugh.

Reviews and articles said almost nothing about Minna's Communism, as if it were an embarrassment or aberration. Yet how did shy little Minnie Nirrenstein become Minna Keal if not through the politics which had energised her, modernised her, educated her? She was writing a second string quartet when she died aged 90 in 1999. All her music was performed and recorded – but have you heard of her? And is the music what makes the life or the life that makes the music? If Minna had lived to 70 only, would her life be worth writing? Are the intervening years merely a filler? What constitutes biographical value? And what kind of biographical evidence or source is music, that most ephemeral of forms?

★

I have been sketching Minna's life because I am currently trying to include it in a memoir of my marriage to her son, my first husband, the historian Raphael Samuel who died before she did, in 1996.[4] Minna and I were very close, despite, or perhaps because of, the forty years between us. I have been thinking about inspiration and idealism, including political idealism, and of the life as exemplum, now a seemingly unfashionable notion. Since those moderns like Lytton Strachey and Virginia Woolf had such fun at the expense of what they took to be Victorian mawkishness, the saccharine and sentimental, all those lives made holier than thou, literary biography has steered clear of what might smack of hagiography.

Yet despite all the debunking, the appetite for role-models and exempla survives. Biography is the bastard child of the saint's life. Like its sister the novel, it began with the secular – the life, faulty, foolish and recognisable: warts and all. No miracles, no martyrdom beyond the ordinary pains of the human, though these biographical subjects were often extraordinary people, poets and artists who suffered from alcoholism, disease, or drugs, but not the outlandish slicing off of body parts or exotic deaths. The saint's life was meant for a mediation. Only a saint could emulate Christ but they could prompt us to be better; their miracle tales were aspirational as well as inspirational. St Francis seeing all animals as his kin; St Martin, the Roman soldier who gave

half his cloak to a beggar: we could not hope to imitate Christ but we might
try to copy the saints.

I think that the need for an intelligible life still matters enormously to
people and according this dignity, the dignity of a life worth knowing, is what
many of us want to do. Humans seem to need to learn *from* lives and not only
learn *about* them. We want to hear about the good life, not just the enviable
life.[5] That tension – between being and having, if you like – feels for many of
us like an opposition and is perhaps even more acute in a hyper-consumerist,
capitalist world. Thinking about the quality of everyday lives decentres those
other narratives of accumulation as well as the Whiggish notion of progress: it
focuses us on what is generated in a day to day life. But that's why, probably,
I am interested in writing about forms of idealism at the moment, in these
lives and in my own.

Let me end, though, with a provocation. Do we not need obscurity? We
live in an extraordinary age of self-exposure. The social media, the internet,
blogosphere and twittersphere, but also the surveillance by corporations and
the state, who harvest the personal data of individuals – all are spotlights on
the biographical, on the self, on individuals and groups. They are part of the
creation of a new social value, which has been called 'the publicity of the private', if you like, 'the private publically consumed'. [6] In fact those categories
of private and public have been, and are being, so profoundly transformed,
they may soon no longer make any sense. Such transformations raise political
questions about the control of information but also ethical questions and legal
issues for life-writers and researchers. If to be obscure is to be in the shade,
out of the glare of scrutiny, I wonder if we will we see a new valuing of the
state of being in the margins. There are political and personal advantages
in obscurity.

I understand that 'obscurity' as Woolf used it, was an appealing literary
concept, and often a condescending one. It sat very comfortably with a conservative, consoling version or vision of the social order. It sounds accidental,
but we know that at its worst obscurity can mean obliteration – the deliberate erasure from the records. In a gentler modulation, the obscure is also the
enigmatic, the ambiguous and complicated. It suggests that which cannot be
understood straightaway and may always remain unintelligible, even at times,
incomprehensible – in our selves and to others. What I take from Woolf's
'Lives of the Obscure' is also *that* sense of obscurity, a sense which might be
cherished in our attempts to write the lives of others: a respect for their ultimate unknowability, for what cannot be labelled or plumbed. After all, a life
does not need to be witnessed or recorded to be a life.

NOTES

1. This is a version of the talk given as the opening plenary at a conference on 'Everyday Matters: Writing Obscure Lives' held at the Centre for Life-writing, Wolfson College, Oxford on May 5th 2018.
2. Michel Foucault, an interview with Stephen Riggins, reprinted in *Ethics: Subjectivity and Truth* (London 1997).
3. https://www.al-monitor.com/pulse/originals/2018/02/turkey-turks-become-obsessed-with-genealogy.html
4. *A Radical Romance: A Memoir of Love, Grief and Consolation* will be published by Fig Tree/Penguin Press in 2019.
5. This distinction is explored by Adam Phillips in his essay, 'On Success', in *On Flirtation* (London 1995).
6. Roland Barthes, *Camera Lucida: Reflections on Photography*, (London, 1984).

Index